MW00354409

AFTER ELIZABETH

AFTER ELIZABETH

Can the Monarchy Save Itself?

ED OWENS

BLOOMSBURY CONTINUUM
LONDON · OXFORD · NEW YORK · NEW DELHI · SYDNEY

BLOOMSBURY CONTINUUM
Bloomsbury Publishing Plc
50 Bedford Square, London, WC1B 3DP, UK
29 Earlsfort Terrace, Dublin 2, Ireland

BLOOMSBURY, BLOOMSBURY CONTINUUM and the Diana logo are trademarks of
Bloomsbury Publishing Plc

First published in Great Britain 2023

A catalogue record for this book is available from the British Library

Library of Congress Cataloguing-in-Publication data has been applied for

ISBN: HB: 978-1-3994-0652-9; eBook: 978-1-3994-0650-5; ePDF: 978-1-3994-0649-9

2 4 6 8 10 9 7 5 3 1

Typeset by Deanta Global Publishing Services, Chennai, India
Printed and bound in Great Britain by CPI Group (UK) Ltd, Croydon CR0 4YY

To find out more about our authors and books visit www.bloomsbury.com
and sign up for our newsletters

Contents

British Monarchs: George III to Charles III

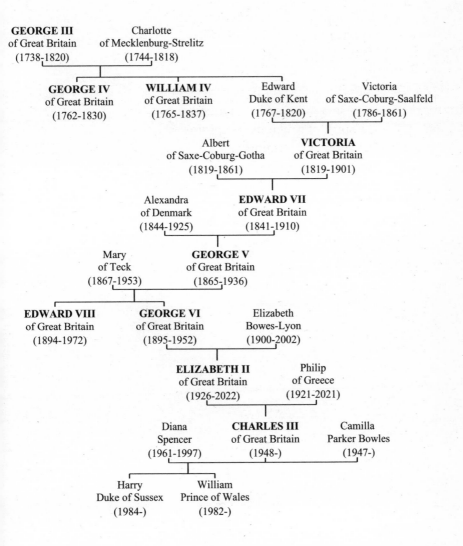

GEORGE III of Great Britain (1738-1820) — Charlotte of Mecklenburg-Strelitz (1744-1818)

GEORGE IV of Great Britain (1762-1830)

WILLIAM IV of Great Britain (1765-1837)

Edward Duke of Kent (1767-1820) — Victoria of Saxe-Coburg-Saalfeld (1786-1861)

Albert of Saxe-Coburg-Gotha (1819-1861) — **VICTORIA** of Great Britain (1819-1901)

Alexandra of Denmark (1844-1925) — **EDWARD VII** of Great Britain (1841-1910)

Mary of Teck (1867-1953) — **GEORGE V** of Great Britain (1865-1936)

EDWARD VIII of Great Britain (1894-1972)

GEORGE VI of Great Britain (1895-1952) — Elizabeth Bowes-Lyon (1900-2002)

ELIZABETH II of Great Britain (1926-2022) — Philip of Greece (1921-2021)

Diana Spencer (1961-1997) — **CHARLES III** of Great Britain (1948-) — Camilla Parker Bowles (1947-)

Harry Duke of Sussex (1984-)

William Prince of Wales (1982-)

For Lisa

Introduction
Crown and country in crisis

The coronation of King Charles III on 6 May 2023 was a triumph for the kind of royal continuity that characterized the reign of Queen Elizabeth II. As the media stressed in the lead-up to the event, the ceremony in Westminster Abbey combined traditional ritual – the symbolism of some of which dates back more than a thousand years to Anglo-Saxon England – with a new emphasis on racial and religious inclusion to mirror the social and cultural diversity of the United Kingdom in 2023. Such incremental modernization has defined the monarchy's evolution since 1952. And, as the archbishop of Canterbury, Justin Welby, made clear, elements of the coronation service were ripe for reinterpretation. When the last one was held, 70 years ago, Britain was an almost entirely white, Christian nation that was outwardly still an empire, and which inwardly remained deeply deferential to the young queen and head of state who then led the country.

The recent coronation was also successful in projecting a dignified vision of a monarchy of a bygone age. At times it verged on pantomime. But by blending pomp and pageantry (all rehearsed to the finest detail) with an emphasis on the divine as conveyed through the often stirring music, the religious ceremony briefly managed to reassert the mystique of monarchy after four years of lurid tabloid headlines that have tarnished the House of Windsor's public image. King Charles and Queen Camilla know only too well how difficult it is to wash away the stain of scandal, having been at the centre of a damaging media storm throughout the 1990s because of their illicit relationship and the sudden death of Diana, princess of Wales. Indeed, it is in light of these events more than a quarter of a century ago that the coronation should be viewed as an improbable personal victory for two people – our new monarchs – who were once deeply unpopular with a majority of the British public.

However, while we may view the coronation as the moment that sealed the beginning of the new king's reign and set out some of the themes he wishes to promote, it was also an opportunity missed, because of how

distinctly backward-looking the whole thing was in terms of the overall
style and content of the performance that was staged for our viewing
pleasure. Yes, there was *some* timely innovation. But the event foregrounded
continuity by essentially following the blueprint of the last four coronations, dating back to 1902. As we shall see, this was when Edward VII
was crowned as part of a new kind of coronation that combined, for the
first time, large colourful military parades with an expertly choreographed
religious service and public celebrations in London and across the country
in honour of the sovereign. Far from representing a moment of reboot,
bringing the monarchy up to date and into the twenty-first century, the
coronation of Charles and Camilla thus revealed a monarchy short of fresh
ideas and fearful of deviating too far from a timeworn script which, until
recently, had served the Windsors rather well.

The problem here is complacency – not just on the part of the royals
and their advisers but also on the part of a British news media, which,
with one or two exceptions, refused during the long reign of Queen
Elizabeth to ask difficult questions about the role played by the monarchy
in the modern world. While the old queen was on the throne, it was taken
as given by most journalists that events such as jubilees, royal funerals
and weddings helped to project outwardly an image of a Britain that was
confident, ordered and resplendent, thus enhancing the country's reputation abroad. But this is simply no longer the case. It doesn't matter how
refined and appealing royal events are if no one's paying attention. For
all its magnificence, televised royal ritual simply cannot buy you the kind
of influence internationally that might be earned through the careful
nurturing of diplomatic relationships, the promotion of overseas trade or
investment in aid and development programmes – all things Britain has
struggled with over the last decade.

We've been conning ourselves. Just as historians of the (royal-backed)
Commonwealth have revealed it to be a hollow organization, devoid of
any clear sense of purpose or direction and which does nothing to enable
Britain to exert real influence abroad, so the monarchy exists as a kind of
screen on to which the UK public has been encouraged to project ideas of
perpetual national greatness that simply don't bear the weight of scrutiny.
Given its loss of real-world economic and geopolitical power, Britain has
comforted itself by focusing on a rear-view mirror that offers a romantic,
rose-tinted vision of past glories.

Meanwhile, the world has moved on. In the last decade we've witnessed:
a return of warmongering authoritarian states; the rise of a new generation

of techno-capitalists equally determined to remake the global system in their image through the introduction of disruptive algorithms and forms of artificial intelligence that are already causing havoc in our societies, economies and political institutions; and an upsurge in anxiety about the damage we've done to the environment, which is making itself felt with far greater frequency in natural disasters such as flooding, drought and crop failure. All of these may in turn lead to war or the mass migration of human populations.

It should come as no surprise that a younger British generation that is more alert to these tectonic global shifts is not as enamoured with the monarchy as their parents and grandparents are or were. This internal disaffection with the monarchy was evident in the lead-up to coronation day. To the alarm of the right-wing media, opinion poll after opinion poll revealed that more than half of the country – including a significant majority of younger people – were uninterested in the royal event. On the day itself, the peak viewership for the British TV coverage of the service in Westminster Abbey was just 20 million, roughly two-thirds the size of the audience that tuned in for Queen Elizabeth's funeral and less than one third of the entire UK population.

The recent polls suggest there now exists a significant minority (about four in ten people) who are either indifferent to the monarchy or who are actively hostile to the idea of retaining a hereditary head of state. That this ambivalence and opposition is again most marked among the under-40s (and particularly among under-25s) is of grave concern to a royal household that has, as we shall see, succeeded since the nineteenth century in devising new public relations strategies that have ensured that the monarchy has remained relevant and meaningful to a large cross-section of society.

Let us be in no doubt. Contrary to some media reporting, the young have not always been as anti-monarchy as they are today. As recently as 2013, 72 per cent of 18- to 24-year-olds wanted to keep the monarchy. If we go further back to 1969 and the so-called years of teenage rebellion, we can find polls where almost two-thirds of 18- to 24-year-olds agreed with the statement that Elizabeth II was 'a symbol of Britain at its best'. The situation was very different in 2023, when one of the UK's leading polling organizations, YouGov, found ahead of King Charles's coronation that only 36 per cent of 18- to 24-year-olds wanted to keep the monarchy compared with 40 per cent who now want an elected head of state.

Again, most of the UK media have failed properly to get to grips with why there has been an upsurge in ambivalence and opposition towards the monarchy. In fact, these shifts in public opinion should not be surprising. While the House of Windsor has had its own problems – namely the duke and duchess of Sussex, Harry and Meghan, and to a greater extent the spectral figure of Andrew, second son of Queen Elizabeth – the young's disenchantment with the monarchy is symbolic of a wider disillusionment among this age group with the social, economic and political status quo in Britain. The 'Millennials' (born between 1981 and 1996) were the adult generation that bore the brunt of the lost opportunities that resulted from the 2008 financial crash. Saddled with sometimes staggering levels of university debt, when they've got good jobs they've found that their salaries haven't increased at anything like the rate they were increasing pre-crash. Meanwhile, house prices have continued to soar, delaying – sometimes permanently – home ownership for a significant section of society, many of whom have had to reconcile themselves to the fact that they'll never have access to the kind of assets or relative wealth enjoyed by so many of their parents' 'baby boomer' generation.

These trends are even more pronounced among members of 'Gen Z' (born between 1997 and 2012), who are much more politically radical than their Millennial elders. They are the generation who, because of the way older sections of society voted in the Brexit referendum in 2016, have been deprived of the opportunity to live and work in Europe. They are the generation who, during the Covid-19 pandemic, spent their daytimes enduring confined schooling by Zoom and their evenings following the activities of 'influencers' like their contemporary, the climate activist Greta Thunberg. And they are the generation who have started to move away from home to university towns and cities only to find they're unable to register with oversubscribed doctors' surgeries and, back in their rundown student homes, having to deal with a cost-of-living crisis brought on by the UK's failed long-term energy strategy and the knock-on effects of Russia's invasion of Ukraine in 2022.

It is this profound sense among the young that Britain is broken – a feeling that polls and studies have regularly captured by revealing a significant loss of confidence among the under-40s in the UK's democratic political system over the last 15 years – that helps to explain why these age groups are much less fussed about the continuation of the monarchy. It is not that the crown is necessarily to blame for the failed status quo (although, as we shall see, it absolutely is part of the problem). Rather, why should the younger generation care at all about a pampered royal elite who want for nothing, when their own lives are, by comparison, so difficult?

In the past, as people got older they tended to become more socially conservative and, the theory went, more *royalist*, turning their backs on their younger radical selves. But this is not the case with the under-40s today, who remain staunchly progressive in their politics. Indeed, helping to crystallize the sea-change in opinion against the monarchy are recent journalistic investigations from the *Sunday Times* and *Guardian* newspapers, which have lifted the lid on the monarchy's shady connections to Middle Eastern billionaires, the immense private wealth of the House of Windsor and the crown's historic links to the slave trade. The young are also more attuned to issues of historic moral injustice, and it is for this reason that they are concerned about the royal family's complicity in the project of empire. From the seventeenth century onwards, the monarchy directly financially benefited from the transportation and sale of enslaved people, while also promoting an extractive (and often violent) imperial system that witnessed huge amounts of colonial treasure and loot flood into Britain, some of which today sits in the crown jewels.

This heady mix of challenges threatens the monarchy's long-term survival and has been seen by anti-monarchists as grist to their mill. Spearheaded by the organization Republic, anti-monarchism seems to be growing more visible in the UK, despite having had no real presence in Britain since the late nineteenth century. The republican cause recently gained momentum as a result of two serious missteps at King Charles's coronation. The first was the failed 'Homage of the People', which revealed the limits of public enthusiasm for the new king. As publicized by Archbishop Justin Welby, all members of the televiewing public were invited as part of the coronation service to swear a pledge of allegiance to the monarch as part of a new ritual. But polls suggest it was roundly rejected by a significant majority, with just 12 per cent of the population pledging allegiance and opponents of the ritual claiming that it was a feudalistic throwback to a hidebound past where individual liberties were limited. The second, more dramatic misstep came about as a result of the over-zealous policing of the event, which saw several of Britain's leading republicans wrongfully arrested so that they were unable to join the peaceful protests against the coronation in London (while several other people who had nothing to do with the event were also wrongfully taken into custody and had their liberty taken away from them for hours). The arrests generated huge publicity for the anti-monarchist movement and

raised questions over the nature of British constitutional monarchy, where
the sovereign is meant to symbolize democratic freedoms, including the
right to free speech.

However, while recent news exposés and events may have hardened the
resolve of the opponents of monarchy to abolish the institution once and
for all, the greatest threat to the crown is not its loudest critics but rather
its slow slide into irrelevance. The last 15 years have witnessed significant
divisions open up in Britain. These divisions have partly come about as a
result of the coarsening of public debate and the polarization of opinion
as promoted by social media. What we are left with is the impression that
the country is undergoing a profound period of crisis. These divisions, as
we've already seen, separate the experiences of young from old. But they
also exist between rural and urban communities, between the south-east
and the rest of Britain, between progressives and conservatives, between
the faithful and faithless and, most fundamentally, between the rich and
the poor, particularly the so-called '1 per cent' super-rich and 'the rest'.
With the UK's political class seemingly unable or unwilling to develop
the kinds of long-term solutions needed to address these divisions, things
are – depressingly – only likely to get worse. And as the prevailing sense of
national malaise deepens, people will simply stop caring about the House
of Windsor. The key question that remains then is, how can the British
monarchy save itself?

In this book I adopt the position of critical friend – or progressive monarchist, as I prefer to call it – in order to argue that the British monarchy
can ensure its survival, overcoming its current difficulties, but only by
embarking on a programme of significant modernization. Radical renewal
might also create a monarchy fit for the twenty-first century, one that plays
a genuinely useful role in national life.

The argument for serious change rests on three ideas. First of all, that
there is significant historical precedent for this kind of royal overhaul.
About one third of this book is devoted to examining the period before
Queen Elizabeth's reign began in 1952 and reveals how, when and why
the crown embraced a modernizing agenda in the recent past. We shall
see how a new kind of monarchy emerged in response to wider social,
economic and political changes in the period stretching from the eighteenth century to the mid-twentieth century. And we'll also see how the

royal household (the monarch and members of their family, their courtiers and advisers) developed new public relations strategies in order to
make the monarchy's media image and role more appealing and meaningful to a wider public, thus ensuring the perpetuation of the dynasty.

By setting Elizabeth's reign in its historic context, we'll be well placed
to understand the second idea at the heart of this book: that while her 70
years on the throne were marked by incremental change and adaptation
to new circumstances, her reign was ultimately one that was characterized by complacency and, in some respects, even regression. At no point
did the queen embrace a progressive programme of modernization;
where major change did occur, it was in relation to her role as head of
the Commonwealth – a subject that lies largely beyond the British focus
of the present study, and which has already been expertly explored by
other historians. Rather, what I reveal in the one third of this book that
focuses on Elizabeth's time on the throne is a queen who, far from proactively innovating, sought instead to consolidate the model of kingship
bequeathed to her by her father, George VI, and her grandfather, George V.
The latter, in particular, had a formative influence on his successors and is
a key character in our story.

Elizabeth's consolidation of the crown's role and position saw British
national life become saturated with a particular version of monarchy that
traces its origins back to the mid-Victorian period and the pen of the
English journalist and political essayist Walter Bagehot. As we shall see, in
his writings Bagehot prescribed a formula for a new kind of monarchy for
an age that was undergoing rapid (and, for him, frightening) change. His
road map for the crown's transformation was, from the early twentieth
century, accepted almost as gospel: the monarchy would exercise limited
political influence, having given over the great bulk of its lawmaking
power to democratically elected ministers in return for a set of attenuated
(or secondary) forms of power. These attenuated powers included the
symbolic leadership of the modern nation: a) as articulated through big
ceremonial events that put on show elite royal power, traditional social
hierarchies and a version of British culture and history that centred on the
monarchy; and b) as exhibited by a royal family who now had a moral role
to play in society, dutifully engaging in service and philanthropy while
acting out a fantasy of idealized Christian family life.

It is Bagehot's royal formula – ceremonial, dutiful, philanthropic, familial, constitutional – that Elizabeth inherited in 1952 and which she made
the centrepiece of her long reign over Britain. These roles – along with an

everyday culture of monarchism made visible on passports, postage stamps and pillar boxes, banknotes and coins, in television documentaries and popular film dramatizations and on the souvenir spoons and tea towels that clutter people's drawers and are sold in their thousands in central London and at other historic sites throughout the UK – have ensured that the House of Windsor has enjoyed a salience as a focal point of identification in national life unrivalled by any other institution. However, the third main idea that this book is based on is that the conventional roles of the monarchy – ceremonial, dutiful, philanthropic, familial, constitutional – are no longer enough to keep it going. By unpicking each one of these in turn, we'll see how each comes with its own, innate historical baggage and set of problematic contradictions, all of which have the potential to further undermine King Charles's monarchy, losing it support among the British public.

It is for this reason that the remaining third of this book is dedicated to arguing that we need to rethink the functions of the monarchy in modern Britain. I make the case for a new kind of democratic kingship (one that is nevertheless rooted in the past) where the attenuated powers of the last 150 years fade away and where – contrary to Bagehot – the monarchy makes a return to the centre stage of constitutional politics. One of the reasons why Elizabeth did so little to modernize the monarchy was that at no point did she have to overcome the kind of existential crises that had faced both her father and her grandfather – George VI having had to navigate the fallout of the abdication crisis and George V the far-reaching consequences of the First World War. Given the scale of the challenge facing King Charles as a result of his predecessor's unimaginative reign, we now require a level of royal reinvention comparable to that which took place in the mid-nineteenth century, under Queen Victoria and Prince Albert, and again after 1918, as Bagehot's model of kingship was more fully implemented by the royal household.

The programme of modernization set out in this book, but in particular in Part Four and the Conclusion, goes well beyond simply downsizing a dysfunctional dynasty disgraced by the recent behaviour of some of its members. It will require concerted action from the monarchy. Queen Elizabeth's legacies are many, but they include a failure to deal with problems when they arose. In her later reign she perfected her long-running (and ineffective) management strategy of 'playing ostrich' – burying her head in the sand at the first sign of trouble, preferring instead to wait for the day when it might go away. This approach explains the queen's failure to keep in check the more outspoken members of her family, who subsequently developed reputations for saying (mostly) the wrong things in public.

Indeed, one of the reasons King Charles has been so cautious since acceding to the throne is that he fears the consequences of putting a foot wrong or, for that matter, overstepping the bounds of what is deemed constitutionally proper, given the criticism that he regularly received as a politically outspoken prince of Wales. But if he does not act now, he will fail to arrest the slide towards royal redundancy. He needs to redefine the raison d'être of his kingship and, in so doing, strip away the most troubling aspects of the monarchy as it exists today. And in this he will need our help.

Many of the current problems facing the crown stem from the fact that, for most of the twentieth century, the institution was not the subject of proper scrutiny, either from the British press, public or academics. Until recently, most history and biography written about the royal family was fawning and sycophantic in the extreme, and the monarchy subsequently became accustomed to not having its activities questioned. However, this has started to change. The challenge facing historians now is that a culture of secrecy was allowed to develop around the monarchy because of the deference once paid to it. This royal secrecy is a deeply embedded, but largely hidden, feature of our national life. As was recently reported in a special edition of the Index on Censorship, this culture of secrecy has had a suffocating effect on our knowledge of the past, restricting the files historians can access in the UK's National Archives in London and in the Royal Archives at Windsor Castle.

I've had the privilege of working in the Royal Archives with its brilliant team of archivists. But strict limits on what historians like me are allowed to see has a profoundly frustrating effect on our pursuit of the truth. It is worth saying that, until researchers and journalists are given full, unfettered access to documents relating to the late queen's reign, any serious appraisal of her behind-the-scenes role in government is impossible. As legal scholars and historians have noted, Queen Elizabeth was doubtless more politically active than she let on publicly – a fact that I discuss in Part Four. However, this crucial part of her reign will evade us until the archives are thrown open.

My point is that if the public want to know the truth, then we have to insist on an end to the culture of royal secrecy as part of a broad programme of renewal focusing on the monarchy but also on our political institutions and values. The secrecy that the crown has strategically woven around itself with the help of obliging politicians and civil servants – most recently when it secured an opt-out from the Freedom of Information Act which applies to almost every other part of government – is simply unsustainable in an age that values transparency and which feels alienated by official mis/disinformation. Historically speaking, the monarchy has reacted (reluctantly and belatedly) to big shifts in public opinion. We thus have a role to play in guiding the transformation of the crown over the coming years, not least because the king's hands are, to a certain extent, tied by the constitutional convention that he must avoid becoming directly entangled in politics. With his own voice constrained, it is up to us as a citizenry and our elected representatives first to demand and then, second, to create a monarchy fit for the future. As I suggest in the Conclusion, the alternative is the rise and rise of republicanism, the appeal of which will grow as a stale monarchy becomes increasingly out of touch with ordinary people's lives, which look set to get more difficult.

I argue in this book that the only kind of monarchy likely to regain the confidence of the Millennial and Gen Z generations (given their disillusionment with the wider political, social and economic status quo) is a reformed monarchy that puts the democratic values of integrity, accountability and transparency at the heart of its existence and ambitions. At the moment these values are not something we naturally associate with the House of Windsor. But we owe it to the next generation to demand better of both our royal rulers and the political system of which they are part. Only through a process where old royal shibboleths are exposed and then demolished, so that they may be replaced by a new type of monarchy which serves a genuinely useful purpose in championing the revival of our democratic institutions and culture, might crown and country undergo the kind of simultaneous renaissance required to restore Britain's fortunes as it hurtles at a speed that would terrify Bagehot into the mid-twenty-first century.

PART ONE

Ceremony, Spectacle and Tradition

There comes now yet another ancient ceremony. The great
officers of state, and the bishops and the nobles who have
borne the swords, the sceptres and other regalia move to the
steps of the throne, which stands upon its dais. This throne,
like the raised floor of the theatre itself, is descended from
those days 1,500 years ago, when the early kings sat for their
crowning upon a mound of earth, and were then lifted high
upon the shoulders of their nobles so that all the peoples
might see them. So today, the queen will ascend the steps
of her throne there symbolically to be lifted into it by the
Archbishop and the Earl Marshal in the sight today of a great
multitude of people. It is at the moment that she is seated
upon her throne that she takes possession of her kingdom and
she is then addressed by the Archbishop with the words of an
exhortation which has come down to us virtually unchanged
from the coronation of William the Conqueror.

RICHARD DIMBLEBY, COMMENTATING
ON THE BBC TELEVISION BROADCAST
OF THE 1953 CORONATION

Perhaps it is time to scale things back. It is often said of our
state ceremonial that we do these things better than anyone
else. And it's true. But is it still something to be proud of? I
wonder. We are after all no longer an empire, as we were when
much of this performance was invented. We are a middle-
ranking power struggling to define our place in a global world,
struggling to come to terms with the result of the Brexit

decision, struggling to hold the country together. Does the
glorification of monarchy, and the obsession with gossip about
the Royal Family, serve a useful purpose? Maybe it is time for
a less ostentatious display: a scaling back of the extravagance, a
redefining of the role.

DAVID DIMBLEBY, *KEEP TALKING:*
A BROADCASTING LIFE (LONDON, 2022)

ONE

Is it still something to be proud of?

Veteran broadcaster David Dimbleby spent much of his career at the BBC interviewing Britain's leading politicians and commentating on royal events. Now retired, his autobiography, which was published in 2022, provides us with his reflections on what he thinks are the problematic elements of 'our state ceremonial'. He notes how, far from having the kind of 'ancient' roots that his father, Richard Dimbleby, described in his coronation commentary back in 1953, much of today's royal 'performance' was 'invented' approximately 130 years ago in the heyday of empire, when Britannia still ruled the waves. The purpose of this ceremonial was to reflect national greatness, and the country's ostensible stability and unity around the focal point of the crown. But, as Dimbleby junior contemplates, is it still something to be proud of in the twenty-first century, when Britain's global power is so diminished and internally the country is so divided, not least over whether the monarchy should continue to exist? Is it time we scaled things back?

Ten days before his book was published, Dimbleby, who had agreed to return to the BBC to commentate as part of its TV coverage of the funeral of Elizabeth II, was left to close the nine-hour broadcast ahead of the private interment of the monarch's mortal remains at Windsor Castle. He described how a 'queen who, in her life and death belonged to so many people, will, for a moment, belong just to her family'. For those viewers who wanted romance, this was a fitting finale that bookended the 70-year reign of the television queen, Dimbleby echoing the sentiments of his father, Richard, back in 1953. His tone was more circumspect, but his words were just as carefully chosen, evoking the idea that a deep, almost eternal bond had existed between Elizabeth II and her subjects.

Then, weeks later, in a remarkable *volte-face*, Dimbleby broke cover. During an interview to promote his new book he condemned the way

Buckingham Palace officials had, behind the scenes, dictated what the BBC could and could not show as part of its television coverage of the funeral. He also expressed frustration with the way his former employer of more than 60 years had readily kowtowed to the royal household's demands. In his autobiography, he enlarges on what he terms the 'incestuous relationship' between the monarchy and the BBC. In a knowing reference to the way he and his father narrated seminal events that marked the reign of Elizabeth II, he describes how, far from being a 'disinterested observer of monarchy', Britain's national broadcaster was instead a 'vehicle for its promotion' and 'enhancement', 'glorifying in the theatre of ceremonial and even helping to create it'.

Such honesty about the relationship between the BBC and the House of Windsor is welcome and long overdue. Richard Dimbleby – a dyed-in-the-wool royalist who was deeply deferential – would never have pulled back the curtain to expose the nature of the palace media operation in the way his son has chosen to. According to David Dimbleby, his father 'relished' the 'details of ceremonial' and 'believed in the importance of tradition as a constructive and unifying force'. As commentator on the BBC's coronation programme on 2 June 1953, Dimbleby senior described the ceremony in ways that made the elaborate rituals intelligible to television audiences across Britain and the English-speaking world. It was the first time royal and religious officials had granted the BBC permission to televise the event live from inside Westminster Abbey.

However, as we can see from his 1953 coronation commentary, Richard Dimbleby's job extended beyond simply reporting on events. He was also a storyteller. His words imbued the ceremony with sacred meaning. He drew links to a semi-mythical past to evoke from viewers a heightened reverence for the crown and its new wearer. For him, kingship was deeply embedded in the spiritual life of the nation and its people, and had been ever thus.

As we saw during the 2023 coronation, esteemed journalists still have a tendency to lose their sense of proportion when it comes to discussing the monarchy. The BBC is not alone in its often fawning coverage of the royal family. The UK media has single-handedly done more to save the Windsors – providing them with immense visibility, while making them appear likeable and repeatedly stressing their importance to the country – than any other national institution over the last century. At the same time, the media has downplayed its central role in this process of popularization. The Times and Telegraph broadsheets, tabloids like the Mail and Express and, more recently, ITV and the satellite news channels have all helped to shore up royal power by unhesitatingly reproducing a version of Britain's past and present that has kingship at its core.

This national narrative has been most loudly championed on big royal occasions such as weddings, jubilees, coronations and funerals. Such events are defined by a kind of 'spectacle': they tend to combine religious ceremonial with colourful pageantry, including military parades, and members of the public participate, either as spectators (in the crowds or via mass media) or by engaging in more informal royal-themed activities at a local level. We are told repeatedly by the media that the ceremonies and pageantry that unfold as part of these events have deep historical roots (à la Dimbleby senior), although, as we shall see, it is not as simple as that. We are also told that these events witness the British uniting around the focal point of the monarchy; but as the public response to Elizabeth's funeral revealed, there are sections of society that remain immune to the pull of royalty.

The estimated viewing figures for the funeral – with 29 million people out of a total UK population of 67.5 million tuning in – reveal that more than half of the country did not watch, despite the media continually stressing the importance of the occasion and the government granting a special bank holiday so that people could watch. The 29 million figure was also smaller than the 31 million viewers who watched the 2020 UEFA Euro final between England and Italy, and the 32 million who watched Princess Diana's funeral in 1997.

Despite these viewing figures, opinion polls suggested over the course of her reign that Queen Elizabeth was widely respected by a large majority of her British subjects (her approval ratings rarely dipped below 70 per cent). Likewise, since coming to the throne, Charles III has enjoyed a lift in his popularity, according to both YouGov and Ipsos MORI. And yet, although individual royals may be quite popular, attitudes to the institution of monarchy are much more mixed, with the UK population divided along generational and political lines. According to recent polls, about two-thirds of the public support the continuation of the monarchy; about one quarter of all Britons (and more than half of all 18- to 24-year-olds) would prefer their country to become a republic – a not insubstantial 17 million of the aforementioned 67.5 million; and the rest are undecided.

The problem here is that, because of the respect accorded the royal family by most media organizations, public expressions of ambivalence or opposition towards the monarchy are not properly reported on, especially during big royal events. News outlets that dare to offer more sober or critical coverage (the *Observer*, the *Independent*, the *Guardian* and Channel 4) tend to be either centrist, or left of centre, in their politics. These perspectives often struggle to cut through to the public because of the market dominance of the royalist media providers.

As a result of these silences, royal occasions tend to be presented almost unquestioningly in positive terms and as a normal part of national life. Yet many non-British people will tell you that they find the UK's apparent obsession with royal spectacle bemusing – if also entertaining. This extends to the other European monarchies too. Although some, such as the Netherlands, have annual holidays to mark royal anniversaries and publicly celebrate moments in the lives of their royal families like weddings, there is nothing on the scale of Britain's celebration of the House of Windsor.

The media reporting of royal events has a 'centring' effect on the monarchy. Because of the emphasis news editors and journalists place on the importance of royal occasions and the way they appear to draw massive public interest, media audiences are left with the distinct impression that the crown exists as a singular focal point of national interest and identification. The monarchy has become absolutely central to the way the British have been encouraged to think of themselves as a national community. And this is not new: as we shall see later on, it is a phenomenon that dates back to the nineteenth century and formed part of a deliberate policy of nation-building in imperial Britain around the crowned head of state.

One of the main arguments of Part One of this book is that the UK media could do a much better job of reporting royal events. Reporters could exercise greater sensitivity towards the diversity of public opinion on monarchy. More newspapers and broadcasters could do like David Dimbleby and acknowledge their complicity in promoting royalist narratives. And harder questions could be asked about the role the royals have come to play in other national events and anniversaries, such as the annual Remembrance Day service and big sporting occasions. With the help of the mass media, these moments have become a national platform for the House of Windsor, once again working to 'centre' the crown at the heart of the national community.

However, royal spectacle hasn't simply been manufactured 'from above' by a monarchy and media that are colluding to indoctrinate the British public. These events do draw significant public interest – even if that interest is exaggerated by the media. Many members of the public do express genuine support for the monarchy and the royal family. The 29 million people who watched the queen's funeral represent a significant minority of the entire population, and their desire to participate needs to be taken seriously. Indeed, on closer inspection, it is clear that these events are often as much about 'us', the British people, as they are about kingship.

For example, many readily joined friends, family or neighbours to mark the 2022 platinum jubilee and 2023 coronation, celebrating with parties, bunting, costumes and games, among other things. The same events also witnessed large crowds pour into London and Windsor to be together in these moments in order to celebrate the monarchy and have fun. And a similar desire to participate – to be part of *something* – was in evidence among the spectators and TV viewers present for the queen's funeral, as well as among the quarter of a million people who joined 'The Queue' in order to see the queen lying in state in Westminster Hall.

As we shall see, there is historical precedent for all of this, stretching back more than a century. The long-standing desire to come together and connect with people is, without doubt, the most powerful argument for retaining some kind of spectacle as we move into the post-Elizabethan age. In our modern (sometimes emotionally constipated) democracy, where social divisions and animosities are more visible than has been the case in decades, there is a strong case for having some symbol or idea that might bring us all together. Having a shared focus, and a chance to celebrate or commemorate it collectively, means there is a common thread that could work to connect the British as a people. Developing an understanding of ourselves by having something that brings us into emotional communion is important, especially if, as part of the democratic process, we are to accept others' opinions and preferences when they do not align with our own.

But should that unifying symbol or idea be the monarchy given its uncertain future? If so, what form should royal spectacle take in order to promote such a symbol? Should there be an emphasis on Anglican ritual, as is currently the case, when the latest UK census data reveals that Christianity is now a minority religion? And what about the echoes of nineteenth-century social hierarchy and empire that remain so central to the big royal events of today?

In this section I argue that royal spectacle needs rethinking urgently. The ceremonial and pageantry of the Second Elizabethan Age were problematic precisely because both were descended from a Victorian era when bombastic royal spectacle was used by a powerful elite to make clear their social authority to the powerless. Not only this, but the vision of a nation united around the crown as engineered and communicated by the media on these occasions has left us with a misleading impression of who we, the British, are as a people.

For too long royalist news outlets have celebrated the monarchy as a symbol of progress and national success, thus smoothing over much of the complex history that in reality defines us. To echo David Dimbleby, the Britain of today is a 'middle-ranking power' that is struggling to maintain its relevance globally. At the same time, the 2016 referendum on EU membership opened up wounds that had been festering for decades and the country now finds itself deeply divided. Meanwhile London, the ceremonial backdrop for so much royal spectacle and display, is a capital city that has been corrupted by the influence of foreign oligarchs and dirty money.

Dramatic change is required. Only by significantly modernizing royal spectacle so that it reflects the diversity, realities and aspirations of twenty-first-century Britain – while retaining the emphasis on emotional communion – might it play a positive, healing role in a sickly society that is crying out for a cure.

TWO

Consecrated obstruction

Spectacle has been used by the monarchy and other elite institutions to promote a vision of the UK that is distinctly royalist in character. The crown has been 'centred' as the unifying force that brings the country together with the sovereign, as head of state, presenting themselves as dutiful servant of their people. However, the monarchy wasn't always viewed as a national symbol in this way. If we go back 300 years to the early Hanoverian period (so-called because of the German princes of Hanover who sat on the British throne from 1714), we discover a king and royal family who were neither very visible nor very popular.

Until the late 1700s, most ordinary Britons would have known little about their royal family and it was highly unlikely they would have ever set eyes on royalty at a public event. This compares to the one-third of today's UK population who reported seeing or meeting Elizabeth II during her lifetime. And, of course, everybody knew who she was from photographs or their TV screens. But back then there were very few opportunities for the common people to engage with the sovereign and royal family. The monarchy was not a 'public-facing' institution. It did not take an active interest in ordinary people's lives; nor did it see the need to outwardly put on a show so that it might be viewed as an important symbol.

The monarchy's need to maintain its relevance in order to survive changed all of this. The crown realized that its existence was only assured if it made itself meaningful to enough British people and so took important steps to popularize its role and public image. Ceremonial, pomp and pageantry all became increasingly key to this process of popularization. Spectacle gave new meaning to an institution that, for much of its history, was invisible and far removed from the lives of ordinary people. Today Charles III and the royals recognize that they must engage with their subjects if they are to ensure public approval. Indeed, there is arguably no institution in national life that is so constantly active in its aim to win hearts and minds than the monarchy. In this respect, we must view the crown as fundamentally reliant for its survival on the goodwill of a majority of the people of Great Britain and Northern Ireland.

To explain how we got here we must travel back in time 250 years, to the late eighteenth century, to see how the monarchy reacted to wider developments in the media and the nation's political affairs. In this period the court became increasingly sensitive to public opinion as reflected in the pages of Britain's nascent national newspaper industry. The then king, George III, the first of the Hanoverian dynasty to speak English as his first language, was not a popular figure during his early reign. Writing in the 1860s, the journalist Walter Bagehot described him as a kind of 'consecrated obstruction': despite 'good intentions' and his interest in the 'business of his country', 'his mind was small, his education limited, and he lived in a changing time.'

The press attacked George's early interventions in politics and the way his government alienated the Thirteen American Colonies, which then fought for and won their independence from the British empire in the American Revolutionary War (1775–83). At a time when the king still wielded considerable political influence, this inevitably led to an upsurge in criticism of the monarch and his ministers. However, the fact that George felt confident enough in 1809 to stage a golden jubilee (the first of its kind, though very small by the standards of today) to mark the 50th year of his reign suggests a change in fortune and indicates that he understood how a celebration could cement support for his monarchy. By this point he was an elderly figure to whom sections of the public had warmed, not least because he had associated himself with the nation's war effort against Napoleonic France. The Times typically lauded how the 'aged and venerable king was celebrated by all ranks of people' who expressed satisfaction 'in the highest degree' with him.

King George's sons ruled after him. First came George IV, who, as prince regent to his ailing father and then as king, was lampooned by the press and in satirical cartoons for his self-indulgent lifestyle and debauchery. Then it was the turn of William IV. He acceded to the throne in late middle age and, quite unlike his older brother, was an abstemious and dutiful fellow. Indeed, he was arguably too serious a king for the times.

He was diligent and interested in affairs of state, but he preferred to keep out of the public eye and his penny-pinching impulses meant he had little appetite for shows of ceremonial splendour.

Today William is remembered for the way he precipitated a political crisis. The middle-class business owners of Britain's newly industrializing towns and cities had been campaigning vigorously for more power and a louder voice in national politics. Only after much obstruction and wrangling did the king concede that things needed to change. This decision generated the momentum for the constitutional updates embodied in the landmark 1832 Reform Act, which extended voting rights to many bourgeois and petty bourgeois men across Britain.

However, the king's initial intransigence and attempts to block these democratic changes left his reputation damaged. When his niece, then just 18 years old, succeeded him as sovereign on his death in 1837, she inherited a crown that was out of step with the shifting public mood and which had been undermined by years of scandal and political misjudgement.

The often inflexible and egotistical Queen Victoria did not initially spot the threat to her throne. But in 1840 she married Albert, another German princeling, this time of the House of Saxe-Coburg and Gotha, and he, as prince consort, rapidly diagnosed the ills that afflicted the institution into which he had wed. (This has often been the case with the British royal family over the last 200 years. Foreigners who have married into the dynasty and brought with them an outsider's perspective have been quickest to detect the malaise that periodically besets the monarchy and they have then set about addressing the situation.)

As we shall see in later chapters, under Albert's stewardship the monarchy became more active in public life and embraced a more impartial political role from which it could work with politicians of all shades – not just those who shared royalty's aristocratic heritage and interests. Together he and the queen also refocused the image of the monarchy around the 'family on the throne', something that carried – and continues to carry – powerful emotional resonance in society. However, for our purposes here, it was the prince consort who was the guiding light in transforming the British monarchy from something that was inward-looking and distant into a public-facing institution fronted by an increasingly recognizable set of 'royal personalities'.

Albert, Victoria and other members of their family began travelling around the country in order to engage with local communities in new ways: for example, by opening civic building projects such as railway stations and hospitals. As part of these trips, Britain's towns and cities drew up increasingly elaborate itineraries which involved some kind of public ritual and procession. The royal visitors embraced these innovations and could soon be seen travelling along crowd-lined streets in open-top carriages designed to give the locals a full view of royalty in action.

These experiments in what the historian John Plunkett has termed 'civic publicness' suggest that royal spectacle grew semi-organically out of local political cultures where there was an appetite for it among sections of the public. Indeed, a very strong argument that can be made in support of the monarchy's embrace of pomp and pageantry is that it is a response to the fact that we want and appreciate such performances. Since the mid-nineteenth century royal spectacle, such as that on display during the Victorian civic tours, has evolved as part of a palace PR strategy that has seen the monarchy use new types of interaction to connect with members of the British public who enjoy the attention they get from the royals.

This type of civic spectacle was notably enhanced by the arrival of the illustrated press. With their engraved images, mid-century periodicals like the *Illustrated London News* made the monarchy more immediately visible to British readers than ever before. In fact, it was this new emphasis on royal visibility that helps us to explain why, having enjoyed a resurgence in its popularity in the 1840s and 1850s, the monarchy again became an object of criticism after Albert suddenly died in 1861, aged just 42, from typhoid fever. Bereft of her consort and closest companion, Victoria entered a prolonged period of mourning, which rendered her invisible to the public eye.

THREE

The seasonable addition of nice and pretty events

It was against a backdrop of mounting complaints about Victoria's neglect of public life that Walter Bagehot penned a series of essays in the periodical *Fortnightly Review* in which he sought to explain how, ideally, the constitution should function in order to ensure effective government. One of Bagehot's crucial elements of the constitution was the monarchy. He argued that, in contrast to elected politicians, who were responsible for devising new laws and running the country through the 'efficient' machinery of state, the crown must instead embody the ceremonial part of the constitution as the 'dignified' symbol around which the nation could gather.

An important event that Bagehot claimed had seen this kind of national coming-together was the wedding of the heir to the throne (later Edward VII) to Princess Alexandra of Denmark. He described how 'no feeling could seem more childish than the enthusiasm of the English at the marriage of the Prince of Wales'. According to the journalist, royal spectacle could serve a serious purpose: 'the seasonable addition of nice and pretty events' enabled the public briefly to feel as though they had participated in the lives of the royal family, creating a shared emotional experience that could unite crown and people.

Bagehot's work theorized that royal spectacle could have a positive nation-building effect on Britain, bringing together all classes and types of people in celebration (or commemoration in the case of funerals) of a national institution that acted as a common focal point. Today the monarchy's website describes how the sovereign is not just the head of state but also the 'head of nation' – 'a focus for national identity, unity and pride' – i.e., the dignified symbol at the centre of Britain.

As we shall see later on, this is not the only part of Bagehot's work that the palace has embraced, reworked and now positively espouses as conventional wisdom. However, on closer inspection we can detect in his essays a much more cynical argument about the nation-building potential of monarchy. And it is this aspect of his analysis that the current royal family would prefer we quietly forget, precisely because it points to the more problematic nature of the monarchy's symbolic role.

The 1860s was a decade unsettled by seismic political, economic and social changes. In the same year that Bagehot's essays on the constitution were published as a collection for the first time, the German philosopher Karl Marx released a searing critique of the nature of mid-nineteenth-century capitalism. *Das Kapital* (1867) distilled the radical thinker's ideas on how the industrial revolution had led to the oppression of the working classes, their labour exploited by a small, greedy and powerful elite.

Marx's criticism of the established economic order had been in circulation for almost two decades already and had helped to energize a growing trade union movement that loudly challenged the status quo by giving voice to workers' demands for the first time. Meanwhile, other political writers such as Bagehot, though progressive by the standards of the day, feared the democratic energies that were being unleashed among what they viewed as the restless, angry masses. It was essential to slow political change by any means possible. Thus, for Bagehot, the monarchy became the symbol to numb the political senses of Britain's labouring classes. He described the monarchy as a 'disguise' that could distract workers from the real business of politics. He thought that, if the masses became emotionally wedded to the monarchy as a digni-fied national institution, such a connection might work to restrain their calls for greater political representation through voter enfranchisement (as seen in the 1867 Second Reform Act) and deter any revolutionary impulses within the population.

In short, Bagehot's vision for the Victorian monarchy was, above all else, about exerting greater control over the nation's increasingly agitated polity. It bears a striking resemblance to the bread and circuses strategy used by Roman emperors to keep unruly citizens content and, therefore, out of politics. Ironically, the big royal celebrations that were orchestrated in the last decades of the nineteenth and first decades of the twentieth century would take the idea of bread and circuses almost literally.

The golden and diamond jubilees of Queen Victoria in 1887 and 1897, followed by the coronations of her son Edward VII in 1902, and grand-son George V in 1911, were staged as major national events characterized more than ever before by ceremony, pageantry and public involvement. Although the main festivities unfolded in London, across Britain village

and town committees were set up to organize events and enable participation. Some of the main beneficiaries of local celebrations included
old-age pensioners and children, who got to enjoy special tea parties,
among other activities. And, to aid the merry-making, the government
extended the opening hours of public houses to ensure a good time was
had among their mostly working-class patrons.

Some of this hasn't changed in more than 100 years. Children continue
to be a focus of official and unofficial activities organized to celebrate
major royal occasions, such as the 2022 'Design a Jubilee Crown' challenge – a subtle but nevertheless significant way of imprinting on young
Britons the centrality of monarchy to the UK. Pub opening hours were
also extended for the queen's platinum jubilee, ensuring it was marked by
many with booze-fuelled revelry – a process repeated for the coronation
of Charles III across a special bank holiday weekend.

Opening hours were not extended for the funeral of Elizabeth II: it
would have been deemed disrespectful. But this didn't stop many, particularly younger, people from taking full advantage of the extra Monday
holiday designated for the event in order to party harder than usual over the
preceding weekend (a fact quietly ignored by deferential media outlets).
It was also notable that attempts to stop the British public from having
fun during the official period of mourning met with visceral opposition,
including the ill-judged decision (that was ultimately reversed) by the
holiday resort Center Parcs to evict guests for the day of the funeral.

This social activity at the grassroots level again points to the way that royal
events only work when *we* participate. It is ordinary people who form the
local committees that organize events, who host the street parties and
the barbecues, who bake the coronation cakes and who get out into their
communities (as per royal instruction) for 'The Big Help Out'. Members
of the public are the crucial, willing actors involved in the celebration of
kingship.

However, we must not overlook the role of elite actors who have, since
the Victorian era, aimed to co-opt the public into acts of celebration and
commemoration where monarchy has been presented as the symbolic
centrepiece of the modern British nation. As royal biographer Jane Ridley
has noted, Edward VII was both a key performer in and the architect of
royal spectacle. He did much to transform events, including the state

opening of parliament, into major public set pieces designed to convey the majesty of kingship and the power of the British state to crowds of spectators and media audiences across the country.

In his experiments with new forms of spectacle, the king was encouraged by the courtier Lord Esher – a friend of the royal family and the organizer of every major state occasion from Victoria's diamond jubilee in 1897 to Edward's funeral in 1910. Esher had a flare for staging pomp and ceremonial and saw royal spectacle as the vehicle through which he could elevate a romanticized vision of Britain that centred on monarchy. His motivations may not have been as cynical as Bagehot's, but he and Edward certainly shared the journalist's concerns regarding the danger posed by a politicized working class and believed the monarchy had an important symbolic role to play in stabilizing a rapidly changing society.

The great state occasions organized by Esher with the support of Edward (first as prince of Wales, then as king) helped to popularize the monarchy through ritual and pageantry. Older forms of ceremonial were revived and updated. And in some cases so-called 'traditions' were invented from scratch. What emerged was a much more sophisticated kind of royal spectacle that drew special attention to ancient precedent, customs and the nation's Christian values. These events played to huge crowds in central London, but were also made accessible to the growing reading public via the national press, including new 'popular' newspapers such as the *Daily Mail* and *Daily Express*, founded in 1896 and 1900 respectively.

A number of historians have highlighted the role played by Esher in reimagining the nation-building role of royal spectacle. For David Cannadine, ceremonial made clear to the public the monarchy's position at the apex of Britain's socio-political order. This was achieved by putting hierarchy on display. For example, in 1902 the eighteenth-century gold state coach was put to new use when for the first time it transported Edward VII from Buckingham Palace to Westminster Abbey as part of a grandiose coronation procession that emphasized royal power. This moment was designed to impress (and intimidate) spectators through its opulent elevation of the crowned head of state.

For the historian William Kuhn, Esher's ceremonies were 'visual sensations' that 'heightened the monarchy's prestige' and similarly 'reinforced ideas about social hierarchy'. For example, the route for Victoria's diamond jubilee procession was extended to include working-class districts in south London for the first time. Esher and the official jubilee committee believed that royal spectacle was an antidote to 'radical agitation' and would, in

Kuhn's words, impress on 'the vulgar and the uneducated, foreigners and Catholics, colonials and black men' the centrality of monarchy to Britain.

As Cannadine noted, these royal events were also imperial occasions. They did not just showcase royal authority; they also put on display the power of Britain's empire. Edward's coronation procession saw marching bands and brightly coloured regiments from the colonies and dominions parade through the streets of London, heralding the king. This self-confident assertion of the military strength of the imperial state reminded onlookers that the monarch's power extended beyond British shores to a vast overseas empire on which the sun never set.

This kind of bombastic exhibition of military might had first been trialled at the diamond jubilee in 1897. Twenty years earlier, in 1877, Victoria had been given the title Empress of India, formalizing her role as the figurehead of empire. When she died, in 1901, Edward succeeded his mother as king and emperor. The inclusion of imperial military parades in the royal events of these years thus reflected the desire of the monarchy and leading British politicians, such as Joseph Chamberlain, to cement the symbolic link between the crown and the imperial state in order to make clear to an imperial public the empire's international strength and success.

Of course, there was another intended audience too: the presence of foreign dignitaries at the coronations and royal funerals of this period, most notably Europe's most powerful kings and queens, as well as the leading statesmen from the republican USA and France, meant that royal spectacle was used to showcase the British empire's ostensible power and unity at a time when other nations, such as Germany, were looking to challenge Britain's global dominance.

In its mission to dazzle, the monarchy was ably assisted by other government figures who oversaw the redesign of central London. As a result, the city became a fitting stage for grand royal-imperial spectacle. From 1906 to 1913 the Queen Victoria Memorial Committee (chaired by Esher) masterminded the building of Admiralty Arch and the widening of The Mall, giving London a ceremonial parade route comparable to those that already existed in Paris, Rome and Vienna. Most importantly, the committee oversaw the creation of the Victoria Memorial and the refronting of the east wing of Buckingham Palace. This led to the construction of a new large balcony, where, for the first time in 1902, following Edward's coronation, the royal family appeared to the cheers and applause of a large crowd of spectators.

The stage managers of royal spectacle welcomed the input of other individuals when it might have a positive nation-building impact. For example, Esher was prepared to accept that London's political elite, including the lord mayor, participate in these royal events, but only on the condition that they dress in spectacular faux Tudor costume, thus adding to the sense of history and tradition. Similarly, for the religious ceremonies arranged for Victoria's jubilees, the officiating clergy dressed in more elaborate, colourful clothing in order to enhance the mystery and theatre of the events. As Cannadine notes, this formed part of a wider professionalization of religious ritual in this period that was designed, in part, to wow the working classes and instil in them a reverence for the status quo. Shortly after the golden jubilee in 1887, the archbishop of Canterbury, E. W. Benson, notably recorded how 'everyone feels that the socialist movement has had a check'.

The main problem with royal spectacle in the twenty-first century is that it remains steeped in the symbolic trappings of the late Victorian and Edwardian monarchies, which used ceremonial and pageantry for the purposes of shock and awe. Although colonial troops no longer parade through London in exhibitions of imperial military might, these events do carry the echoes of empire, with regiments from the Commonwealth realms participating. Perhaps most notably, the British armed forces continue to play a central role in royal events. In so doing, they project an image of national strength that disguises what the head of the British Army, General Sir Patrick Sanders, described in 2023 as the 'dire state' of the UK's military capability.

Think back to Queen Elizabeth's funeral procession through Westminster. Her coffin was borne on a gun carriage drawn by a division of highly drilled naval officers in a custom that dates back to Queen Victoria's funeral in 1901. This was British military precision at its best. Alternatively, recall the glittering military parade that escorted Charles III on his return to Buckingham Palace after his coronation. It was an impressive demonstration of marching prowess, but at the same time a strikingly smaller affair than in 1953, and a reminder of how far the number of British service personnel has fallen since then (it was 870,000 seven decades ago, compared with 150,000 today).

Just as misleading is the emphasis that organizers and the media routinely place on the 'traditional' nature of these events. The type of spectacle popularized more than 125 years ago by Edward VII and Esher made visible and meaningful a royal-centred narrative of the nation's past. The media helped to propagate this narrative, stressing that the British shared a common national identity that was centred on the monarchy and anchored in historic forms of ceremony. In particular, royal elites and their allies used pomp and ritual to try to inculcate respect for the established order among an ill-educated, politically restless proletariat who they feared might challenge the status quo.

The fact that kingship remains key to the way many members of the public continue to think about national tradition suggests that this royal-centred narrative has had some impact. But, as we've seen, many so-called royal 'traditions' are nothing of the kind. Some were plucked from the past and deliberately updated with a modern audience in mind; others were invented from scratch. We saw the results of this in 2022, with the official proclamation ceremonies of Charles III, two days after Queen Elizabeth's death. The brightly coloured medieval tunics and felt hats with plumes of feathers, the heraldry and trumpets – much of this 'ancient' performance was in fact perfected during the first half of the twentieth century in order to convey a sense of historical authenticity to the new media audiences of the photographic press and newsreels.

Britain's history is so much richer and more varied than the embellished story of kingship that takes centre stage on these occasions. But the disproportionate level of interest that the monarchy continues to command from the British media means that our national conversation about our past has been distorted. Perhaps most disturbing of all is the way the emphasis on tradition, as manifested through royal spectacle, continues to help legitimize elite power and outmoded forms of social hierarchy.

Put simply, royal spectacle projects an anti-egalitarian vision of modern Britain. The gold state coach – the most nauseating symbol of the immense inherited wealth that separates the Windsors from so many of their subjects – continues to be one of the main focuses of big royal celebrations. And, although there have been attempts to make events like the funeral of Elizabeth II and the coronation of Charles III more inclusive by ensuring a diverse range of 'ordinary' members of the public are invited to reflect multicultural Britain, the fact that so many peers ended up playing ceremonial roles at both events demonstrates how royal ritual remains steeped in the hierarchies of the past.

FOUR

An alien and uninspiring court?

During the reign of the late Queen Elizabeth's grandfather, George V, much of the symbolism of his predecessors' reigns was consolidated and new forms of royal spectacle pioneered in order to strengthen the vision of a nation united around monarchy. The need to embrace innovative forms of spectacle that promoted a new set of messages stemmed from the fact that the king's 26-year reign was marked by a series of crises that raised questions about the crown's survival and in turn required the royal household to search out new roles so that the monarchy maintained its relevance.

When George succeeded to the throne, at the age of 44, in 1910, political unrest on the Celtic fringes threatened to undermine the idea of British unity. Irish home rule (self-government) had been a thorny issue in national politics for most of the king's life (see Part Four). Politicians from Britain's Liberal Party had tried to accommodate demands for greater Irish autonomy by legislating to devolve power to Dublin and, when that failed, by actively reimagining Britain's national identity so that it was less Anglo-centric and more inclusive in character. A phrase used by many in the party at the time was 'unity in diversity'.

This theme of 'unity in diversity' was promoted by one of the most prominent politicians among the Liberals in this period, the Welshman David Lloyd George. After the king's accession, Lloyd George turned his attention to what he saw as another destabilizing issue in the Celtic fringe: the disestablishment of the state-backed Church of England in religiously nonconformist Wales. In keeping with the Liberals' commitment to unity in diversity, Lloyd George wanted to incorporate Welsh cultural identity more fully into an inclusive vision of Britishness. And to achieve this he persuaded the new king to stage a formal investiture of his eldest son and heir, the future Edward VIII, as prince of Wales at Caernarfon Castle in the north of the country.

The historical record suggests that the first prince of Wales was Edward II, who was born at Caernarfon in 1284. His father, Edward I of England, had recently completed his conquest of Wales and presented his infant son to the Welsh chieftains as the human embodiment of the new union between the two nations. From this moment onwards, kings of England gave their eldest sons the hereditary title of prince of Wales. But there had never been a formal investiture ceremony at Caernarfon; hence, in July 1911, there was no blueprint to follow.

Into this vacuum an eclectic group of stage-managers, ranging from the monarch and his advisers to churchmen, journalists and local and national politicians, poured forth their ideas for the form such a royal spectacle could take. The result was invented tradition par excellence. The investiture was staged as an early modern pageant – more akin to the kind of performance one would expect to see in the age of Henry VIII, given its extravagant use of ermine-lined costumes and tarpaulin pavilions, than in the twentieth century and a monarchy that led one of the world's greatest industrial powers.

The new medium of film ensured that the investiture played to cinema audiences across Britain, as well as to large crowds that gathered in Caernarfon to witness it in person. This had been the king's intention when he granted newsreel companies permission to film the event. (Thankfully for historians, clips of the investiture survive and can be found online.) Particular attention was paid by the media to the young prince, then aged 17, who later described how he hated dressing up in the satin breeches and purple velvet surcoat made for the event. In his embarrassed description of the 'preposterous rig' he was forced to wear, Edward made very clear early on his disdain for the ritualized 'tradition' that had become so central to the monarchy's public image.

For those reporting on events, though, the young prince was the human symbol of Wales. He briefly spoke in the Welsh language as part of an elaborate ceremony that placed emphasis on 'ancient' aspects of Wales's cultural heritage, including poetry, song, nonconformist religion and a deep spiritual connection to the land's mythical history. Thus a vision of modern Wales that was firmly rooted in an imagined past was staged and made meaningful to a wider public who were encouraged to celebrate the inclusiveness of a British nation that was made up of a group of distinctive countries apparently united in their diversity.

Royal spectacle has been used to give expression to the identities of all four parts of Britain and to the idea of a multifaceted Britishness. As with the Welsh investiture, there is much performative mythmaking here. For example, from the moment Prince Albert bought Balmoral Castle in 1852 and he and Queen Victoria began regularly holidaying there, the royal family have adorned tartan kilts and led a Scottish-themed existence whenever north of the border. Today royal participation in annual events such as Holyrood Week (known locally as Royal Week) and the Highland Games forms part of a deliberate strategy by the Windsors to publicly convey an interest in Scotland's culture and an affinity with its people.

It is precisely because of the fuzzy nature of Britain's imagined national past as envisioned by royal events that the crown and its allies have been able to reconfigure royal spectacle to address the specific needs of the day over the last 150 years. However, over time some events have quietly fallen into abeyance, owing to a concern within the royal household that they might backfire if restaged in the present.

One such example is the prince of Wales's investiture, which was last reimagined in 1969 for the then Prince Charles. As in 1911, the event presented the monarchy as the link which connected the rest of Britain to Wales, with the spectacle articulating a sense of Welsh history and cultural identity. But the 20-year-old prince also served another purpose, specific to the moment. He embodied the monarchy's hopes that such an event might offset the recent rise of a Welsh nationalism that resented the control exerted by Westminster politicians over Wales and rejected the monarchy as a symbol of English power within the union.

Like his great-uncle Edward, Charles spoke Welsh as part of the ceremony, having learned some of the language during the term he spent at Aberystwyth University in order to prepare for the investiture. Whereas in 1911 Lloyd George was key to orchestrating the event, both as a politician and as constable of Caernarfon Castle, the Welshman in charge in 1969 was Queen Elizabeth's brother-in-law (the husband of Princess Margaret), Lord Snowdon. A natural when it came to royal stage-management, he possessed an eye for colour and design because of his professional career as a photographer and film-maker. He crafted a picturesque spectacle that retained 'traditional' pomp and pageantry, including a dazzling procession through Caernarfon and an ermine-lined cape for the prince. However, he also introduced modern twists befitting the late 1960s.

For example, whereas tarpaulin and heraldry had dominated the scene in 1911, now the castle's imposing interior was stripped back, and it had at its centre a circular stage and seats carved from Welsh slate for the principal performers. Above this minimalistic platform hovered a Perspex canopy designed to keep the royals dry in the event of rain and to enable a better view of proceedings for television audiences. The prince, meanwhile, was allowed to wear military uniform beneath his cloak, and his investiture coronet was of a uniquely modern style, having been specially crafted for the occasion by architect and goldsmith Louis Osman (Fig 1).

The updated glitter and ceremony met with some approval among the Welsh population, opinion polls suggesting that three-quarters of the country supported the royal investiture. Of course, the extra day off granted by many businesses and schools to their workers and pupils helped to generate enthusiasm as well. However, the investiture was most notable for the way it became a lightning rod for nationalist protests against the monarchy and the British state. This included a failed bomb attack – the latest in a series of such incidents staged by Welsh nationalists through the 1960s.

As the historian Martin Johnes has suggested, Charles handled the pressure admirably, saying the right things in public in order to placate opposition feeling. In a BBC interview at the time, he said, 'I don't blame people for demonstrating like that … I've hardly been to Wales, and you can't expect people to be over-zealous about the fact of having a so-called English Prince come amongst them.' Charles's outward humility and thoughtful recognition of Wales's political concerns would continue to serve him well during his long tenure as prince of Wales. Though nationalist sentiment would find a more formal outlet with the steady rise of the independence party Plaid Cymru, the prince gained a reputation for taking a serious interest in Welsh society.

The same cannot yet be said for his eldest son and heir, William, the new prince of Wales. Beyond fleeting visits to the Welsh Senedd (parliament) and Principality Stadium in Cardiff to publicly cheer on the national rugby team, he has shown little interest in the country's politics or culture, and has faced similar criticism to his father for his 'Englishness'. This helps to explain why William has announced publicly that he will not undergo any formal investiture ceremony. In the twenty-first century the British monarchy is much more attuned to public opinion than ever before and deliberately limits engagements that might lead to opposition protests against the crown. Thus this particular piece of royal spectacle has, for now, fallen by the wayside.

We must ask ourselves: how justifiable is the allocation of royal titles like 'prince of Wales' when the recipient lacks an authentic connection to the region in question? If William and his wife, Catherine, the new princess of Wales, were truly determined to shore up their links to the Welsh people, they could do worse than relocate their family to Cardiff. Polling data suggests they would meet with a warm reception from a large majority of their Welsh subjects. But, as with the UK-wide picture, they would meet with less enthusiasm from younger people, who are not as enamoured with the tokenistic royal symbolism of a bygone age. Unfortunately for Welsh monarchists, it seems that at this stage this is a risk the couple are unwilling to take.

One thing is for certain: the example of the Welsh investiture reveals that the monarchy can, should it so choose, easily transform royal pomp and pageantry, even dropping aspects of it altogether, to better reflect the realities and needs of today. Survival has regularly necessitated innovation. Just as Edward VII used spectacle to enhance the crown's prestige, while also trying to strengthen the identity and cohesion of the modern British nation through the themes of a romanticized royal past and imperial strength, so his heir, George V, oversaw changes designed to address the crises he encountered during his reign.

The UK's royal-centred national story is characterized by such imaginative flexibility that the royal family – a group of people more ethnically German than any other modern nationality – have successfully managed to recast themselves as the personification of the best of British. The key moment came during the First World War, when George found himself aligned against his first cousin, the German Kaiser Wilhelm II. Under fire from critics like the writer and republican H. G. Wells, who described the British monarchy as 'an alien and uninspiring court' and argued that it must sever itself 'definitively from the German dynastic system with which it is so fatally entangled by marriage and descent', George finally acted.

The king took the extraordinary decision to change the name of his dynasty from the House of Saxe-Coburg and Gotha to the more British-sounding 'House of Windsor'. According to the biographer Kenneth Rose,

George thought himself 'wholly and impregnably British', despite his close ties to Europe. Though he was warned by a former prime minister that the royal family faced 'ridicule' if it renamed itself, the monarch's private secretary and closest adviser, Lord Stamfordham, pressed for the change to 'Windsor', believing it suitable because it evoked tradition and history (Windsor Castle was the monarchy's oldest residence and the final resting place of all British sovereigns since George III).

A file uncovered by historians in the Royal Archives at Windsor Castle titled 'Unrest in the Country' helps to provide further context for this and other important developments that took place at this time. The king and his counsellors were receiving intelligence constantly from local officials (often churchmen and politicians) which reported growing public discontent with the royal status quo and, specifically, the crown's close family links to imperial Russia and Germany. The king was also a cousin to Tsar Nicholas II, with whom Britain was officially allied. But such was the level of hostility felt towards the Russian ruler by the British working classes, who saw him as a cruel, oppressive tyrant, that George felt the need to cut ties with him too.

When the tsar was forced off his throne in 1917 by the first of two Russian revolutions, George rejected the British government's proposal to offer asylum to his 'dear Nicky'. This was about self-preservation: sheltering the exiled Romanovs would fan the flames of revolution among his own people. There had already been an attempt at internal insurrection the year before, when a group of Irish republicans revolted against British rule by seizing strategically important buildings in Dublin. Although the 'Easter Rising' was crushed, it deeply alarmed the king and his aides and, in the words of historian Heather Jones, led to 'a rise in republican ideology across the island of Ireland', which, in this period, was still in its entirety part of the so-called United Kingdom.

In 1918 the tsar and his family were murdered by Bolshevik revolutionaries and the kaiser was forced to abdicate as part of Germany's surrender. While the British empire and its allies were victorious, the spectre of social upheaval and dynastic collapse would haunt George V for the rest of his life. The king also knew there was still a battle of ideas to be won. In February 1918 all British men over the age of 21 and all women over 30 were given the vote, partly in acknowledgement of their war service and partly because of a longer-term campaign for full suffrage. It was now crucial for the royal household and its allies to win the hearts and minds of a mass electorate which, endowed with new political power, could, if it wanted to, vote to overturn the status quo and abolish the monarchy.

The interwar period that followed would be marked by the strengthening of the Labour movement but also by the rise of radical political factions, including fascists and communists. The many social and economic challenges of these years – most notably brought on by the Great Depression of the early 1930s – radicalized some groups in society who looked to the European dictators for inspiration. In order to navigate these difficult waters and ensure the survival of his dynasty, George V and his advisers developed a public relations strategy that put the House of Windsor on display as part of new public events that were staged as national occasions. These events took two forms: celebration and commemoration.

As part of the effort to decouple the British monarchy from its closest blood relatives in central and eastern Europe, the king allowed his children to choose partners for marriage from the English and Scottish aristocracy. Before 1914 young royals would have been matched with spouses from the continental cousinhood that both Victoria and Edward VII had looked to in order to identify suitable partners for their children. (George himself had married Mary of Teck, his second cousin once removed and the daughter of a German prince.)

Now it was crucial for the House of Windsor to burnish its British credentials. To this end, Queen Elizabeth's father, Prince Albert, the duke of York ('Bertie' to his family and later King George VI), chose as his bride a Scottish noblewoman, Lady Elizabeth Bowes-Lyon. Their engagement met with an ecstatic response from the press, who saw it as an opportunity to celebrate the historic unity of England and Scotland ahead of the nuptials in April 1923. It was the second of four royal weddings carefully staged by the monarchy as 'national' events between the wars, with Westminster Abbey – Britain's spiritual centre – playing host to the marriage ceremonies of young royals for the first time in more than five centuries.

In 1922 Bertie had noted the change in dynamic when he wrote to his brother, the prince of Wales, who was abroad, recording some of the reporting on their sister's wedding: 'it is now no longer Mary's wedding but (this from the papers) it is the "Abbey Wedding" or the "Royal Wedding" or the "National Wedding" or even the "People's Wedding".' What Bertie's words reveal is his awareness that a new type of royal spectacle was emerging. As part of a concerted effort to make the monarchy as meaningful as possible to a wide cross-section of the public, George V agreed to new types of media coverage that elevated his family as the symbolic focal point of the nation and empire. And working closely with favoured news editors and journalists, the royal household choreographed these events in order to have maximum public impact.

The most notable innovations came in 1934 with the wedding of the king's youngest son, the duke of Kent. For the first time ever, George V agreed that the BBC could broadcast a royal marriage service live via the radio airwaves from the abbey to listeners gathered in their homes across Britain and the world. The outcome was a triumph for modern mass communication: special listening parties were held up and down the country – not just in people's front rooms but also in shops, churches and tearooms. One female listener from north-west England wrote to the BBC describing how: 'I don't think I should have heard so well had I been in the Abbey itself.'

As with big royal events like weddings, the UK's annual commemoration of its war dead is seen today as an intrinsic part of British national life. Remembrance Sunday is held on the second Sunday of November every year to mark the armistice that ended the First World War on 11 November 1918. Communities across Britain stage ceremonies at local war memorials, and a national service of commemoration takes place in Whitehall, central London, in front of the Cenotaph – the empty tomb first erected in temporary form in 1919 in honour of the British empire's war dead.

The House of Windsor continues to act as the focus of Britain's national commemorative activities, having played a central role in the first 'Armistice Day' events that were held in the immediate years after the war, including the unveiling of the permanent Cenotaph in 1920 and the funeral and interment of the Unknown Warrior in Westminster Abbey in the same year. Whether it is laying wreaths or speaking at special events to mark the UK's involvement in past conflicts, the royals have been a constant presence in the national culture of remembrance. The main difference today is that, with Elizabeth II now gone, the British public lacks a royal link to the world wars which gave meaning to this culture. Charles III may have taken on the role of Commander-in-Chief of the

Armed Forces when he acceded to the throne as king and head of state, but unlike his mother he does not have a direct personal connection to this part of the national story.

We have to ask ourselves: who benefits from the continuation of these commemorative practices? Given the significant media coverage it continues to command, the annual service of remembrance certainly works to establish the monarchy at the heart of national life. One can argue that, so long as British military personnel are fighting and dying on the field of battle, their sacrifice requires that we, and the head of state, honour them. This is the view I take. But we must question whether the best way to honour them is through commemorative ceremonies where the royal family take centre stage. And we need to consider the possibility that the way we currently memorialize the world wars actually works to obscure – rather than illuminate – a deeper historical understanding of these seminal events.

The post-1918 culture of commemoration was very important, given the huge loss of life during the First World War. New forms of what historian Jay Winter has described as 'collective remembrance' helped to ease the psychological shock experienced not just by the bereaved families and the wounded soldiers who returned to Britain from the front but by a society left reeling from the brutality of the conflict. The war had cost the lives of more than a million men from across the empire, and commemorative rituals helped the public to come to terms with mass grief while simultaneously creating a moment where the nation could honour those who died.

At the centre of many of these commemorative rituals was George V. Presenting himself as 'mourner-in-chief', the monarch came to be seen by many of the bereaved as the figurehead who connected them to the family members they had lost. Heather Jones has explored how, in the first years of the war, many British men had joined the army to fight, as they saw it, 'for King and Country'. This phrase, which was used in recruitment publicity, reinforced the image of the sovereign as the emotional rallying point of the nation: for those joining up, he was not just a respected paternalistic king but the very embodiment of the modern British state.

During the conflict George played an increasingly important role in honouring those who were killed or injured. He engaged much more actively and intimately with the casualties and the bereaved than any monarch before him, meeting them and acknowledging their suffering and loss at a personal level. As Jones points out, these acts of honouring his people's sacrifices 'sacralized' the figure of the king: he came to be seen as the human intermediary that linked a grieving and traumatized public to the millions of dead, missing and wounded servicemen.

Significantly, the shared experience of war also boosted the image of the king and the royal family by providing them with a role that was relevant and emotionally deeply meaningful. Jones notes how the commemorative practices of the post-1918 period worked to shore up this link between crown and people, consolidating George's reputation as 'accessible, democratic and caring'. The monarchy 'innovatively and successfully became central' to acts of collective remembrance and the grieving public were 'relegated to the place of spectator, rather than actor, in national rituals of commemoration at which the royals took the key roles'.

This was partly by design and partly because the public seem to have been quite content to commemorate their dead by focusing their attention on the king and senior members of his family. We can detect this royal focus in the way many of the war memorials that were funded and constructed in the 1920s at the local grassroots level bore the justificatory phrase 'For King and Country', evoking a shared British identity that centred on the monarchy. And such emphasis was also clear from letters written by the bereaved to the king where they positioned him as the symbolic link between them and their dead relatives. In one especially moving letter a mother wrote to George wondering whether the unidentified body taken from the Western Front to be interred in Westminster Abbey as the 'Unknown Warrior' (intended to symbolize the 100,000 British soldiers whose remains were either never recovered or never properly identified) might be 'my dearest Boy'. Her son had been killed in 1917, aged just 19, and now she wrote to her king asking for information, including whether it was true that 'all mothers are to com [sic]' to what she termed 'the Funeral of a Brave Life at London'.

In this way, then, George V and the royals helped their subjects come to terms with mass grief, their active promotion of commemoration working to channel public emotion into the therapeutic process of remembrance. Inevitably, the crown's public standing was enhanced by all this attention, and the Windsors have, ever since, been at the centre of commemorative activities for the world wars.

But herein lies the problem. Although these practices appear to be about the past, they are, as the historian Dominic Bryan has pointed out, 'actually about the present and the future. Commemorations are a way of capturing the sacrifices of the past for the legitimation of the political present and the imagined political future.' Taking this idea as a starting point, we can argue that the royal family's commemoration of the war dead and those wounded in the present – as well as their active celebration of the less complex, less emotionally fraught victory of the Second World War – has embedded the monarchy's authority in society and rendered the House of Windsor essential to the way we think about these events today.

Under the impotent leadership of George VI the monarchy struggled to assert itself as part of the conflict. Compared with the First World War, where his father had played such an integral public role, the House of Windsor was sidelined from 1939 to 1945. The crown's status, influence and visibility were all reduced as part of a conflict which instead valorized the sacrifice and effort of ordinary soldiers and citizens back on the home front. This was a 'people's war' which witnessed an upsurge in antipathy and indifference towards the royal family, who were seen by many as privileged and out of touch, and which saw George VI consistently overshadowed by his prime minister, the charismatic Winston Churchill.

However, this is not the way we are encouraged to remember the Second World War today. Watching popular television documentaries, one would be forgiven for thinking that the monarchy played a key part in the Allied victory – boosting public morale, acting as a symbolic focal point for national unity and setting an important example by enduring the same material hardships and sacrifices as their people. This is a fanciful yet familiar narrative, and it is one the House of Windsor has actively sought, with some success, to promote ever since 1945.

Indeed, when the then Princess Elizabeth joined the Auxiliary Territorial Service (ATS) in the last year of the war and posed for photographs and films in her new military uniform, she did so with the backing of a royal household that knew exactly how such scenes would play for posterity. Like her father and grandfather before her, it was crucial that she was seen to have played her part in a war that would come to be viewed as the foundational moment in Britain's twentieth-century history. When she succeeded to the throne seven years later, in 1952, Queen Elizabeth was thus well placed to present herself as the symbolic focal point for the memorialization of Britain's victory over fascism and the commemoration of its war dead – a role she continued to play on VE Day anniversaries and Remembrance Sundays until the end of her life.

In the twenty-first century we have to contend with the fact that many people in Britain, particularly the young and migrants who have come to the UK and made it their home, have no direct personal connection to the world wars. Nor would they have memories of watching TV images of elderly veterans of the two conflicts gather on the second Sunday of November in central London to honour their fallen comrades. Seeing those old men in their berets with their service medals pinned to their chests, some walking side-by-side through Whitehall, others wrapped in blankets as they were pushed in wheelchairs, was always one of the most moving aspects of Britain's national commemoration service. In these brief moments the focus was firmly on the ordinary participants of war – not on a royal family intent on embellishing and consolidating its symbolic power at the centre of the modern nation.

It was these ordinary people who gave meaning to the idea of sacrifice. But now that they are gone and fading from memory, we ought to think again about how we honour them and those with whom they served. Their stories must be kept alive and meaningful for all members of the public. And, just as importantly, their stories must not be lost behind a highly misleading, propagandist royal-centred narrative of Britain's victory in 1945.

The state visit of Charles III to Germany in March 2023 saw him publicly pay his respects to the victims of the Allied bombing raids killed in Hamburg during the Second World War. The symbolic emphasis was firmly on reconciliation between two countries that were once great adversaries – a theme that has similarly long characterized joint Franco-German commemorative practices. This is the kind of remembrance service that plays a positive role in encouraging greater understanding of shared histories, with the bigger aim of promoting international cooperation in order to ensure future conflicts are avoided.

In their role as the custodians of remembrance in modern Britain, it is incumbent on the House of Windsor to continue to rethink their roles in commemorative activities so that these events speak to the needs of today, while respecting the experiences of those who participated in the wars of the past.

FIVE

The bride waves, the crowd cheers

Crowds are vital to the British monarchy. In the absence of a vote or referendum on the House of Windsor's existence, crowds work to legitimize the monarchy's place in society by making it appear popular. In the case of parliament, the legitimacy of politicians as our decision-makers comes from the way we, the people, elect them as our representatives. Today this process is repeated as part of periodic general elections which give legitimacy to the politicians who gain the most votes in their local constituencies.

Similarly, the British prime minister's legitimacy stems from the fact that he or she is the leader of the political party which, usually as a result of winning a majority of seats in the House of Commons, is in the strongest position to form a working government. When a premier loses the support of his or her colleagues, this normally leads to a change of leader, as was the case with Conservative governments in 2019 and on two occasions in 2022. Hence a direct link can be traced between our power as an electorate and the political administrations we select to make and pass laws on our behalf. The legitimacy of our elected representatives to rule in this way is anchored in our right to vote as part of Britain's 'representative democracy'.

So far in Part One we have seen how the monarchy used spectacle to become a pervasive part of national life and how, through pomp, ceremony and pageantry, it has positioned itself as the unifying symbol of Britain's shared history, traditions and culture. This symbolism made the crown meaningful and powerful, crystallizing its place at the centre of society. But power is not the same thing as legitimacy. Legitimacy is about consent. Legitimacy comes from us, the people, and is something we confer on our leaders in an act of recognition which gives them the right to represent us. In light of this equation, we must ask ourselves: why has the crown's legitimacy gone largely unchallenged when it has never faced a public vote? And what role has royal spectacle played in helping to enhance the crown's outward legitimacy?

The British people have never had a vote on whether a monarchy should continue to preside over the UK. Other European monarchies, such as Denmark, Spain and Luxembourg, have been the subject of referenda, with their publics invited to decide on questions concerning the continuation of dynasties or on the style of monarchy they want. As I suggest in the Conclusion of this book, the upshot of a referendum for a monarchy is that, when a public vote in favour of retaining a crowned head of state, it settles the question of legitimacy for a generation. But in the absence of a formal vote, the legitimacy of monarchies must be established in other ways.

Over the last 50 years, opinion polls have contributed to the impression that the British monarchy commands broad popular support. And in the last three decades two of the UK's polling organizations, YouGov and Ipsos MORI, have regularly tested public opinion on support for the crown, as opposed to abolition in favour of a republic. Two-thirds of the population continue to express support for kingship, while support for a republic has recently increased from 20 per cent to about 25 per cent. Meanwhile, the proportion of people who are undecided sits at about one in ten.

The fact that two in three people continue to express support for the monarchy does not equate to democratic legitimacy. Polls are blunt instruments in the way they measure opinion. And psephologists have readily admitted that their polls have the unintended consequence of shaping opinion, as well as measuring it. The media tends to commission and report on polls in ways that frame debates – for example, by offering just two options, such as retain or abolish the monarchy, with 'reform' rarely listed as an option. Just as problematically, when the results of opinion polls are published by the press, readers' attitudes are shaped by the knowledge of what their fellow citizens are thinking – in other words, polls can work to reinforce opinion in one direction or another.

Despite the flawed nature of opinion polls, they are often presented by the British media as irrefutable evidence of the monarchy's legitimacy and of the public's desire to stick with the royal status quo. The same applies to journalists' treatment of crowds. Since the 1920s the media has paid

special attention to the cheering masses that have turned out to celebrate royal events, presenting them as evidence of popular support for the
monarchy. Descriptions and photographs of crowds in newspapers and
the sounds and images of crowds gathered on royal procession routes as
communicated by television and radio are all part of a familiar repertoire
of scenes that we today associate with royal spectacle. For the coronation
of Charles III in May 2023 the procession route through central London
was significantly shorter than had been the case at his mother's coronation in 1953. There was less public enthusiasm in 2023 and, with fewer
people travelling to the capital to see the event unfold in person, it was
crucial to at least create the impression that the crowds were big, and
packing them into a smaller space was key to this.

The problem is that the British media's almost singular focus on the
vocal enthusiasm of the minority of dyed-in-the-wool royalists who readily take to the streets has contributed to a misleading impression that
the country as a whole consents to the crown's position and power. This
is because journalists working on these events have tended to conflate
royalist enthusiasm with a broader enthusiasm that is imagined extending
across the entire UK. The media theorist Marina Dekavalla has shown how,
for example, at the wedding of the then duke and duchess of Cambridge
in 2011, UK broadcasters focused exclusively on positive expressions
of support for the couple from the public and emphasized throughout
their televised coverage that it was a 'must-see' event that had drawn huge
crowds of people from across the country into central London.

I've witnessed this kind of reporting first-hand when working as
a historical commentator on royal occasions. However, in recent years
some international media organizations have begun to acknowledge that
many members of the British public do not join in with royal events and
resist being typecast as deferential monarchists. The change in approach
can partly be explained with reference to the way social media platforms
like Twitter have created a space for the expression of dissenting views,
which are suddenly much more visible. But we should also explain the
shift with reference to the recent challenges the House of Windsor has
faced, including the humiliating behaviour of Queen Elizabeth's second
son, Andrew, and the damaging accusations levelled at the royal family and
household staff by the duke and duchess of Sussex.

I noticed the change in tone while commentating on Queen Elizabeth's
funeral in 2022. British broadcasters spent the day with their cameras
trained on central London and Windsor, their commentators solemnly

describing how a nation was paying its final respects to a much-loved queen. However, one of the international television channels I was working with interspersed its coverage of the funeral with reports from a correspondent who had been sent to northern England to take the temperature of members of the public there. In many cities in the north, including Manchester, Sheffield, Leeds and Newcastle, big screens were erected outdoors to enable mass spectatorship. The aforementioned journalist ended up in Newcastle and revealed that just a small gathering of viewers had come to watch the funeral in public on what was a sunny day in September; and, perhaps most significantly, many of the other people he spoke to in the city centre expressed a lack of interest in the event.

This was the first time I had ever seen a major broadcaster, albeit an international news provider, focus attention on public ambivalence towards a big royal event. The British media tends to be much more cautious and deferential in the way it choreographs its interaction with crowds. It uses carefully staged vox pop interviews in order to lend credibility to the idea that the entire nation is joining in. When BBC and ITV journalists go out into the crowds looking for interviewees, they are searching for regional accents and expressions of a pro-monarchy point of view from people who are clearly from different class, religious and racial backgrounds in order to build an imagery and soundscape of faces and voices that might reflect the imagined nation at large.

Experiments in this kind of socio-cultural profiling began in the 1930s, with BBC reporters interviewing what they identified as 'typical' working-class people for the first time in an effort to convey to media audiences the impression that all sections of society were united in support of the monarchy. For the 1934 royal wedding, special arrangements were made to capture for listeners not just the 'crowd noises and general effects' but also the voice of a 'bright Cockney' (code for sensible working-class Londoner) who could be relied on in a live interview to express enthusiasm for the event. The newsreels followed suit when, in 1937, they filmed interviews with the four working-class people specially selected by Buckingham Palace to represent their class at the coronation of Queen Elizabeth's father, George VI.

Today attempts by journalists to capture the royalist sentiments of a 'loyal citizenry' can ring hollow and seem tokenistic. But this has not prevented the monarchy and media from experimenting more widely with the theme of 'popular monarchy'. Ordinary members of the public were specially invited to the funeral of Elizabeth II and the coronation of

Charles III, their selection based on the voluntary work or service they
had performed within their communities. At these events, these guests
were allowed to blend in with the rest of the congregation: in a symbolic
moment designed to capture the ostensible unity of the nation around
the focal point of the crown, the ordinary guests were, in effect, indis-
tinguishable from the royals, dignitaries and celebrities with whom they
sat. This felt much more appropriate than in 2013, when, at the televised
ceremony held at Westminster Abbey to mark the 60th anniversary of the
coronation of Elizabeth II, one of the ordinary guests – a lollipop lady
whose job it is to help children cross the road safely next to school – was
required to wear her fluorescent 'high-viz' jacket in an overt (and jarring)
display of royal inclusion.

It is no surprise that the 1930s witnessed the UK media engaging more
seriously with the idea of 'public opinion' by attempting to capture the
views of ordinary citizens in new ways. This was a period when the new
mass media – comprising the press, newsreels and BBC radio – loudly
claimed to speak on behalf of the British people. If the media was going
to present itself as the authority on the views of the public, then it had to
at least try to reflect these views as well. Of course, this was also a period
when the elite figures who ran the big media organizations saw it as their
national responsibility to shape public opinion so that their audiences
came to think of themselves as one people.

No individual was more ambitious in his aims to create a unified
British citizenry than the first director-general of the BBC, John Reith.
His view was that mass communication must be used to 'educate, inform
and entertain', and he was instrumental in aligning the BBC with what
he, as a patriotic monarchist, saw as Britain's most significant institution.
Like many figures in the media and politics at this time, he felt that it
was his duty to promote kingship. Against a backdrop of social and political upheaval, elite anxieties about Britain's stability and the survival of
the crown ensured that the media collaborated with Buckingham Palace
to popularize royal spectacle to engender the loyalty of the masses and
ensure the continuation of the status quo.

Media organizations including the BBC constantly pushed for new
kinds of access to royal ceremonies and events in order to bring their
audiences closer to the monarchy, thus helping to 'centre' the crown as

the institution at the heart of the modern nation. Events like the annual commemoration of the war dead (first broadcast in 1928), the weddings of the children of George V, the royal family's attendance at the annual FA Cup final, the king's silver jubilee in 1935 and his funeral in 1936 were all transformed into moments of national importance. Radio, in particular, worked to conjure the sense among its audience that the crown was at the centre of a British national community: it enabled a mass listening public to feel as though they were simultaneously joined around the focal point of big royal events.

The sounds of the crowds at such events were carefully captured by the audio engineers who worked for the BBC and newsreels companies in order to amplify the emotion experienced by listeners and viewers. The British media's choreography of big occasions was in keeping with the way media organizations in other countries reported on major events between the wars. But it is also clear that the royal household and British media drew some inspiration from what they saw going on abroad, most notably from the continental dictator Benito Mussolini, who had pioneered new forms of public spectacle in fascist Italy in the 1920s.

As a former journalist, Il Duce was the master when it came to orchestrating mass media events. Although he was a short man, he carefully positioned film cameras so that he could be seen standing proud on the balconies of imposing buildings above large crowds to whom he delivered explosive orations designed to encourage interaction – especially cheering, applause and waving. Mussolini would also repopularize the Roman salute – what we think of today as the fascist salute. When Mussolini lifted his straightened arm in front of crowds, it evoked a reciprocal gesture. Captured by the newsreels and set to hyperbolic commentary, the dictator was able to convey the impression to cinema audiences that the Italian public – as symbolized by the crowd – was united in its displays of loyalty to him.

Against this backdrop, new types of interaction between members of the royal family and the British public were trialled. Beginning with the wedding of the duke and duchess of Kent in 1934, the Windsor family started to wave from Buckingham Palace's balcony to crowds that gathered below them following big royal events. 'The bride waves, the crowd cheers' ran a headline in the popular newspaper the Daily Sketch, which juxtaposed a photograph of the duchess of Kent with her arm upraised with a much larger image of the massed crowds outside the palace gates. This kind of juxtaposition was intended to communicate to media audiences the bond between the monarchy and people – just as was the case with Il Duce and the Italian people.

For the UK media the Buckingham Palace balcony appearance has become the seminal moment that is meant to symbolize the ostensible unity between the crown and British public (Fig 2). The BBC presenter Kirsty Young indulged in fantasy on the final afternoon of Queen Elizabeth's platinum jubilee festivities in June 2022, when, over televised scenes of the queen and royal family emerging onto the balcony to the cheers of Union Jack-waving crowds, she described how 'this is the moment when London, when the UK, when the Commonwealth says thank you to Her Majesty'. Such commentary might at first seem inconsequential. But Young, like many journalists before her, was conflating the enthusiasm of the crowds on The Mall with a much wider imagined enthusiasm which, she claimed, extended nationally and internationally.

The impact of royal spectacle in creating a misleading impression of royal popularity is perfectly illustrated by the 1937 coronation. The British media loyally presented the new king, George VI, as the symbolic focal point of a national and imperial event which – according to news reports – drew massive crowds into London that turned out to celebrate the monarchy's success, the empire's strength and the vitality of the UK's parliamentary democracy. And yet, when we look at personal testimonies left behind by ordinary members of the public who were in the capital and other British towns and cities on the day, there is an overwhelming sense that the events organized in honour of the new king felt like a huge anticlimax. Despite the media narrative, it is clear that he was not very popular and, for some of his subjects, he lacked legitimacy because he came to the throne unconventionally, replacing his brother Edward VIII, who had abdicated in December 1936.

Until his departure, Edward was probably the most well-liked public figure in national life and had one of the most recognizable faces in the English-speaking world. His decision to renounce the throne in order to marry the woman he loved left some sections of the public devastated. On the day that George was crowned in his place, the social research organization Mass Observation recorded how members of the public felt an enormous sense of loss and an uncertainty about the new king's physical strength, having been made uncomfortably aware of his speech impediment. According to a working-class man who had been at the coronation celebrations in Leicester and Nottingham, there was 'not much heart in it this time, not like the Jubilee. [Edward] was very popular ... [he] took all the shine out of it ... I practically loved him.' And of the new king he continued: '[George] didn't really want [the crown]. I saw him once in Halifax. He looked dreadfully tired.'

The monarchy was tarnished by Edward's abdication, and public concerns persisted over the legitimacy of his younger brother. It would take years (and a new monarch in the figure of Elizabeth II) for the House of Windsor to fully recover its reputation. However, the example of the 1937 coronation reveals how one-sided media coverage which deliberately ignores dissent in favour of a misleading narrative of national unity, as conveyed through a visual emphasis on large crowds, can distort how we interpret the past, disguising the complexity of public opinion and smoothing over divisions regarding the legitimacy of a reigning monarch.

SIX

The new Elizabethans

The coronation of Elizabeth II in 1953 represented the apogee of royal spectacle in the twentieth century. It was the moment when the symbolism, drama and ritual of the previous 60 years came to its culmination as part of a mass media event experienced by a much larger media audience than ever before. But it was also the last time that a royal state occasion would ever be staged on such a scale and in such a way that commanded mass public interest and enthusiasm. Arguably Britain had never been – and has never been since – so united in its focus and royalist fervour as it was on 2 June 1953. The 70 years that have elapsed since have seen a return of social and political division and an inexorable decline in Britain's standing in the world. And yet royal spectacle today is not all that different in terms of its style and performance from what it was at the start of Elizabeth's reign. How should we account for what has often been a royal resistance to change? And, where the monarchy *has* cautiously innovated, why has it done so and to what effect?

We saw, at the beginning of Chapter 1, how officials and the British media presented the queen's coronation as a momentous occasion, with the ceremony carefully orchestrated and reported on in order to emphasize the 'traditional' – almost mythic – qualities of royal ritual. However, as we've seen throughout this section of the book, much of the ritual was renovated, refined or invented in order to transform royal spectacle into something that was visually arresting, emotionally moving and which elevated the authority of the central royal performers through its emphasis on splendour and hierarchy.

As with the coronations of 1902, 1911 and 1937, the pomp and pageantry of the queen's crowning were also designed to showcase British power and unity: brightly coloured military divisions from across the country and empire (now rebranded the Commonwealth of Nations) marched through central London as part of the coronation procession. The media, meanwhile, continually stressed in the lead-up to the big day how the public was rallying around what was described as a 'historic' moment: cities, towns and villages across the UK were organizing their own celebrations and people were busily making plans either to watch the coronation together or, if they had the motivation and means, to travel to London to join the crowds.

Of course, this was all about nation-building. The emphasis in the media coverage on the momentous nature of the coronation not only centred the crown as the institution at the heart of British national life but also heightened the feeling among media audiences that the event represented a crucial milestone in their national story. Many believed that this was something of which they needed to be part, not least to be able to tell others 'I was there' – the monarchy capturing their attention and inspiring a desire to celebrate.

However, the jubilation served another purpose too. The Second World War had not only seen the UK leapfrogged as a global superpower by the USA and Soviet Union, but the everyday economic hardships experienced by the public during the conflict had persisted into the late 1940s and early 1950s. The coronation – with its flash of fun and colour – seemed to spell the end of rationing and controls. And the spectacle that marked the occasion projected a triumphant national narrative, invoking the spirit of the empire's recent wartime victory and acting as a comforting balm for those who hoped the so-called 'New Elizabethan Age' might lead to the restoration of Britain's greatness.

The sense that the nation united around the event (and that the UK was, albeit fleetingly, back at the centre of the world) was enhanced by the way BBC television enabled a new kind of mass participation for the first time. TV had been trialled at the coronation of George VI in 1937, with BBC cameramen allowed to capture some of the outdoor procession. But in 1953 UK and international viewers were granted access to Westminster Abbey to watch a coronation service for themselves. The BBC estimated that more than 20 million people across Britain 'tuned in' from their living rooms or crowded into the homes of family, friends or neighbours, and into public venues like churches and ballrooms, in order to watch the event unfold. In total, 56 per cent of the adult population saw some of the coronation, many as part of what were described as 'tele-viewing parties', and this figure was double the size of the radio audience.

The grainy monochrome images that were projected through TV screens, most no bigger than 25 cm across, quite literally brought home the spectacle and sounds of monarchy. This had been a point of contention during the initial negotiations between the BBC and the palace: the queen, her advisers, Prime Minister Winston Churchill and religious leaders had all at first rejected the idea of televising the coronation ceremony, as they felt it would put intolerable pressure on the lead protagonist, who was then only 27 years old. They also feared it would undermine the sacred dimensions of the ceremony, with its spirituality lost on viewers at home who might joke, eat and drink their way through the service.

On the day these initial fears were proved partly correct. There is a wealth of evidence in the Mass Observation archive that reveals how many viewers watched the coronation irreverently: for example, making fun of what they saw, which included the moth-eaten robes of the aristocrats who, as the so-called 'representatives of the people', had various special roles to play in the service. Other viewers, meanwhile, expressed frustration when the BBC broadcast cut away from the anointing of the queen – the only part of the ceremony that was not allowed to be televised – or used the sudden break in the programme to light cigarettes. And some people found their coronation viewing was interrupted by the ebbs and flows of domestic life: chit-chat, the doorbell, meal preparation, children playing, babies crying, piles of ironing and so on.

But other groups watched attentively, sometimes in complete silence and often in awe of the religious ceremony they were witnessing. Many later expressed how they were deeply moved by the singing of the choir in the abbey, the blaring of trumpets that accompanied the moment of crowning and the cheerful sounds of the large crowds and marching bands on the processional route. Clearly the royal spectacle that had been perfected over the course of the first half of the twentieth century had its intended impact on many in the audience on 2 June 1953. The orchestrators of the event who ultimately bowed to public pressure and agreed to let the BBC television cameras inside the abbey had been absolutely right to do so.

Significantly, it also seems that the event helped to crystallize the emotions felt by some members of the public towards the royal family who featured in many viewers' comments at the time. Some people recorded how they enjoyed seeing the Windsors up close, including the then Prince Charles, aged four, who watched from a balcony as the archbishop of Canterbury placed the crown on his mother's head. Of course, the majority of comments were reserved for Elizabeth herself, with TV viewers commenting how impressed they were by her composure, given the challenges of performing live as part of a mass media spectacle. In advance of the coronation, much had been made of how the queen wanted her people to pray for her so that she might have the strength to carry out her role on the day. Many of her subjects seem to have taken these words to heart, notably expressing sympathy and respect for a young monarch whose ostensible burdens and sacrifices were given new meaning by a live televised coronation that played to a global audience.

Never before had the British been given front-row seats to a coronation. Irrespective of how attentively they watched the televised ceremony, it was a moment that transformed the relationship between monarchy, media and public forever. The day of national celebration was followed by highly publicized royal trips to all three Celtic nations and then a six-month tour of the Commonwealth, designed to reaffirm the unity of Britain and its former empire. This was again about visibility, the queen presenting herself in person to her different peoples as head of state and then as head of the Commonwealth – a new role created in 1949 for George VI to help ease the process of decolonization, but which urgently needed imbuing with meaning.

For many people, these first years of Elizabeth's reign seemed to herald a fresh start for the monarchy after the difficult years of her father's reign, which had been scarred by war and overshadowed by the abdication of his brother, Edward VIII. However, while the coronation acted as a moment of reboot for crown, country and Commonwealth, the sense of optimism and confidence that characterized the media's descriptions of a New Elizabethan Age would not even last to the end of the decade.

In the 70 years that have elapsed since Elizabeth was crowned, the UK has changed almost beyond recognition. The queen's reign was a period marked by what economic historians term 'relative decline': the economy performed quite well, but it was outstripped by comparable developed nations such as Germany, Japan and the US. The deindustrialization and privatization of large sections of the economy – processes accelerated by

Prime Minister Margaret Thatcher in the 1980s – led to the disappear-
ance of much of Britain's manufacturing sector and with it many jobs in
regions like southern Scotland, north-east England and south Wales.

The subsequent failure of central government to invest in the communities most affected by these policies, combined with the unwillingness of
successive Conservative administrations to support public services properly and their refusal to curb the excesses of market capitalism, has led
to a deepening of social divisions within the UK and a surge in hostility
towards London. The capital city has been at the centre of national decision-making and wealth creation in what has been, since the 1980s, a
service-led economy. But London's role as a hub of global finance has also
seen it corrupted by an influx of foreign money that has bought political
influence and had the knock-on effect of driving up house prices to such
an extent that home ownership in the capital is now harder for young
people than it has been at any point since 1945.

Since the 1960s regional frustrations have spilled over into the politics of nationalism in the Celtic fringes, enabling the rise of the Scottish
National Party (SNP) and Plaid Cymru, which both aim to break the union.
Meanwhile, the process of decolonization, which began when India won
its independence in 1947 and led to the creation of the Commonwealth
as a way for the UK to maintain ties to those former colonies that wanted
to become republics, has reduced British power on the global stage. The
Commonwealth initially helped the UK to maintain some international
connections and, in the 1940s and 1950s, facilitated the immigration of
people from south Asia and the Caribbean to the UK in order to assist with
post-war reconstruction. But today the organization lacks purpose and, in
the era of the 'Black Lives Matter' movement, the British government's
mistreatment of members of the Windrush generation has enflamed
tensions with Caribbean nations.

Most worryingly, since losing an empire, Britain has struggled to find a
new place for itself in the world. In 2016, 52 per cent of the voting public
decided that the UK would relinquish its hard-earned position as one of
the three key players in European politics. And, while some supporters of
Brexit hoped that leaving the European Union would see Britain regain
sovereignty over its affairs, the interdependence that characterizes global
politics means that the country cannot develop an autonomous international role without further damaging its existing relationships.

This reliance on other countries is clear from the UK's defence strategy.
Governments have reduced military spending to such an extent that today

Britain is unable to act unilaterally, instead having to look to its allies, such as the French and the Americans, to help implement its defence priorities at a time when authoritarian states menace the world again. Interdependence also means Britain is reliant on other nations for some of its core needs, such as energy supply. The rapid inflation experienced by the UK population following Russia's invasion of Ukraine in 2022 was proof of how destabilizing dependence on international energy markets can be.

Writing from the vantage point of the summer of 2023, it is clear that the optimism and sense of renewed purpose that characterized the 1953 coronation are in short supply as uncertainty instead grips the country. And here the monarchy hasn't helped. Royal spectacle has acted as a façade. It has disguised Britain's growing problems (the origins of which can be traced back decades) behind a comforting fantasy of national unity and enduring greatness. By failing to move with the times and resisting the need to update its ceremonial, the monarchy has helped to create an illusion which conceals the divisions and inertia that we're confronted with today. A reality check is overdue. But we must ask ourselves: why has the crown been so reluctant to modernize its pomp and pageantry?

We can explain the monarchy's reluctance to significantly change royal spectacle partly with reference to a suspicion of innovation within Buckingham Palace. Elizabeth II and her advisers followed the example of the ever cautious George VI and his private secretary, Alan 'Tommy' Lascelles, whom the queen inherited from her father when she came to the throne. However, the resistance to change must also be explained with reference to the success of Elizabeth's coronation and a complacency that subsequently set in at the palace. As royal biographer Ben Pimlott noted, 'popularity is not normally seen as a reason for self-appraisal – it is more likely to encourage a belief that the existing formula is a successful one'. And such was the popularity of the queen in the years immediately after her crowning that the monarchy 'wasted its most bountiful years – taking what it was given in mindless admiration as its due'.

The jubilees that celebrated the landmark years of Elizabeth's reign and the big public weddings involving both her children and her grandchildren all reworked aspects of the spectacle of 1953. These events sought to reinforce the crown's position as the symbol at the heart of British national life. At the same time, the way they unfolded was clearly shaped by a growing awareness within the royal household and media that the country faced grave problems that were fuelling political and social discontent. But aside of small gestures designed to shore up the reputation of the sovereign and her family, there was no concerted effort by the palace to transform royal spectacle so that it acknowledged the challenges the country faced. Despite a growing sense of uncertainty about the future, the diminution of Britain's overseas power, and the emergence of new fissures that divided public opinion, the monarchy continued as before, splendid and backward-looking, with a firm emphasis on the need to keep calm and carry on.

This sense of uncertainty was evident in the lead-up to and during the 1977 silver jubilee. A Labour government which was unwilling to splash out on celebrations at a time of national economic hardship had to be persuaded by the palace that it was in the best interests of Britain to mark the occasion properly with full fanfare. The aim of palace officials was, as ever, to shore up public support for the monarchy and push back on those forces that threatened to undermine the crown and the political integrity of the United Kingdom.

Amid growing calls for Scottish independence from the SNP, the queen included in her jubilee address special mention of the benefits the union had conferred on all parts of Britain, which inevitably further infuriated nationalists north of the border. In addition to the usual pomp and pageantry Elizabeth also sought to demonstrate publicly that she possessed a more personal touch by embarking on a carefully staged 'walkabout' through central London, making small talk and engaging more intimately with the assembled crowds. This kind of routine had been popularized by the royals earlier in the decade and was intended to counter accusations that they were aloof and out of touch. This also seems to have been something of a concern to Charles III when he became king in 2022, the monarch using intimate walkabouts in the days after his accession in order to present himself in front of the cameras as a kindly, popular king.

In the context of the silver jubilee celebration, the queen's walkabout met with a positive response. Ten days before the festivities began the British punk band the Sex Pistols released their infamous hit single 'God Save the Queen', one lyric of which protested that Elizabeth was 'not a human being'. After the main event, the monarch and duke of Edinburgh would repeat this kind of intimate interaction as they set off on a series of tours, first around the UK, including to Northern Ireland as a way of showing concern for the country at a time when it was beset by the Troubles, and then on to Canada, which was in the process of updating its constitutional relationship with Britain and the crown.

The wedding of the heir to the throne, Prince Charles, to Lady Diana Spencer in 1981 was also staged by the monarchy and media as a moment of national unity and rejoicing, despite a despairingly gloomy backdrop. Unemployment soared between 1979 and 1983 from 1.3 million (5.7 per cent of all workers) to 3.2 million (14 per cent). At the same time, trade union militancy highlighted the hardships experienced by those who did have jobs, while in poverty-stricken districts of London and other British cities riots broke out in April and July 1981, mainly involving young black men who were fed up with the way they were being discriminated against by a racist police force.

By way of contrast, the wedding promoted a narrative of popular royalism. The UK media paid particular attention to the refreshingly informal style and charming character of the bride-to-be, who was celebrated (disingenuously, given her patrician origins) as a Cinderella figure – an everywoman-turned-fairy-tale-princess. This new strain of popular royalism would define the princess of Wales as she rapidly became one of the best-known public figures in the world. In fact, her media image became so powerful that the dramatic failure of her marriage to Prince Charles, followed by her sudden death in 1997, saw the House of Windsor's reputation plumb new depths. Over the course of the first half of the 1990s it became evident that the royal family had failed to look after Diana as her loveless marriage collapsed. It was ironic then that, after her death, the monarchy looked to harness the kind of popular royalism she had inspired in order to reassert its relevance at the beginning of a new millennium.

Elizabeth's golden jubilee in 2002 followed the pattern of earlier events, drawing on the same time-worn royal spectacle to which the public were now so well accustomed. However, there was one notable innovation that sought to highlight how the royal family were much more in touch with the interests of ordinary people. The 'Party at the Palace' included performances from the former Beatle Paul McCartney, the boyband Blue and disco queen Annie Lennox, in what was an attempt to connect with the viewing public through a televised pop concert that showcased the best of British musical talent.

Drawing on the huge success of the UK's music industry in the second half of the 1990s and early 2000s, as well as the renewed sense of national optimism that was briefly stirred by Tony Blair's first years as prime minister at the helm of New Labour, the monarchy wanted to demonstrate how it was 'in tune' with popular culture. There had been earlier attempts at this, for example with the annual Royal Variety Performance – and further back with the Windsors' attendance at the annual FA Cup final. However, the connection with pop music and musicians – almost all of whom were huge global stars – presented the monarchy as a modern, vibrant institution, which could play host to the so-called 'party of a lifetime'.

The presence of Spice Girl Emma Bunton, the winner of the inaugural series of TV talent show *Pop Idol*, Will Young, as well as of older favourites including Shirley Bassey and Cliff Richard, ensured that the event carried an inter-generational cultural appeal. Indeed, so successful was the pop experiment in making royal spectacle appear more accessible and mainstream that the palace decided to stage repeat concerts for Elizabeth's diamond and platinum jubilees, and for the coronation of Charles III (although many leading musicians notably declined the invitation to perform at the latter event).

The two decades that followed the golden jubilee also continued to see the reinvention of monarchy as more down to earth. Princes William and Harry were the key protagonists who led this remodelling. Before they fell out, the brothers' weddings in 2011 and 2018 captured something of the popular royalism first seen at the time of their parents' nuptials, with the UK media highlighting the scale of public interest. As before, these weddings took place against a troubled political backdrop bookending an almost decade-long period of Conservative-backed austerity, which predictably intensified pre-existing social and economic divisions in society. Of course, the media coverage of the royal events paid little heed to these wider problems, with journalists instead loudly (and misleadingly) celebrating the national unity supposedly created by the weddings and the way Britain had become the centre of much of the world's attention because of these episodes in the Windsor family saga.

There was also significant international interest in the queen's death and the coronation of her successor. The televised scenes of both events played to viewerships that some of the more outrageous estimates put at several billion. A more realistic estimate would be in the hundreds of millions. Media outlets engage in wild exaggeration around royal events like these because they have no method for measuring the viewing patterns of a global media audience, and troublingly it leads to the widespread reproduction of misinformation. What is beyond doubt, however, is that royal spectacle in its modern mass mediated format has, since the 1953 coronation, been made more accessible to an international viewership through TV, which has done more than any other medium to present to the world a United Kingdom that has kingship at its heart.

SEVEN

The glamour of backwardness

The Scottish political theorist Tom Nairn described in his famous polemic against the British monarchy how, since the age of George III, the institution had functioned as a popular national symbol, pushing back on the forces of democracy and republicanism in a 'counter-revolution' that entrenched old class privilege and elite power. He argued that during the reign of Elizabeth II the crown had become more – not less – important to a UK that had been 'disintegrating'. The monarchy benefited from the 'glamour of backwardness': in direct contrast to Britain's steady decline, a royal-centred national identity had 'constantly brightened and extended its radiant appeal' by acting as a symbol of 'continuity and reassurance' in a rapidly changing world.

I don't share Nairn's republicanism, but I broadly agree with his analysis. The monarchy remains at best backward-looking, at worst reactionary. Even when it is trying to modernize, for example, by staging royal pop concerts, it is doing so in order to remind us of its continuing relevance, despite it embodying an elite power that is rooted in dynasty and rests on hierarchy. I also share Nairn's concern that, in presenting itself as the ceremonial focal point of Britain's shared history, culture and traditions, the crown has promoted a deeply misleading narrative of national unity and strength when there is currently an urgent need for level-headed realism about how the country best responds to the challenges of the twenty-first century.

The good news is that the monarchy *can* refashion royal public spectacle so that it better speaks to the needs and ambitions of today if it so chooses. This would require innovation. But as we saw with the period from the late nineteenth century to the mid-1930s, the monarchy actively and repeatedly transformed its ritual and pageantry in response to a shifting political, social and cultural landscape. Having innovated once, why shouldn't it do so again? The reigns of Edward VII and George V saw the crown modernize its spectacle primarily in order to survive, embedding royal power at the centre of British society. The difference now is that a new type of royal spectacle could facilitate a process of nationwide healing, requiring us to take a more rounded look at the UK's recent history, while working to promote unity around an optimistic vision of a future that puts democratic renewal unambiguously at the centre of national life. This is certainly preferable to having the palace and its allies in the media continue to promote a stale, propaganda-laden narrative of a glorious royal-centred past, which is both misleading in its simplicity and dangerous in the way it ignores other aspects of the national story which do not fit the rose-tinted perspective.

The risks of failing to innovate were made clear when the then duke and duchess of Cambridge toured the Caribbean as representatives of Elizabeth II in her platinum jubilee year. This was a classic case of the monarchy failing to heed wider political and cultural trends, meaning that the royal couple's advisers didn't anticipate the kinds of problems that were likely to arise. The fact that William and Catherine (who are usually so careful with their public relations strategy) were caught off guard also suggested a lack of awareness on their part of the crown's historic links to colonialism and the royal family's role as the advocates and envoys of empire.

The growth of the Black Lives Matter movement over the last decade has done much to draw attention to forms of racial prejudice and discrimination that were previously less visible in public life. Unfortunately for the Cambridges, modern royal spectacle has, since its inception, been imbued with the symbolism of hierarchy and power which, in the context of the empire-turned-Commonwealth, has long had an added racial dimension. And one of the reasons why the couple's Caribbean tour flopped was that they agreed to participate in types of royal spectacle that were badly outdated.

As we've seen, the royal spectacle that emerged out of the last decades of the nineteenth century and first decades of the twentieth put hierarchy and royal power on display in order to instil in spectators a respect for the socio-political status quo and a belief that they belonged to a United Kingdom that had monarchy at its centre. However, this kind of spectacle was not just performed for the benefit of the British. Whenever members of the royal family travelled to parts of the empire in these years, they used ceremony and pageantry to imprint on the local populations the power of the imperial state and the role of the crown as the symbol to which loyalty and deference was owed.

In the so-called 'white dominions' (the original settler colonies, which included Australia, New Zealand and Canada) royal tourists represented for many the human link back to Britain, embodying the fraternity that emigrants and their descendants felt existed between them and their relatives in the UK. However, in Britain's African and Asian colonies that were inhabited by majority black or brown populations but administered by white colonial administrations for the benefit of the imperial economy, royal tours served a different purpose. Here the emphasis was on shock, awe and the celebration of an empire that claimed to be a force for good – equally benevolent and 'civilizing'.

Royal spectacle provided the splendour and symbols of hierarchy that could be used to win over local elites who might help the British run their colonies. This was the case with the 1911 Delhi Durbar attended by the new king–emperor, George V, so that he could personally receive homage from the princes of India. As historians and media theorists have explained, there was an implicit racial dimension to this, which would outlast the king's reign and continue to inform how his successors interacted with colonial peoples they encountered when touring the empire. Royal spectacle created a vision of white British power symbolized by the visiting royal, which was designed to imprint on the local non-white population the strength and authority of the imperial state.

It is important to mention that earlier royal tours did not always have their desired effect. In front of the 100,000 Indian spectators who gathered in Delhi's 'Coronation Park' for the 1911 Durbar, one local prince, the Gaekwad of Baroda, disloyally turned his back on George V, refusing to pay homage to his emperor as convention dictated he should. The impression that imperial control over India was slipping was reinforced a decade later, when, as prince of Wales, the future Edward VIII was dispatched to the subcontinent in order to shore up political ties between Britain and the so-called 'jewel in the crown' of empire. However, as historian Chandrika Kaul has noted, Mahatma Gandhi called for a nationwide boycott of the prince's tour as part of his 'non-cooperation' resistance campaign against the British, and this made it hard for journalists who accompanied the royal tourist to present his visit as a success.

It is also worth mentioning that the royals have sometimes been victims of circumstance, finding themselves used by local organizers of events who have their own political agendas. This was the case in 1947, when another future monarch, Princess Elizabeth, was confronted by a complex racial situation in pre-apartheid South Africa. She and the three family members with whom she travelled may have been 'colour blind', but, as historian Hilary Sapire suggests, the spectacle that was staged during their visit was organized in such a way as to present black South Africans as inferior to their white counterparts. For example, the princess was allowed to dance with men she met at 'white only' events that were held in her family's honour, but at ceremonies involving black communities, distance and hierarchy were carefully maintained, and no dancing was allowed.

Although the royal family were active participants in the performance of royal spectacle that unfolded across the empire, the vision of white power that these events constructed was also a product of the imagination of British officials intent on using the royal visitors to maintain an image of imperial authority. Ironically, this was especially the case when the empire was in retreat. Independence ceremonies would become an increasingly regular occurrence after the Second World War – the first took place in India in 1947 – to mark the transition made by individual colonies from imperial possessions to self-governing sovereign states. Politicians and civil servants back in London ensured that a member of the royal family attended almost every independence ceremony, acting as representative of the monarch and the British government. The royals most regularly called on included Prince Philip, Princess Margaret and members of the Gloucester and Kent families.

After 1949 all former colonies automatically joined the Commonwealth on gaining their freedom from the empire. But as the historian Philip Murphy has discussed, independence ceremonies were staged in such a way as to emphasize continuity. Drawing on a familiar repertoire of pomp and pageantry, they represented a 'rearguard action' to 'uphold the notion of hierarchy' at the very moment when power was being transferred from Britain to the newly sovereign countries. The focus on the royal family member throughout proceedings ensured there was an emphasis on British power and dignity, both of which seemed to be in short supply after the international humiliation of the Suez Crisis in 1956. And the official narrative that was widely reproduced in the media coverage of independence ceremonies – that Britain was willingly handing power to the new states, having guided them as colonies to political maturity – helped to embellish a story of national noblesse.

Restrictions on full access to documents in both the UK National and the Royal Archives means that it is currently impossible to know just how involved the monarchy was in the orchestration of independence ceremonies. However, we do know that Elizabeth II was much more supportive of decolonization than her father, George VI, recognizing, in Murphy's words, 'the need to reach an accommodation with the forces of colonial nationalism'. During the first 30 years of her reign, all of Britain's former colonies became self-governing states. The independence ceremonies and the continuation of royal tours to what had once been the far-flung outposts of the empire, but which were now 'equal members' of the 'Commonwealth of Nations', helped to smooth over the often violent process by which imperial control ceased to be by making it appear as though the former colonies had naturally evolved to become part of the new international organization.

The queen's encouragement of these changes gave meaning to her new role as head of the Commonwealth, a title created specially for her father in 1949 so that he might retain some symbolic link to India after it decided to become a republic. Queen Elizabeth's unwavering support for the new international organization throughout her reign conferred on it a prestige it would have otherwise lacked. Indeed, as we shall see in Part Four, the monarch increasingly found herself at odds with British politicians and government officials who, in the last decades of the twentieth century, struggled to see any real value in the organization.

Tom Nairn did not discuss at any length the monarchy's historic role as the symbol at the centre of empire. However, his arguments about the 'continuity and reassurance' offered by the monarchy to Britain apply here as well. Put simply, after the war royal spectacle continued to be staged in the former colonies in order to embellish the crown's role as the symbol that held together the empire-turned-Commonwealth, and to present media audiences back home in the 'motherland' with a comforting fantasy that its monarchy (and implicitly the British nation) retained global influence at a time when their country's real power on the international stage was rapidly diminishing.

The problem for the British monarchy today is that the history of empire has undergone significant revision in the last two decades. Empire is no longer something that the crown wants to necessarily be linked to, because much greater attention is now being paid by historians and the general public to the injustices of modern colonialism, including its legacies of violence and exploitation. When the duke and duchess of Cambridge visited the Caribbean in the spring of 2022, they were unprepared for the criticism they would receive from sections of the local population alert to these legacies who saw the royal tourists as symbols of Britain's historic oppression of the peoples of the islands – including its role in the transatlantic slave trade.

Perhaps most problematic of all was the Cambridges' participation in a military parade during the Jamaican leg of the tour. They were clad mainly in white – the duchess in a stylish summer outfit, the duke in the 'tropical dress' uniform of the Blues and Royals regiment, which men of the House of Windsor have historically worn while on tour or presiding at independence ceremonies in the former African and Caribbean colonies (Fig 3). Together the couple rode in the back of the same open-top Land Rover that had transported Elizabeth II and Prince Philip during their tour of Jamaica in 1953, before the country gained its independence in 1962. But what was intended as a colourful and poignant piece of pageantry instead led to a media storm. Critics complained that the Cambridges looked like imperialists, the choreography of the event elevating them visually above the local people and country as if it was still an 'infant colony'.

Following the public criticism, William made it known via the press that he had expressed reservations about this particular piece of royal spectacle to his team of advisers before it took place. However, it was too late. It became one in a series of PR missteps that marred the trip and led the duke to admit in his speech at the end of the tour that 'relationships evolve'. This was a nod to the fact that many of the Commonwealth realms in the Caribbean – nations that gained their independence from the empire, but which chose to retain the British monarch as their head of state, including Jamaica – are on the pathway to becoming republics.

Some realms may soon decide to become republics with a new elected head of state. But this does not mean they will leave the Commonwealth. When the new king visited the former realm Barbados in 2021 to speak at the ceremony that celebrated its transition to a republic (the moment it simultaneously got rid of Elizabeth II as head of state), he did so as heir to the throne and as future head of the Commonwealth. Charles's trip was about continuity. He stressed in his speech the importance of Barbados and the UK continuing to work together as members of the Commonwealth. And, in another significant move, he described how the 'appalling atrocity of slavery ... forever stains our history'.

Although Charles refrained from directly implicating the British state through his careful use of the word 'our', he nevertheless acknowledged the historic injustice perpetrated against the people of Barbados in a symbolic act of remorse. This was an important shift in tone. Royals have generally been reluctant to acknowledge the wrongdoing of the imperial state in the past. But these words suggest that Britain's monarch seems to have accepted that a new approach is required, whereby his family must work to address some of the social and political tensions left over from the age of empire.

The shift in tone towards contrition is a welcome step from the new king and the royals as they help the UK come to terms with its complex past and, indeed, the historic role played by the crown in the empire and Commonwealth. It has notably shaped Charles's interactions with other communities who suffered at the hands of the imperial state, with subsequent tours emphasizing low-key events that have stressed the themes of reflection and reconciliation, as opposed to ritual and pageantry. Of course, this change in behaviour from the Windsors has been *reactive* rather than proactive, and comes at a time when the royals know they need to connect to younger members of the British public who are more attuned to issues of injustice. However, importantly the shift in attitude suggests that the monarchy *can* refashion its public spectacle so that it better speaks to the needs and aspirations of today if it chooses to do so.

Such a change in royal public spectacle could also help to ensure the survival of the House of Windsor in a new guise. I explore this theme in greater detail in Part Four, but as part of this shift to a new status quo it is crucial that we also get to learn about the roles Elizabeth II played as queen and head of the Commonwealth in the process of decolonization after 1952. Writing in 2022, Murphy noted how our understanding of decolonization has been constrained by the 'obsessive secrecy' of a royal household which has prevented historians from accessing archival records that detail Elizabeth's international activities. It is in the interests of transparency and of democratic values for Charles now to grant researchers access to the official archives so that we might finally learn about the role his mother played in the rise of the Commonwealth out of the ashes of empire.

One area where the monarchy has developed an unusually proactive policy of change in terms of its public spectacle is in relation to religion.

Elizabeth's reign saw the royals publicly engage with religious communities in new ways in an effort to foster social cohesion through inter-faith dialogue. Social cohesion should be the theme that informs the royal household's creation of a new type of spectacle designed to bring the British public together in order to encourage greater social interaction and the development of a deeper understanding of ourselves. There is a strong argument for having a shared focal point in modern democracies – a symbol or set of ideas that works to knit us together despite often conflicting views – in order to ensure long-term social and political continuity. The crown could play this role in twenty-first-century Britain. However, for this to happen, the meaning of kingship within national life must change, and royal spectacle needs to be reinvented so that it projects a new set of messages.

To begin with, the Anglican church should be disestablished and, if new reigns are to start with a formal coronation, then it should be a secular affair. This is not to say that the monarch should lose their role as supreme governor of the Church of England. Historically, this function has at times allowed the sovereign to play a useful part in national life: the king or queen should be allowed to retain this position, but it should not be central to their public function, as is meant to be the case today. Attitudes towards organized religion in the UK are rapidly changing, and pragmatic constitutional experts have admitted that having an Anglican state religion is untenable when demographically there is no longer a majority of the population that belong to that faith.

It is important to note that a move to disestablishment and a secular coronation would not necessitate a wider cultural shift towards secularism in modern Britain. Rather, this change would simply acknowledge that the UK today is a multifaith society. The 2021 census revealed how Christianity is now a minority faith in England and Wales, with the number of self-declared Christians having dropped from 59.3 per cent of the public to 46.2 per cent in a decade – a significant decline that is likely to continue. Meanwhile, 10 per cent of people identify as belonging to one of Britain's other minority religions – Islam, Hinduism, Sikhism, Judaism and Buddhism.

The historian John Wolffe has noted how the 'monarchy has been looking towards a Christian Britain giving way to a religiously plural rather than a secular one'. This process accelerated during Elizabeth's reign in recognition of wider developments in British society. Her coronation set the tone when she imaginatively reinterpreted her role as head of the Church of England in order to extend the hand of friendship to other religious communities in the UK as part of a royal policy of social cohesion. Although the queen was crowned in the sight of a Christian god in the spiritual centre of Anglicanism, Westminster Abbey, she recognized that as monarch she had a responsibility to all of her subjects, which required her to promote religious inclusion as the country underwent demographic change.

In 1953 the moderator of the Church of Scotland was thus specially invited to participate in the coronation as the representative of Britain's second established church in a telling sign of the queen's readiness to accommodate other faith traditions. As decolonization gathered pace during this decade, so increasing numbers of migrants arrived in the UK from the former colonies in search of opportunities, bringing their cultures and religions with them. Recognizing how her country was evolving, Elizabeth played a leading role from the mid-1960s onwards in attending and promoting multifaith church services to foster religious pluralism. This included the annual Commonwealth Day service, which has been staged in London since 1966 in order to bring together faith leaders and religious groups from across the UK and former empire. Then, in her diamond jubilee year, the queen declared in a key intervention that it was not her and the established church's role 'to defend Anglicanism to the exclusion of other religions'; rather, both had 'a duty to protect the free practice of all faiths in this country'.

While the monarchy's active engagement with non-Christian faiths has been politically expedient (it has helped to create royalists out of the UK's newest citizens), its approach has also helped to make Britain more open to religious diversity than would have otherwise been the case. Leading advocates of multiculturalism, including Tariq Modood, Bhiku Parekh and the chief rabbi, Lord Jonathan Sacks, have notably argued for the continuation of the establishment of the Church of England precisely because they see it as a force for the promotion of faith in British national life and the defence of religious and ethnic minorities.

This attitude has underpinned King Charles's conception of his role as head of the Anglican church. At the time of his coronation, much was made of how the new king was, by divine right, defender of the faith but, by choice, 'defender of faith', in the abstract – a phrase he first invoked on his 60th birthday to describe his future religious role. In a symbolic act to reflect Britain's modern multiculturalism, the 2023 coronation also witnessed the new monarch invested with pieces of regalia by four peers, each representing one of the UK's other minority religions. As a passionate advocate of the UK's multifaith culture and the right to practise one's reli-gion freely, Charles is notably building on foundations established by his mother almost 60 years ago.

Although the British monarch's championing of religious pluralism is in keeping with the times, the changing patterns of worship in the UK suggest that the 2023 coronation should be the last to have an explicitly Christian dimension. In keeping with his millennial generation, the heir to the throne, Prince William, has shown no great interest in religion, in contrast to his father and grandmother. Unless this changes, or there is a resurgence in Christian worship in Britain between now and when he accedes to the throne, it wouldn't be right for him to be crowned symboli-cally in the sight of a Christian god as part of a national coronation service.

For Anglicans to whom it matters, a smaller, more modest religious service could take place whereby William was anointed with holy oil – if he felt compelled to undergo this ritual. But in line with the central arguments of this book, we can make the case to scrap the formal coronation ceremony entirely (such a move would do away with a lot of invented tradition and flummery), or to turn it in to a wholly secu-lar service designed to celebrate the sovereign's role as defender of our democracy (see Part Four). The location for a secular ceremony would have to be Westminster Hall in the UK's Houses of Parliament because of its pre-existing connections to royal spectacle, but also because it was the site where, in the mid-thirteenth century, a more democratic House of Commons originated.

The British monarch is the only crowned head of state in Europe who still undergoes a coronation. The UK is behind the times. Even in the Scandinavian countries, where the royal families maintain close ties to their national Lutheran churches, there is no formal coronation. Indeed, although the national churches of Norway and Sweden were recently disestablished, the monarchs in these countries continue to act as reli-gious figureheads, which demonstrates that disestablishment need not be incompatible with the continuation of a sovereign's spiritual activities.

I think that most existing royal spectacle should be scrapped or, at the very least, dramatically modernized. But I also think that the British public deserve to have more – not fewer – royal-sponsored opportunities to come together to celebrate our national culture. The history of royal spectacle shows how much of it was introduced for what we would consider today to be suspect purposes, including propping up a reactionary class system while trying to contain the democratic energies of the masses by winning them over to the status quo. But at the same time there has been a consistent enthusiasm at the grassroots level for participating in forms of national celebration. There is clearly a feeling among large swathes of the public that we stand to gain something from coming together around a shared focal point. And as anyone who has attended a big music concert or sporting fixture knows, there is a profound emotional power to being part of a large crowd of people. But what story should Britain be celebrating? And what might the monarchy do to promote a new narrative through renovated royal spectacle?

Other interpretations of Britain's national story have long been staged as part of public spectacle. The political left continues to use pageantry to celebrate a narrative of class struggle and the successes of the labour movement in winning rights and power from an uncooperative capitalist elite. Political demonstrations have promoted this story, as have annual events such as International Workers' Day staged at the start of May, which sees sections of the British left rally to celebrate the global struggle of labour as it continues to challenge social inequalities. This kind of partisan narrative would, of course, be completely unsuitable for Britain as a whole, given the country's plurality of political opinion; but the example reveals how other stories gain traction when they speak to the experiences of enough people.

In terms of more mainstream examples of popular spectacle, the most significant to have been staged in recent memory was the opening ceremony of the 2012 London Olympics – an event that is much better remembered today than Queen Elizabeth's diamond jubilee the same year. As historians and sociologists have noted, director Danny Boyle drew on old mythologies and newer themes such as multiculturalism in order to construct a complex, multifaceted vision of the UK that might resonate with different audiences' understanding of the past and present.

The opening ceremony was markedly different from royal spectacle in terms of its content and style. However, the queen did perform a small, playful part in proceedings, when escorted by James Bond (played by actor Daniel Craig) to the stadium in a helicopter from which the two British icons then parachuted, their stunt doubles landing centre stage to the astonishment of spectators. This performance from Elizabeth (much like her tea party with Paddington Bear ten years on, at the platinum jubilee) was in keeping with the shift to a new popular royalism that was reassuring and entertaining in its wider references to shared cultural reference points.

But apart from this spectacular royal entrance, the ceremony was much more democratic and transgressive in its portrayal of Britain's history. The highlights included the transformation of the country through the industrial revolution, with the arrival of towering factories and new technologies developed by engineers such as Isambard Kingdom Brunel. Throughout the spectacle the focus was on the workers whose back-breaking toil drove industrial expansion. Boyle thus raised moral questions about the impact this period had on ordinary Britons. Indeed, he drew direct inspiration from the famous William Blake poem 'And did those feet in ancient time' – better known today as the hymn 'Jerusalem' – which criticized the oppressive impact of the 'dark, Satanic mills' on both working-class people and the nation's 'green and pleasant land'.

Boyle's progressive politics shone through his opening ceremony again in the section that celebrated Britain's NHS and valorized the work of its nurses. The funding of the NHS had become a particularly contentious political issue after a new government came to power in 2010 pledging to cut investment in public services. Hence this part of the ceremony was poignant and embellished the reputation of the health service as the UK's 'secular religion' – or what critics have disparagingly called its 'sacred cow'.

That the NHS featured so prominently in the spectacle reveals how Boyle and his team tapped into the feelings of the British public, a large majority of whom identify with the health service's social democratic values, including the idea first set out in 1948 at its founding that it would provide care 'free at the point of delivery'. Today the NHS desperately requires reform and proper financing if it is to serve the needs of the country as it enters the mid-twenty-first century (see Part Two). But its popularity indicates that there is a significant social democratic consensus that underpins national life that the monarchy could tap into via royal spectacle.

My argument is that a new type of royal spectacle could be staged to create opportunities for the public to celebrate the values and ideals to which modern Britain aspires. Abandoning the current pomp and pageantry with its trappings of elite power and Edwardian hubris, the focus of a new, more modest royal spectacle could be the monarch as a symbol of democracy. This theme could take centre stage as part of an annual 'King's Day' celebration (or 'Queen's Day' when the sovereign is female) to coincide with the official birthday of the monarch on a Friday in mid-June, which could then be followed by a weekend of special events up and down the country. Our neighbours in Europe tend to have at least three more annual bank holidays than us on average. So why shouldn't the British government create a new public holiday for the specific purposes of promoting a shared understanding of our democratic culture which might also enable us to learn more about ourselves?

The appeal and impact of King's Day would depend on the success of the new democratic and constitutional programme that is set out in Part Four of this book. In brief, the king would become the constitutional arbiter tasked with strengthening Britain's democratic institutions. With the help of a special non-partisan 'Crown Committee', the monarch would be responsible for upholding integrity, transparency and account-ability in public life, with the express aim of strengthening Britain's democratic culture, while boosting participation in the political process. The role of the Crown Committee would also extend to encouraging cross-party cooperation on issues that require long-term planning (i.e., beyond the short-term electoral cycle). Finally, the sovereign would be tasked with promoting a democratic educational programme to help equip learners of all ages across the UK with the kind of critical thinking skills they will need to make sense of the increasingly complex world in which we live.

As I suggested in the first chapter of Part One, bringing people together as part of a public event, around a focal point they care about and identify with, can inspire a kind of emotional communion that works to remind us that we have much in common. This is crucial in modern democra-cies like Britain where it seems there is so much that separates us. By doing away with opulent, backward-looking, anti-democratic fantasies, royal spectacle could instead project a vision of an inclusive country bravely embracing democratic renewal at a pivotal moment in its national story. To help achieve such a vision, a King's Day ceremony (again in Westminster Hall) could highlight the role of the monarch as defender of our democracy and give pride of place to ordinary citizens – not tokenis-tic representatives of the public specially chosen to represent a particular constituency that the crown is trying to win over.

What about the programme of special events that might unfold over the weekend after King's Day? The overarching theme has to be social cohesion; and the aim of such a project would be to enable and encourage new forms of public interaction, so that people get to learn things about one another and their national culture. The result could be that we, the British, get to develop a deeper understanding of ourselves as a citizenry and country. Of course, there would be no pressure on people to organize parties or, for that matter, feel as though they must have fun. Rather, opportunities for social interaction could be created across Britain by staging events and opening up public spaces in innovative ways.

The House of Windsor might look overseas to see how other nations do things differently. There are many countries that no longer have a monarchy which have had to invent new forms of spectacle and special events as a way of communicating national political symbols and ideas, while also encouraging popular participation in public life.

Take, for example, the two great eighteenth-century republics: the USA and France. Just as a coronation is used to mark the start of a new reign in Britain, so the Americans and French (having got rid of their ties to monarchy) had to devise an inauguration ceremony whereby the president, as head of state, is formally invested with his or her power. Like a monarch, the US and French presidents both pledge to uphold the political system and values of their countries; there is a symbolic emphasis on the interaction between the incoming and outgoing presidents in order to highlight the peaceful transition of power and strength of their democratic systems (although Donald Trump was conspicuously absent at US President Joe Biden's inauguration in January 2021 claiming, falsely, that the election was 'stolen' from him); and crowds play a key role in the modern media orchestration of inaugurations, helping to convey the legitimacy of the new US or French president – the main difference from kingship being that the presidents have participated in and won a democratic election in order to gain legitimacy and power.

What is most relevant to us here is the various public holidays the Americans and French have created to give meaning to their politics, culture and identity as nations. For America, the Fourth of July – the day the USA declared its independence from the 'tyranny' of King George III and the British empire in 1776 – is a national holiday marked with parades, festivities and other, more low-key, events, including picnics and family gatherings. Similar to another US holiday, the birthday of founding father George Washington, which witnesses the annual celebration of the office of the presidency every February, the Fourth of July creates a moment for Americans to rally around some of the defining episodes and themes that are central to their country's story – in this case, liberty and republicanism.

France shares in these political traditions and celebrates them with a public holiday on 14 July. The *fête nationale française* (commonly known as Bastille Day) marks the revolution that led to the founding of the French republic and sees villages, towns and cities put on special festivities for their inhabitants. It also witnesses Europe's largest military parade along Paris's procession route, the Champs-Élysées. This kind of military spectacle takes centre stage every 8 May (VE Day) too, when the French celebrate the end of the Second World War. These public holidays project a romanticized narrative of the revolutionary past, as well as national strength and unity. In this respect, the French engage in a similar kind of mythmaking to the British, once again distracting from the fact that the country has suffered a significant diminution in its global influence and a loss of internal social cohesion in ways comparable to the UK.

Interestingly, in another European republic, Germany, because of its violent and sometimes shameful national past, there is much less public spectacle designed to promote narratives of strength and greatness. Since the fall of the Third Reich in 1945, there has been an active rejection of the kind of pomp, pageantry and military parades that continue to play a key part in the national life of other modern nations. Instead, a distinct mood of anti-jubilation has prevailed, with post-war Germany suspicious of flag-waving and self-glorification precisely because such activities were encouraged by the Nazi regime.

German patriotism tends instead to be quieter and more introspective, with an official government emphasis on the need for atonement for past sins, including the Holocaust. The closest the country gets to national celebration is the annual Day of German Unity, which takes place every 3 October to commemorate the reunification of East and West Germany in 1990. Each year a different city plays host to the national *Bürgerfest*, with other celebrations taking place in the federal capital, Berlin, and in other major regional cities. However, it is significant that many Germans either claim not to actively engage in the celebrations or mark the day in any special way, preferring to treat it like any other public holiday.

The three republics discussed here demonstrate that, just like Britain, other nations have used spectacle – or, indeed, an absence of spectacle – to tell a story about themselves, their history, culture and values. For our purposes, it is notable that public events have also been introduced to respond to the needs of today. For example, in the USA the birthday of

Dr Martin Luther King has been celebrated annually since 1986 with a national holiday in mid-January that commemorates the achievements of the Civil Rights Movement and its leader's campaign to end racial discrimination. Given the growing salience of identity politics in the US in recent years, MLK Day has become an opportunity for anti-racist groups and organizations to increase awareness of inequality and minorities' rights, something that also features as part of the USA's Indigenous People's Day, formerly the public holiday known as Columbus Day.

France, meanwhile, hosts the annual fête de la musique every 21 June, which has aimed, since 1982, to bring the country together around the focal point of the nation's musical culture. Tens of thousands of events that are free to attend take place all across France at a grassroots level. This event was originally launched by the French culture ministry in order to foster social cohesion by creating an opportunity for the country's increasingly diverse population to share and celebrate the many varied genres of music they enjoy. Today, 21 June is popularly known as World Music Day, the French fête having taken on a life of its own, becoming an international phenomenon.

As we saw at his coronation, Charles III has a deep love of music, having commissioned 12 new pieces specially for the event. One of the main features of the weekend after 'King's Day' could therefore be a national celebration of music, comparable to the fête de la musique, with a multitude of free local events taking place to highlight the UK's diverse musical culture. As part of this celebration, one regional city could be chosen each year to host a bigger festival, attended by the monarch, in order to showcase the range of musical talent that exists within Britain. It could also have a multicultural dimension and be broadcast on TV and radio in order to give those people who are unable to attend in person the opportunity to share in the event.

The primary aim of such a national celebration of music would be to bring people into Britain's towns and cities in order to interact with one another socially, together experiencing the country's varied musical cultures, while simultaneously inspiring the next generation of musicians. Holding a big festival in one of the UK's regional capitals could also have a positive, de-centring effect on London and the south-east, which for too long have had a monopoly on royal spectacle.

The other main focus of the weekend after King's Day could be Britain's rural heritage. This would fit with the regional dimension of the events already discussed, and the countryside is again one of King Charles's great passions. Copying the European Heritage Day model, attractions including stately homes, historical sites and museums, agricultural and craft centres, and even the king's own country residences, could all be opened up to members of the public for free in order to enable maximum participation. King Charles could lead the campaign to get urban dwellers into the countryside for at least a day a year, sponsoring specially chartered buses designed to transport disadvantaged social groups. Such an innovation could equally be used to get people from the countryside into towns and cities so that they might partake in the aforementioned musical events that would be taking place there.

Although such royal-led events might at first seem contrived and even deeply 'un-British' in the emphasis on organized social activity, they would be celebrating at the grassroots level the UK's diverse culture. At the same time, such events would enable the crown to build on its past efforts to bring individuals from different backgrounds together in an effort to foster social cohesion through experiences that encourage us to develop a deeper understanding of ourselves as a people.

Such a move would also see the monarchy acknowledge the divides that have opened up in British society over the last 70 years, which it has so far helped to disguise behind a narrative of national unity. Rather than trying to paper over the cracks, the crown could aim to transform Britain by helping to generate a renewed sense of social solidarity in a post-Elizabethan Age. Such a move could even ignite genuine enthusiasm and hope for the future, while leaving a positive legacy that might be felt long after the end of the twenty-first century.

PART TWO

Duty, Service and Philanthropy

There is a motto which has been borne by many of my
ancestors – a noble motto, 'I serve'. Those words were an
inspiration to many bygone heirs to the Throne when they
made their knightly dedication as they came to manhood. I
cannot do quite as they did.

But through the inventions of science I can do what was
not possible for any of them. I can make my solemn act of
dedication with a whole Empire listening. I should like to make
that dedication now. It is very simple.

I declare before you all that my whole life whether it be
long or short shall be devoted to your service and the service
of our great imperial family to which we all belong.

But I shall not have strength to carry out this resolution
alone unless you join in it with me, as I now invite you to do:
I know that your support will be unfailingly given. God help
me to make good my vow, and God bless all of you who are
willing to share in it.

PRINCESS ELIZABETH
SPEAKING TO RADIO LISTENERS ON HER
21ST BIRTHDAY, 21 APRIL 1947

Tomorrow, 6th February, marks the 70th anniversary of my
Accession in 1952. It is a day that, even after 70 years, I still
remember as much for the death of my father, King George VI,
as for the start of my reign.

As we mark this anniversary, it gives me pleasure to renew
to you the pledge I gave in 1947 that my life will always be
devoted to your service [...]

I was blessed that in Prince Philip I had a partner willing
to carry out the role of consort and unselfishly make the
sacrifices that go with it. It is a role I saw my own mother
perform during my father's reign.

This anniversary also affords me a time to reflect on the
goodwill shown to me by people of all nationalities, faiths and
ages in this country and around the world over these years.
I would like to express my thanks to you all for your support.
I remain eternally grateful for, and humbled by, the loyalty and
affection that you continue to give me.

QUEEN ELIZABETH'S MESSAGE TO MARK THE

70TH ANNIVERSARY OF HER ACCESSION,

5 FEBRUARY 2022

EIGHT

Devoted to your service

On 21 April 1947 the then Princess Elizabeth delivered a special broadcast message to the people of Britain and the empire to mark her 21st birthday and coming of age as a full working member of the royal family. She spoke from South Africa, where she had just finished a tour with her parents and sister. As we can see from the excerpt above, her message included a 'solemn act of dedication' which emphasized that a challenging job lay ahead of her as heiress presumptive to the throne and, one day, as monarch. She told her audience that she required their support if she was to successfully carry out her pledge to serve her people – something she made clear was a daunting and difficult task.

Today the film footage of the princess's message that was recorded for release as part of the newsreels is regularly incorporated by broadcasters into television documentaries in order to tell the story of Queen Elizabeth's sense of duty (Fig 4). It is presented as the moment when a long life of service began. More often than not, these documentaries use a section of the film that doesn't include the reference to the empire, given that it carries problematic connotations today. Rather, the reproduction of this scene on TV, usually accompanied by loyal commentary from royalist talking heads, has helped to burnish the queen's legacy as a selfless figure who, in devoting her life to the service of her people, consistently put the good of the nation and Commonwealth ahead of self-interest.

Of course, there is much evidence to support this story of duty. Elizabeth II was a highly visible public figure because of the many roles she performed. She undertook civic visits to all parts of the UK; she carried out daily political functions overseeing (with the help of her private secretaries) the business of state while diligently playing her part as the lead representative of Britain and the Commonwealth on the international stage; she willingly participated in the kind of large, highly publicized events discussed in Part One of this book, despite her reported aversion to fuss; and, as the nation's patron-in-chief, she supported the activities of charities and philanthropic organizations that were set up to do good in the UK and other parts of the world.

This non-exhaustive list of Queen Elizabeth's official roles – which have now transferred to King Charles – reveal a queen who took her responsibilities seriously. In a carefully worded public message issued to mark the 70th anniversary of her accession in 2022, she renewed her pledge of service from 1947. In this moment she helped to crystallize in the minds of her people her dutiful character – the theme that would subsequently define the media coverage of her reign after her death. Notably, she also emphasized in the 70th anniversary message that she had been sustained in her role by the 'loyalty and affection' given to her by her subjects. Thus, the ailing queen made clear once again that a special bond connected her to her people. She performed her duties and had, along with her husband, Philip, accepted the personal sacrifices that came with being a member of the royal family in return for the support of the public.

The vision of monarchy that was articulated throughout the Second Elizabethan Age was one rooted in an almost sacred relationship between crown and people where we were encouraged to see our royal rulers as sacrificial victims of their unique circumstances. For many royalists one of the most compelling arguments in defence of the crown throughout the queen's long reign was that she could be viewed as the 'ultimate public servant'. For them, her performance of her duties on behalf of the country enriched community life, strengthened the UK's voluntary culture and, most significantly of all, set a positive moral example of selfless service that the rest of us could follow.

The idea that the sovereign puts the interests of country ahead of his or her own interests is a powerful one precisely because it seems to deny the crowned head of state the one thing that we, in modern Western societies, have come to value above all else: the individual's desire for self-fulfilment and self-expression. Indeed, Elizabeth's identity as constitutional sovereign was also rooted in the concept of self-denial: more than any king or queen before her, she was – at least in public – the consummate politically voiceless monarch, refraining from articulating almost any opinion and acting (as far as we know) only on the advice of her ministers.

The new king has so far tried to uphold the model of constitutional monarchy embodied by his mother, as have those around him.

For example, the new prayer book that was published by the Church of England for Charles's coronation described him as God's 'chosen servant' – an important reminder that the idea of the sovereign as a figure of duty carries with it strong religious undertones. But having at various times throughout his life struggled to accept the idea of royal self-denial, it is uncertain whether Charles will stick to the Elizabethan blueprint or embrace a more confrontational style of kingship given his well-known opinions and record as someone who believes his voice must be heard. Let us be in no doubt: the consequences of such a change would be seismic, resonating beyond politics and transforming the relationship between a monarchy and people which has, for over a century, been anchored in the concept of self-sacrifice – rather than self-expression and personal fulfilment.

This second section of the book reveals how the idea of the selfless monarch, with its echoes of Christian sacrifice, was deliberately elevated by royal officials and their allies as part of a new palace-led public relations campaign that began in the years after the First World War. It was first given meaning by Queen Elizabeth's grandfather, George V, who sought to enhance his public image as a benevolent sovereign dedicated to promoting the welfare of the British nation and empire. Then, following the abdication of Edward VIII – the man who was unwilling to forego love in order to perform his kingly duties – the concept of self-sacrifice as embodied by Elizabeth's father, George VI, was crucial to winning the new monarch emotional support from his subjects and to securing the monarchy's place in national life at a time when the royal family found themselves out of favour with sections of the public.

Importantly, while the language of duty, service and self-sacrifice has consistently worked to evoke sympathy and affection for the main protagonists of the House of Windsor, it has also helped to distract from some aspects of royal life that Buckingham Palace would prefer we did not dwell on. These include practical concerns about the role played by an elite monarchy in a modern democracy, as well as the power, privilege and immense wealth enjoyed by the royals at the public's expense.

As social psychologist Michael Billig first noted, we, the British public, have rationalized the material inequalities that separate our lives from those of the Windsors with reference to the ostensibly 'unenviable' nature of royal existence. Billig interviewed more than 60 families in the UK in the late 1980s, with his research revealing that there existed a popular perception that royal life was governed by restrictions. For example, one mother he spoke to sympathized with the royals by describing how 'their lives aren't their own, their lives belong to the people'.

The impression that royal life centres on self-sacrifice was, of course, at the core of the message Elizabeth delivered to her subjects on her 21st birthday: 'I declare before you all that my whole life whether it be long or short shall be devoted to your service.' The men tasked with writing the princess's message were alert to the fact that, after the Second World War, the monarchy was the focus of growing public criticism because of its cost, but also (as we shall see) because of certain personal choices made by members of the royal family. These men were Alan 'Tommy' Lascelles, the king's private secretary, and Dermot Morrah, a leader writer at *The Times*, who became an unofficial member of the royal court as the secret architect of the language the Windsors used to communicate publicly with their subjects as it evolved through the 1940s and 1950s.

Both of these men knew that Elizabeth's dedication to lifelong service had the power to evoke from her listeners a deep feeling of sympathy that might help ease wider public concerns about the monarchy's role in society. While working on the speech, Lascelles told Morrah how he anticipated that it would make 200 million listeners 'cry when they hear [Princess Elizabeth] deliver it, and that is what we want'. It was ironic that a message which at first glance seems to be about royal self-sacrifice was in fact about self-preservation and the survival of monarchy at a time when it was coming under increasing public scrutiny.

Throughout the reign of Queen Elizabeth a language of self-sacrifice was consistently invoked to awaken in us sentiment that easily translated into affection for (and loyalty to) the monarch. And her heirs have inherited a royal public language that continues to emphasize the ideals of duty and service. However, the queen's long reign taught us that, when members of her family struggled publicly to put the national good ahead of self-gratification – whether it was Princess Margaret, the new king during his often troubled tenure as prince of Wales or, more recently, his second son, Prince Harry – it has led to real difficulties for the crown.

This begs the question of whether duty and service should continue to define the public image of the House of Windsor now that Elizabeth is gone. Both carried a wider resonance in British society, notably coming to underpin the UK's honours system in the second half of the twentieth century, with the queen acting as the embodiment of these values and as the 'fount of honour'. But today the ideal of public service seems to have been lost in an honours system corrupted by political nepotism. Surely we therefore need to rethink the values at the heart of our society, including those espoused by the royal family? In keeping with the wider arguments of this book, I believe there is a better model of monarchy available that wouldn't require the royal family to carry on the story of self-sacrifice, which I interpret as often disingenuous (given the self-indulgent behaviour of certain Windsors) and as a distraction from the privileged lives they continue to enjoy.

We must never forget that the life of a 'working' royal is a life where, materially speaking, one wants for nothing: large entourages of servants at one's beck and call; vast palaces that one calls home with one's relatives living gratis nearby in 'grace and favour' accommodation; access to the best private healthcare from cradle to grave; the best private schools followed by a job for life which mainly involves touring the country and Commonwealth to be hosted as a guest of honour at parties and special receptions; when one wants them, the best seats from which to publicly enjoy live sports and music events; and, when one is not 'on the job' so to speak, considerable playtime out of the public eye to spend enjoying oneself quietly in the British countryside or on holiday abroad where private jet travel, yachts, ski chalets and the best hotels beckon.

Part Two also focuses on the theme of philanthropy. In keeping with the emphasis on duty and public service, the royals have used their patronage of charities and voluntary organizations as a means of presenting themselves as a force for good. Philanthropy has offered the royal family an opportunity to exercise their altruistic instincts by demonstrating a compassionate interest in the lives of their fellow men, women and children. This is something we see today with, for example, Queen Camilla's work raising awareness of violence against women, and in the prince of Wales's Earthshot Prize, which has supported innovative solutions to the climate crisis that is already doing so much damage to the natural world.

However, we must not be blind to the public relations opportunities created by civil society and philanthropy for a royal family who want to look as though they care. Since it took off during Queen Victoria's reign, royal philanthropy has served another, more subtle purpose. Put simply, it has been used by the crown as a means of trying to maintain social and political stability. It is not in the interests of the House of Windsor for the public to suffer. Such personal suffering could lead to civil strife and difficult questions being asked about the inequalities that characterize life in the UK, possibly even generating the momentum required for revolutionary political change. Better for the monarchy that it is seen as though it is on the side of the people and that it has their best interests at heart.

As we shall see, this was exactly the line of thinking of Prince Albert in the mid-nineteenth century and George V after the First World War. Both men developed proactive approaches to engaging publicly and sympathetically with a poor and downtrodden proletariat at precisely the moment when their dynasties seemed threatened by popular political discontent. And, crucially, the idea of a crown with a social conscience, or what historian Frank Prochaska calls the 'welfare monarchy', has informed the royal family's approach to philanthropy ever since.

Although I'm sure most members of the House of Windsor are genuinely well-meaning in their promotion of charity work, what perhaps they fail to realize is how profoundly political royal philanthropy can be – contrary, I'd suggest, to the underlying principles of a non-partisan constitutional monarchy. Since 1945 the Windsors have developed philanthropic roles which have sometimes complemented and at other times undermined the role the British state has played as provider of key services to the public. They have been able to do this because, with the exception of Prochaska's work, there has been an absence of serious discussion about the nature and aims of their philanthropy, including whether it is compatible with the social role of government.

In carving out these spheres of influence for themselves (most recently in the fields of children and young people's development, mental health and environment) the royals have as advocates and patrons increased the visibility of certain social issues in national life. But at the same time their philanthropy has normalized a situation where these issues are no longer seen as a primary responsibility of government; rather, they've been left to a patchwork of charities and voluntary organizations that have neither the resources nor the reach to address the problems properly.

It is my argument here that royal philanthropy is not always good for society because of the way it enables government inaction on key issues. It is notable that most other European monarchies do not engage in philanthropy the way the Windsors do in the UK. This is because these royal families today accept that matters relating to public welfare belong to the sphere of state and government. They are of real political importance, and royal activism on these issues could jeopardize a monarchy's neutrality. Indeed, both the Swedish and the Danish monarchies have had to distance themselves from social issues such as supporting vulnerable communities, as royal interventions in these areas have led to public accusations of interference in politics.

Positive points of comparison are often made between the House of Windsor and the Scandinavian monarchies, especially regarding the relative stability of the societies over which they have presided, with the assumption being that kingship has something to do with it. I'd suggest that what has had a greater impact in ensuring stability is the fact that, until recently, the UK, like its Nordic neighbours, had a functioning welfare state that created opportunities for people in all sections of society, while addressing some of the bigger social problems that resulted from poverty. The benevolent reach of the British state in relation to education, health and children's lives has been curbed over the last decade because of deep cuts to public services. This has in turn created space for the return of piecemeal voluntarism and charity.

Constitutional monarchies run the risk of becoming entangled in politics when politicians or the people suddenly decide that a social issue is of grave importance. The House of Windsor can avoid such entanglements by distancing itself from a culture of royal philanthropy which has, too often, capitalized on the gaps left exposed in a broken welfare state. Of course, much good work has been done by royal-backed charities in the past. But today there are simply too many issues of great importance to be left to royal philanthropists and their allies in civil society to deal with. However well intentioned, the monarchy is a hostage to fortune when it decides that it is going to promote children's development, or that it will lead the country to a greener, more climate-friendly future.

There is one final practical benefit to decoupling from philanthropy. Such a move would enable a timely downsizing of the number of working royals after continued criticism of the costs of the House of Windsor to the nation. During the first 50 years of the reign of Elizabeth II, Walter Bagehot's argument about the importance of visibility to the royal family was taken to the extreme as the monarchy became bloated with royal cousins, aunts and uncles who all undertook various civic engagements on behalf of the queen.

In the last two decades the situation has started to shift, with the new king slowly reducing the number of working royals. Although some recent studies have advocated a return to a bigger royal family, with a bigger programme of civic and charitable activities, it is my view that a serious streamlining of the House of Windsor is long overdue. Crucially, giving up philanthropy need not entail royal redundancy. Rather, it would free up the sovereign and the heir to the throne to play a number of other valuable roles in public life that would come at no additional cost – social or financial – to the country.

NINE

Benevolence sweetens authority

The role of the monarch and royal family as performers of duty and public service has evolved over 250 years to become the central occupation of the House of Windsor in the present. The fact that we today even associate the concept of 'work' with members of the House of Windsor attests to the success of a royal public relations strategy that has deliberately drawn attention to the constant programme of engagements carried out by the royal family, thus highlighting their impact on British society. This is key in a capitalist age which demands 'value for money', as seen in the annual reporting by the UK press of the number of activities undertaken by each of the royals, in order to ascertain whether they are 'worth it' or 'workshy'.

Notably, the emphasis on work also points to the complete transformation of a monarchy which, shorn of the governing powers it once exercised, has had to seek out new roles in order to ensure its relevance and, ultimately, its survival. Gone are the halcyon days when, after a long morning spent lawmaking, a king might pass his afternoon hunting wild animals and his evening in pursuit of other pleasures. The British royals discovered a new meaningful function as part of the philanthropic and civic cultures that emerged in the mid-eighteenth century and which have remained key to public life ever since.

The French Revolution that began in 1789 was led by a coalition of middle-class radicals and common people, known as the *sans-culottes*, who aimed to bring about the end of a feudal political system led by a king and aristocracy deemed to be decadent and out of touch. The social upheaval that ensued witnessed the abolition of the monarchy and the execution of Louis XVI at the Place de la Révolution in Paris in 1793, sending shockwaves through Europe and a warning to all royal elites to be *en garde*. But this didn't put an end to the poverty of the plebeian classes. France was one of several Western nations undergoing industrialization and urbanization in these years, and the millions of people who flocked into the growing towns and cities of northern Europe in search of work often faced extremely desperate living and working conditions.

Back in Britain, George III, of the House of Hanover, was the first monarch to take royal philanthropy seriously as a way of addressing the plight of the poor and containing the terrifying political passions that had been unleashed on the opposite side of the English Channel. A tradition of 'royal giving' already existed whereby kings, queens and their families handed out 'alms' – for example, with Royal Maundy at Easter, which dates from the thirteenth century – to some of those poor in need of help. But George recognized that he could generate good publicity by casting himself as a kindly paternalist who took a real interest in the lives of his subjects through supporting a range of charitable causes. On the relationship between altruism and his role as king, he wrote how 'Authority should dignify Power and Benevolence Sweeten Authority.'

The late eighteenth century witnessed the expansion of Britain's voluntary culture spurred on by the growing activity of the increasingly relevant and ambitious middle classes, who participated in public life through new forms of voluntary civic action. The king recognized that this group were becoming a key constituency in society whose backing the crown would need if it was to maintain a broad social appeal. What better way, then, to cultivate their loyalty than by becoming benefactor to organizations led by middle-class altruists who sought to do good? The maths was simple: this connection with the middle classes might guarantee their support for the monarchy but also encourage respect for the traditional social hierarchy among those further down the ladder who were on the receiving end of royal-sponsored charity.

Queen Victoria and Prince Albert benefited from a very close relationship with middle-class civil society as it continued to expand through the nineteenth century. In his plans for the popularization of Britain's monarchy, the prince consort decided that it would take on the 'headship of philanthropy'. As Albert's most recent biographer, A. N. Wilson, has noted, this came naturally to him as he was deeply moved by the 'vile condition in which many of his fellow citizens were compelled to live'. Victoria and her husband saw philanthropy as a way of expressing their deeply held Christian conviction that they had a moral responsibility to care for their fellow man.

The prince consort's concern for the British working classes was, however, also motivated by the politics of the day. He believed that popular discontent with the status quo had fuelled the burgeoning Chartist unrest of the 1830s and 1840s and the anti-elite revolutions that lit up parts of Europe in 1848. It was thus against another dramatic backdrop that Albert agreed to take on the presidency of the Society for Improving the Condition of the Labouring Classes. This was one of many such roles he embraced in order to do good – for example, by drawing up plans to improve the working and living conditions of the poor – while also courting publicity that highlighted the monarchy's compassion for those at the bottom reaches of society. Such a move appealed to pious middle-class Victorians because, in a world without the kind of safety net of state social welfare (as introduced by the Liberal-led governments of the early twentieth century and built on by Clement Attlee's post-1945 Labour administration), philanthropy was, to quote Frank Prochaska, seen as a 'moral obligation' and a 'test of faith'.

Victoria meanwhile was influenced by Albert's pragmatic vision for a compassionate monarchy and her own mother's generous sponsorship of voluntary societies and charities. By the end of her reign in 1901 she was patron to approximately 150 philanthropic organizations, doing much to raise funds from elite benefactors. The royals played host to special charity balls, banquets and dinners in order to drum up donations. In return, those who gave could expect to receive invitations to garden parties and special honours that were conferred in recognition of services to philanthropy.

Many institutions that benefited from the monarch's patronage renamed themselves accordingly: there were Queen Victoria voluntary hospitals, Queen Victoria infirmaries, Queen Victoria maternity homes – and a multitude of other institutions that took her name outside the medical world too, all of which embellished her image as a benevolent maternal figure. The queen was also extremely generous at a personal level, giving upwards of £650,000 to charity from her own purse over her lifetime, roughly equivalent to £100 million in today's money. (This figure dwarfs the £600,000 a year given away by Elizabeth II to charities towards the end of her long reign – a very small proportion of her personal wealth, which was estimated at £277 million in 2022.)

The philanthropic links that connected the crown to the voluntary medical sector (in this period the main provider of public healthcare) were particularly important to a monarchy that wanted to appear compassionate. Indeed, to coincide with Victoria's diamond jubilee in 1897, her heir, the future Edward VII, launched the Prince of Wales's Hospital Fund for London, so that he might carry on the work begun by his mother. On his succession this became the King's Fund – today a health think tank but back then a charitable organization which raised vast sums for, and helped to coordinate, the medical treatment offered by the large network of voluntary hospitals in Britain's capital city.

Outside London, the Victorian royal family pioneered another kind of public activity that was designed to demonstrate their interest in the lives of their ordinary subjects. Royal civic tours were carefully planned to provincial cities such as Glasgow and Manchester because they were hotbeds of political radicalism where support for the crown was not assured. The royal visitors would meet and greet the local great and good; they would probably lay a foundation stone to inaugurate some new civic development such as a town hall or museum; and then they would demonstrate their support for the city's philanthropists by spending time with local voluntary and charitable societies.

As I noted in Part One, this kind of tour proved a hit and would, in turn, encourage the monarchy to embrace new kinds of public spectacle. The success of these tours also gave Victoria and her family the confidence to experiment with more low-key visits designed to bring the royals into much closer contact with their poorest subjects. From the 1880s onwards the queen's advisers let her visit economically depressed areas in the East End of London, Birmingham and Liverpool in the hope that her presence might raise spirits and help quell political unrest in these parts of industrial Britain.

The Victorian royal tours of the provinces and working-class districts provided a blueprint for George V, heir to Edward VII, who as monarch adopted a more direct approach to try to counter political discontent, beginning with Ireland. The growing pressure for home rule generated by Irish nationalists increased tensions between them and Ulster unionists loyal to Britain, its monarchy and the Westminster parliamentary system. George and his consort, Queen Mary, visited Ireland in 1911 with the dual aim of reassuring Irish loyalists of their concern, while also trying to assuage anti-British feeling among nationalists. Historians have suggested this was partially achieved with moderate home-rulers appreciating the royal attention, although the king and queen failed to slow the slide towards self-government, which finally made it into UK law in 1914.

Meanwhile, in England, Scotland and Wales, the growth of a new political movement that demanded greater equality, improved working conditions and the redistribution of material wealth and opportunity had gained traction in the form of a buoyant and expanding Labour Party. Its first leader was James Keir Hardie, a vocal republican and a figure whom George V and his father loathed and feared in equal measure. A growing dread of Labour and progressive socialist politics witnessed the king, queen and their courtiers develop a new policy of active social engagement. The historian Frank Mort has explored how, as part of special 'good will' tours to Labour strongholds, including mining villages and industrial towns and cities, the royal couple engaged more intimately than ever before with some of their lowliest subjects, visiting their homes and workplaces, shaking their hands, conversing and expressing concern for their communities.

This royal PR strategy evoked royalist feeling among those people most predisposed (owing to their difficult circumstances) to the politics of radical change. Of course, some resisted the royal charm offensive. But these widely publicized tours built on a tradition of royal concern for the least fortunate, and enabled the monarchs to establish relationships with their working-class subjects. This in turn helped to promote social cohesion and political stability, with the proletariat developing an affection for and loyalty to the monarchical system as embodied by their king and queen. That the tours were made visible to the nation and empire via the press, photography and new medium of film was also key: journalists and cameramen accompanied the royal couple on their regional excursions and focused especially on the emotions and informality displayed by George and Mary during their cross-class interactions, thus making clear the direct human bond that connected crown and people.

TEN

A living power for good

The First World War was a seminal event for the British monarchy, leading to a permanent recalibration in the relationship between crown and people. The sheer scale of human suffering witnessed during a war where so many died fighting 'for King and Country' demanded that George V recognize the sacrifices made by his British and imperial soldiers. We saw in Part One how, after 1918, this led to the emergence of new rituals of commemoration, where the king acted as the symbolic emotional focal point for a grieving nation and empire. However, during the war he came to see it as his duty and responsibility to honour those who were killed and wounded on the battlefield, as well as those of his subjects performing crucial war work back on the home front in Britain.

As discussed by the historian Heather Jones, these years saw a new sacred bond take shape between George and his people, with the king readily enduring personal hardship and emotional suffering himself, as a way of outwardly sharing in the burdens and sacrifices of war. Probably the most explicit example of this shared experience was the way the king's eldest sons – Princes Edward and Albert – engaged in active war service. Edward, prince of Wales (later Edward VIII), was already a well-known public figure and was desperate – like so many other young patrician men of his generation – to prove his mettle on the Western Front. In the event, he was prevented from doing any actual fighting: it was seen as too risky, because if he was killed or captured it would have been a devastating blow to the empire's war effort. However, he nevertheless did his best to muck in with his comrades and quickly came to be seen as the symbolic 'soldier prince', embodying the monarchy's and the nation's shared sacrifice.

As representative of his father, Edward spent much of his time in France visiting soldiers from Britain, the dominions and colonies in the trenches and hospital wards in order to honour them through his presence and by decorating them with medals in recognition of their valour. The king himself made six trips across the English Channel to the Western Front for the same purposes, undertaking inspections of his troops and investing men with medals. At this point, the pre-1914 experiments with royal tours to working-class communities were finessed. In full sight of an accompanying press pack, George V engaged caringly – but stoically – with injured soldiers whose bodies had been broken in the fighting, thus demonstrating a readiness to share in the emotional hardship of the conflict with his people.

Back on the home front, the king and his advisers also publicized the fact that the royal family had willingly embraced the material challenges of war. For example, George V insisted that an austere rationing policy was implemented in the royal household; he led by example in taking the 'King's Pledge' to abstain from alcohol for the duration of the conflict; and from 1917 he insisted that his family members and all of those who lived at Windsor Castle work on the surrounding farmland for two hours a day to help with food production. These measures meant the monarchy could present itself outwardly as in touch with the public's concerns and willing to forgo the privileges of royal life in order to demonstrate exemplary leadership.

The emphasis on shared sacrifice, where the monarch and his subjects endured wartime hardships together, became more important to the crown from 1917 onwards. The previous year had witnessed the Irish nationalist-led Easter Rising and then, in February 1917, the Romanov dynasty was forced into exile following revolution in imperial Russia. King George's reaction to these events was to distance his monarchy from its cousins in central and eastern European in an effort to offset a perceived rise in anti-royal sentiment among sections of the British proletariat.

The following year George was advised by his private secretary, Lord Stamfordham, that the monarchy had to convince the temperamentally unpredictable working classes that it was a 'living power for good'. What the king's counsellor meant was that the House of Windsor needed to present itself publicly as promoter of working-class social and political interests. To this end, George and his aides made it known that the king endorsed the full enfranchisement of working-class people as part of a new mass democracy. The change made it into law with the Fourth Reform Act, which gained royal assent in February 1918. Unbeknown to the public, this move represented a significant reversal in royal thinking. Before the war the king had expressed strong opposition in private to mass working-class enfranchisement, fearing its impact on the country and its political system.

The monarchy also made clear its support for the working classes by directly celebrating their service on the home front. Beginning in August 1914, the king, Queen Mary and members of the royal family criss-crossed Britain visiting factories and industrial centres where essential war materials such as munitions, coal and food were being produced. Then, in 1917, George expanded the honours system, notably introducing the Order of the British Empire, so that he could confer decorations on all sections of society, including his humblest subjects for the work they had performed on behalf of the country – what David Cannadine has called the 'order of chivalry of British democracy'. And it created a new way for the monarchy to interact altruistically with a much wider cross-section of society at a time of significant social and political change that could, if not managed carefully, undermine the crown's position.

A revamped honours system was initially meant to strengthen the symbolic links connecting George V as British head of state to power-ful figures in the dominions and colonies: honour was reconceived as something that could help to tighten the personal bonds of empire. But the system was rapidly democratized, and honour became something conferred by the sovereign on ordinary people in recognition of special services or deeds performed. Honour thus had significant potential to incentivize 'good' behaviour among the British public: for example, you might be honoured for engaging in philanthropic work that directly bene-fited your community.

While the monarch as symbolic 'fount of honour' played a key part in democratizing the honours system after 1917, the British state was the main driving force behind these changes. In the early 1920s a small central honours committee was set up in government and overseen by civil servants who came to judge nominations on a case-by-case basis. Much like the king and Stamfordham, the Westminster elite tended to view honour as a useful way of promoting a certain set of values, includ-ing the culture of voluntarism. They also saw how it could be used to recognize the contributions of working-class people to public life in order to try to reconcile them to the political status quo. Thus the political estab-lishment, as much as the monarchy, saw honour as a useful tool of social control at a time of great change in British national life.

When we look at the way the honours system works today, we can see how the House of Windsor's public image is enhanced through a positive association with some of the famous people they get to honour. High-profile, highly publicized honours investitures carried out by the new king or by close members of his family tend to be the focus of media coverage of royal honours investitures. This reminds us that the Windsor conferring the honour and the recipient of the decoration inhabit an exclusive world far removed from most people's everyday lives.

The collision between the realm of popular celebrity and the more traditional realm of royal authority follows a long line of such interactions that began when The Beatles were made Members of the Order of the British Empire (MBEs) in 1965. This moment turned into something of a controversy for the prime minister, Harold Wilson, with some members of the public claiming he had cheapened and trivialized the value of honour by nominating the 'Fab Four'. He was also notably criticized by some of his political colleagues who accused him of using the honours system to bolster the image of his Labour government. Wilson had sought to project his administration to the public as modern and forward-thinking – qualities he clearly thought it shared with The Beatles, who were viewed as similarly cutting-edge in the field of pop music.

Wilson would continue to use honours in innovative and sometimes cavalier ways. Eleven years later, in 1976, when departing as premier for the second time, he prepared a resignation honours list that sparked outrage in some quarters. His 'Lavender List', so-called because of the purple notepaper on which his nominations were compiled, included popular celebrities and entrepreneurs whom others thought morally suspect and therefore unworthy of honour. And yet Wilson ultimately got his nominations through, revealing how an outgoing prime minister could in effect nominate whoever they wanted to, provided they had sufficient determination and their successor did not veto the selection.

The historian Tobias Harper has recorded how, since the 1990s, most honours given out by the royal family have been in recognition of voluntary and charitable service. This is doubtless seen as cause for celebration by a monarchy which values its continued leadership of Britain's philanthropic culture: under Elizabeth II, the crown set the standard for service and duty, and the public, it seems, followed. But in the same period there has been a growing concern throughout Britain that its governments and prime ministers have been abusing the honours system by rewarding political allies – including party donors – with decorations. It is the nepotistic use of honour that has the potential to tarnish the monarch's position as 'fount of honour' while also undermining the very idea of honour if we agree that it should be used to recognize exemplary forms of public service.

Concerns about unworthy recipients of honour were expressed by a number of journalists and commentators in 2023 in connection with the resignation honours lists of former prime ministers Boris Johnson and Liz Truss. Johnson was accused of rigging the honours system to suit his own ends when he controversially nominated a number of his key allies for honours despite the fact that most were undeserving of such recognition. He was also accused of lobbying (unsuccessfully in the end) for a knighthood for his father, Stanley Johnson (despite the latter having done nothing to merit such an honour), and, worse still, for a peerage for the editor-in-chief of the Daily Mail, Paul Dacre, after he used his newspaper to defend the disgraced premier against the charges brought against him during the 'Partygate' scandal.

Truss, meanwhile, with her equally dishonourable record as one of Britain's worst ever prime ministers (forced out of office after just 44 days in the job, having sent the UK's economy into a needless tailspin), nevertheless decided that she deserved a resignation honours list – itself a symptom of her tone-deaf, morally vacuous style of politics. Indeed, according to one source, the fact she kept her list quite short was to avoid the king embarrassment – the implication being that her crass political nepotism could critically damage the concept of honour and King Charles's role as 'fount of honour' in the process.

These examples reek of cronyism and continued the undermining of public confidence in an honours system that has historically tried to recognize achievement based on merit. Of course, honours scandals are nothing new. For more than a century, politicians of all stripes have got in trouble when they have played the system. The Liberal prime minister David Lloyd George was accused of 'selling' honours to wealthy party donors in what was the original modern honours scandal. This led to the introduction of a new law – the Honours (Prevention of Abuses) Act – in 1925, designed to stop the financial exploitation of the system through payment, bribery or any other such means. Other premiers were subsequently accused of bending (if not breaking) this law, including Labour's Tony Blair after he tried, unsuccessfully, to nominate four businessmen for peerages after they supported his party with generous loans in 2005. But to be fair to Blair and his successor, Gordon Brown, neither prime minister requested resignation honours lists on leaving office, their Labour Party having campaigned against political honours throughout the 1990s, notably scorning them as a fixation of the rival Conservative Party.

It is clear that the behaviour of our elected representatives has the potential to discredit the honours system. The simple answer to this problem is to get rid of prime ministerial resignation honours once and for all while increasing central oversight of the nominations process. However, there are other pressing issues that could have a more direct impact on the reputation of the monarchy, given the current state of politics, if the crown is not careful. The first of these is the anachronistic name of that democratic order of chivalry, the Order of the British Empire. The reference to Britain's imperial past is at best outdated and at worst offensive to British citizens whose ancestors suffered at the hands of the often violent and rapacious imperial state. The crown played a crucial role in the nineteenth and early twentieth centuries as the symbol at the centre of the imperial system, and this is something the House of Windsor is currently having to come to terms with, as we learn more about the troubling legacies and histories of empire. In this respect, it is significant that some recipients of OBE honours have decided recently to hand back their awards, citing new concerns about the empire.

The fact that even Prince Philip, duke of Edinburgh (who was not known for holding very progressive social views), thought the OBE in need of renaming should give us pause for thought here. The good news is that there is a simple solution on offer, as has been noted by various commentators, and that is to change the word 'Empire' for 'Excellence', with the OBE therefore becoming the 'Order of British Excellence'. It is a small change but one that would mark a decisive break with the past as a new reign begins. And it would make clear to the British public and world that, having been instrumental in both the formation of the imperial system and the creation of the OBE, the monarchy is re-examining its links to empire seriously and sensitively.

The other main challenge facing King Charles is the ongoing investigation by the Sunday Times into what the newspaper has, since 2021, termed a 'cash for honours' scandal involving a close aide of the new sovereign. The journalist Gabriel Pogrund and his team have uncovered how, when the monarch was still the prince of Wales, he received significant donations totalling £1.5 million from a Saudi Arabian billionaire for his charity the Prince's Foundation. Charles then invested the billionaire with the honour of Commander of the British Empire (CBE) in a private ceremony in Buckingham Palace in 2016, which was not disclosed in the court circular that tracks the daily activities of the Windsor family. As a result of the newspaper's investigation, the Metropolitan Police launched an inquiry and one of the king's closest advisers, Michael Fawcett, who was also head of the Prince's Foundation, was revealed to have overseen the process by which the Saudi billionaire (who, it turned out, liked collecting honours and also wanted UK citizenship) got his gong in return for the donations.

Fawcett resigned in disgrace in late 2021. Since then, the police inquiry into whether he or others in the royal household were guilty of breaking the 1925 Honours Act has stalled. The new king has pleaded ignorance, emphasizing publicly that he was unaware of Fawcett's shady dealings on behalf of his charity. However, in the wake of the *Sunday Times*'s original reports, more evidence has come to light of King Charles having previously met with businessmen, often from the Middle East, in order to receive from them large cash donations (as much as €1 million in one go) for his charities.

It is crucial to remind ourselves that there have been no further allegations of impropriety relating to 'cash for honours'. However, these stories point to the way the new monarch has, in fundraising to support his philanthropic endeavours, put his reputation at risk. It is equally important to remember that if the king *was* ever accused of knowingly accepting large sums of money in return for conferring honours, he would not face criminal prosecution because his role as monarch means that, so long as he is in office as head of state, he is the only person in Britain whose conduct and behaviour are legally beyond reproach. And yet at the same time it's clear that investigative journalists are not going to stop asking difficult questions that could potentially be embarrassing for him and the monarchy as he tries to turn over a new leaf. All the more reason, then, to make positive changes that focus on the future rather than the past.

After the guns fell silent in 1918, George V continued in his mission to present his monarchy as a 'living power for good'. The theme of royal public service, performed on behalf of his subjects in acknowledgement of their wartime sacrifices, would define the remainder of his reign, with the king presenting himself as a symbolic servant to his peoples. The notion that the king and his family were public servants worked to evoke affection, sympathy and loyalty towards the House of Windsor among the British population. Of course, such public service was also crucial in ensuring the survival of the crown in a new useful guise in an interwar period punctuated by a succession of social, economic and political crises.

George's five adult children – four men, one woman – led the campaign of public service. Each embarked on a busy programme of regional civic tours, goodwill visits to working-class areas and philanthropic and fund-raising engagements – all on a scale never seen before. This activity was aimed at promoting the monarchy's role as a benevolent force in society, with the House of Windsor trying to relieve some of the worst social distress experienced by poorer working-class communities because of the economic turbulence of the period. The hope was, as before, that royal philanthropy might stop anti-monarchical voices from taking root in these communities and offset some of the criticism levelled at the crown by its loudest opponents, who, between the wars, included the far-left Communist Party of Great Britain.

The king is recorded as having meticulously mapped those places he and members of his family visited to ensure all parts of the country received attention from the crown. Poverty-stricken areas that were most susceptible to the lure of political extremism remained the king's priority and, ever the strict taskmaster, he insisted that his eldest two sons, Edward and Albert, engage particularly energetically with these communities. Edward, prince of Wales, had a star appeal rooted in a modern informality and ease when it came to meeting peoples of different social backgrounds. He had mastered his approach to public engagement during his long tours to the far-flung outreaches of the empire in the early 1920s, travelling to the dominions and colonies as the representative of his father to thank the peoples there for their service and sacrifice during the war.

Both Edward and Albert became patrons of special funds designed to help men who were out of work and therefore struggling to feed, clothe and house their families. Albert, as duke of York, also lent his name to a new annual summer camp initiative that brought together upper- and working-class boys as part of an experiment designed to foster social cohesion between different sections of society. In reality, the impact of the duke of York's camps was limited because of the small numbers of boys involved. But the publicity for the annual event presented Albert – later George VI – and the British monarchy as a caring and relevant institution engaged in important social work that was helping to ease tensions within the nation. Crucially, the camps also paved the way for Prince Philip to launch his 'Duke of Edinburgh Award' in 1956, which was similarly designed to bring together diverse groups of young people from across society as part of a programme of self-improvement that continues to celebrate values including self-reliance, teamwork and physical fitness – all against the backdrop of the great outdoors.

So preoccupied was Albert, duke of York, with his mission to engage with the industrial working classes that his siblings took to calling him 'the foreman'. Royal biographer Jane Ridley records how he 'went down coal mines, drove locomotives [and] inspected new machinery'. Of course, the attention he and other members of his family devoted to the British proletariat was key, given how these were years that witnessed significant socio-economic dislocation, first with the industrial unrest of the mid-1920s which culminated in the General Strike of 1926 and then with the severe distress created by the Great Depression, the full impact of which struck Britain in 1930 and lasted into the middle of the decade.

It was against this backdrop of high unemployment, hunger and misery that King George V was finally persuaded by the BBC's director-general, John Reith, to speak to his people live for the first time by way of a special radio greeting on Christmas Day 1932. His message was written for him by the famous poet and novelist Rudyard Kipling, who captured some of the key themes of the king's 22-year reign. The monarch spoke of his pleasure at being able to address all parts of the British empire; he expressed sympathy for his people as they weathered the fallout of the economic recession; and he articulated his desire for them all to rally together to get through a period of difficulty. But most important of all was George's emphasis on his duty. He told listeners how 'my life's aim has been to serve'.

As the historian Philip Williamson has noted, the interwar period was marked by a notable increase in royal public addresses and speeches through which members of the House of Windsor gave meaning to the monarchy via a new public language that coalesced around the theme of service. When the archbishop of Canterbury, Cosmo Lang, took over as George's speechwriter he used the king's radio broadcasts to re-empha-size a connected theme that has also persisted to the present day: that the service performed by royalty on behalf of the nation and empire was onerous and imposed a heavy personal burden on those engaged in it. Modern royals were thus self-sacrificing figures – a key element of the public image of George V in his final years on the throne and the theme that would come to define the reign of his granddaughter, Elizabeth II, more than any other.

ELEVEN

The heavy burden of responsibility

The fact that the themes of service, duty and self-sacrifice came to define the British monarchy under Elizabeth II had as much to do with the errant behaviour of her uncle Edward as it did her morally upstanding grandfather George. To be a member of the modern royal family you have to at least appear to put duty and public service ahead of personal fulfilment. While this aspect of the public image of George V won him the support and affection of many of his people, younger generations of his family have, ever since, found it difficult to live up to his example. This began with his eldest son and heir. By the time Edward succeeded to the throne in 1936 he was one of the best-known and most beloved public figures in the English-speaking world. His early work on behalf of the crown as prince of Wales included time spent on the Western Front with British and imperial soldiers during the First World War, and a series of empire tours to Canada, Australia, New Zealand and India in the early 1920s.

These activities transformed him into a modern media celebrity. His boyish good looks, athleticism, sociable personality and love of the fast life meant he was perfectly suited to the hedonistic age of the so-called 'Bright Young Things'. He also had a reputation for informality when engaging with the ordinary people he met during his tours around Britain and the empire – a trait fêted in press and newsreel reports as setting him apart from earlier generations of royalty. His interactions with the British working classes and the concern that he displayed for them during the depression as the founder of various royal relief funds won him plaudits and much support from all sections of society.

However, despite his great show of sympathy for the poor and unem-ployed, Edward's official biographer, Philip Ziegler, noted that he was not always as conscientious or consistent in his approach to public service as his father would have liked. These shortcomings became increasingly evident after he became king because he had another private preoccupation: the American socialite Wallis Simpson, with whom he had been having an extramarital affair since 1934.

That the two were in a relationship was common knowledge within the royal family and in London high society. But the British establishment kept it a closely guarded secret from the rest of the country because Wallis was deemed to be an unsuitable match for a king, no matter how modern and popular he was. She had already been divorced once and was formalizing her separation from her second husband so that she could marry again. And not only was Edward supreme governor of the Church of England – a role that required him to uphold the highest standards of moral rectitude – but as a young Windsor he was expected to marry someone who was from a respectable and ideally British family untainted by divorce or marital irregularity.

Edward's determination to flout convention and marry the woman he loved flew in the face of the concept of public duty that had been so diligently promoted by his father and the royal household ever since the First World War. He was ready to put personal fulfilment ahead of all else, his behaviour threatening to break the sacred moral bond that had existed between crown and people whereby the monarch and royal family performed service on behalf of their subjects in return for their past sacrifices and, more importantly, their loyalty in the present. But at the same time, his pursuit of self-fulfilment was in keeping with an interwar emotional culture which celebrated, more than ever before, the idea that happiness could be achieved through true romance. And, in fact, when Edward's affair with Wallis was finally revealed to his subjects by the press at the start of December 1936, many members of the public sided with him in the belief that he should be able to marry the woman he loved *and* stay on the throne.

However, another section of public opinion – more traditional, pious and middle class in character – led by Prime Minister Stanley Baldwin, argued that Edward must give up the throne if he wanted to marry Wallis. In the end, the king as a constitutional monarch had to heed the advice of his premier and was thus forced to choose love over duty, abdicating his position to be replaced by his younger brother, the duke of York. In his abdication broadcast to the public, Edward (now with the new title of duke of Windsor) made clear to his listeners how modern kingship required a kind of dedication that, without Wallis by his side, he was simply unwilling to consider: 'You must believe me when I tell you that I have found it impossible to carry the heavy burden of responsibility and to discharge my duties as King as I would wish to do without the help and support of the woman I love.' His message brilliantly crystallized the idea that to be royal was to live a life restricted by onerous duty: if Edward could not marry Wallis, then he would be unable to bear that 'heavy burden of responsibility'.

Edward's abdication was without doubt the most earth-shattering episode in the history of the modern monarchy. It demonstrated spectacularly the problem of a personality-led royal family where, after years of adulation and positive media coverage, a huge sense of public expectation came to rest on the shoulders of one person, who, it turned out, was not up to the job. It also made clear to the public the idea that there existed a 'good' version of kingship – anchored in duty, service and self-sacrifice – and a 'bad' version, where personal fulfilment and self-gratification won out. The good version also emphasized the virtues of Christian family life, which was something Edward was unwilling and unable to embody. While many in Britain and the empire were sorry to see the old king go, one thing the duke of York had that the duke of Windsor did not was a young family. And although the abdication changed the life of the new king for ever, it also changed the life of his eldest daughter, Elizabeth, by bringing her into the direct line of succession.

———

The man once known as Prince Albert, duke of York, took the name George VI to convey to his subjects a sense of continuity with his father's reign. Palace officials and a mostly compliant media promoted the message that the new king had come to the throne reluctantly but had ultimately accepted the burden of responsibility as someone who, unlike his brother, put duty before personal desire. In truth, the story of George's accession was more complex. Behind closed doors, there were deep concerns about his readiness for the role because of his nervous disposition and speech impediment. He was not a showman like Edward. And because of this, their youngest brother, the duke of Kent, was briefly considered as a potential successor to the former king because, as a good-looking prince charming and family man who was popular with the press and public, he was deemed to be better suited to the role of modern monarch.

Nevertheless, this plan was scrapped probably at the insistence of Elizabeth, duchess of York (the future queen mother), who helped to persuade her husband that he could be king and she queen consort at his side. The two found themselves out of favour with the public to begin with, the new queen recognizing this when she told a confidante that 'I fully expect that we may be moderately unpopular for some time.' The shadow of the duke of Windsor notably hung over them both on the day of their crowning and dampened the festivities.

While it is clear from comments made by the public at the time of the 1937 coronation that many saw George VI as an inferior substitute for his older brother, it is also significant that many took pity on him, seeing him as someone who had taken on the 'difficult job' of monarch despite his personal misgivings and physical shortcomings. Typical was the comment of one 'northcountry-man' who spoke to Kingsley Martin, editor of the *New Statesman*, after the event:

> If it had been Edward the nation would have gone mad. As it is, we would still prefer to cheer Edward, but we know that we've got to cheer George. After all, it's Edward's fault he's not on the throne, and George didn't ask to get there. He's only doing his duty, and it's up to us to show that we appreciate it.

This sense that the new king was simply 'doing his duty' earned him a degree of respect, if not necessarily affection. Over time, the palace PR narrative that George VI was, above all, a responsible and self-sacrificing figure would cut through, defining early biographies written about him which celebrated how his commitment to public service helped to stabilize the throne after the turbulence of the abdication crisis.

Central to the narrative of kingly duty was the role of George VI during the Second World War. The conflict witnessed a rise in popular criticism of privileged sections of society, including the royals, owing to the way the initial privations of war – rationing, conscription and evacuation – affected working-class people disproportionately. It was also the case that, separated from family and friends and with their everyday lives turned upside down, most people cared little about news that was not war-related. This posed a problem for the royal family, who found themselves sidelined in the first year of the conflict. Worse still, the shadowy activities of the duke of Windsor, who, it was rumoured at the time, had got himself involved in a treacherous Nazi plot, threatened to again bring the crown into disrepute.

The Luftwaffe's Blitz of British cities, which began in September 1940, thus proved to be an opportunity for George VI and Queen Elizabeth. For the first time since the war began, the royal couple were able to demonstrate a benevolent interest in the lives of their subjects. They undertook carefully organized visits in London and around Britain to meet the ordinary people whose homes and communities had been torn apart by the bombing raids. And much like his father and mother before him, the king went on special trips to industrial communities in order to try to boost morale and embed royalism among those people he encountered.

Carefully choreographed media arrangements meant that the king and queen could be seen in photographs and newsreel films engaged in informal conversation with their subjects, offering words of encouragement and, crucially, symbolic leadership at a time of national crisis. Problematic encounters where the royal couple met with a cool or hostile reception from their subjects, as was the case when they were booed during a visit to part of the East End of London just after it had been heavily bombed at the start of the Blitz, did not get reported by a media that was required to self-censor throughout the conflict.

As had been the case with the First World War, the House of Windsor also sought to lead by example. Rationing came into force again in the royal household. And the aerial bombing of Buckingham Palace in September 1940 was seen as an excellent PR opportunity by courtiers to publicize how the king and his subjects found themselves 'on the front line together' – even though, unbeknown to the public, George VI and Queen Elizabeth spent most evenings holed up in Windsor Castle, 25 miles from central London and out of harm's way.

I mentioned in Chapter 4 how Princess Elizabeth donned the uniform of the Auxiliary Territorial Service in the spring of 1945 as part of a propaganda exercise designed to present her as an exemplary figure who symbolized the royal family's leadership of the war effort. Film crews and photographers were given special access to the training camp where she was based in order to capture scenes of her in uniform – the same uniform she would wear for the famous photos that show her and her family on Buckingham Palace's balcony flanking Britain's war leader, Winston Churchill, on VE Day in 1945. It is a key image of celebration that is still used in British TV documentaries to immortalize the narrative that in wartime monarchy, parliament and people dutifully came together to serve and defend the nation and empire (Fig 5). As we know now, the reality was more complex. The royals had often struggled to generate positive publicity as part of a conflict that witnessed an upsurge in criticism of the old British elite, including the House of Windsor. And yet, to this day, documentary film-makers have refrained from telling this other side of the story, preferring to repeat *ad nauseam* a version of events that emphasizes instead how class differences and political tensions were briefly put aside by a British public which rallied around the symbols of crown, country and democracy in the fight against fascism.

TWELVE

Come on Margaret!

We have so far seen how royal public relations strategies that centred on duty and public service, including philanthropic work, developed over the course of more than 150 years mainly in response to concerns about self-preservation on the part of the monarchy. Dramatic social and political shifts witnessed the power of the crown challenged by new groups, as well as by a series of crises, including the world wars, the Great Depression and the abdication of Edward VIII, which required resolute responses from the royal family if they were going to remain meaningful and relevant to the public.

One of the main challenges the crown had to contend with after 1945 was the rise of a new style of media coverage that was becoming less deferential. Many journalists had expressed concern after the abdication that they conspired in misleading the British population by keeping the king's affair secret when what they should have done was publish a story that was very much in the public interest. The Second World War increased the feeling among more progressive elements in the media that the job of news reporters was not to protect Britain's elite establishment but to provide an outlet for ordinary people's concerns and to scrutinize the actions of the powerful. Foremost among these progressive voices was the *Daily Mirror*, which, with its brash populist tone and left-wing agenda, blazed a trail for other newspapers by critiquing the behaviour of the royals and holding them to account for their actions as part of the more democratic post-war age.

If we briefly return to Princess Elizabeth's 21st birthday broadcast in April 1947, we can now appreciate more fully why the message drew on the language of duty, service and self-sacrifice in order to evoke sympathy from her listeners. However, there was a hidden twist to this story. Back at the beginning of the year the British press had published the (true) rumour that Elizabeth had become secretly engaged to a Greek royal called Philip. The public had no idea who this Hellenic prince was and, when invited by the Mirror's sister paper, the Sunday Pictorial, to give their views as part of a daring opinion poll on the suitability of the relationship, 40 per cent of respondents out of a total of 6,100 judged that Philip should not be allowed to marry Elizabeth.

The result was panic in the royal household, the poll representing an audacious attempt to challenge the princess's desire to marry the man of her choosing. Courtiers would have also been worried by some of the reasons respondents to the poll gave for opposing the marriage. Some judged Philip too foreign and insisted Elizabeth marry a nice young British man instead. Others thought the relationship could lead to a dangerous political alliance between the House of Windsor and the Greek royal family, which at the time was fighting for its survival in a civil war involving rival monarchist and communist factions.

What followed was a big royal PR campaign designed to transform Philip's public image and, as we shall see in Part Three, it was ultimately successful. Elizabeth's 21st birthday broadcast formed part of this PR effort, with its conscious attempt to generate sympathy for the princess in the hope that, when her engagement to Philip was officially announced, it would translate into support for her desire to marry the man she loved. From the evidence that is available, it seems it may have had its intended impact. One woman from the south of England writing about Elizabeth and Philip shortly after their marriage for the social research organization Mass Observation described them as an 'attractive couple' and noted how she felt 'that after her "dedication" of herself to our service on the occasion of her 21st birthday the princess is deserving of the best that this country and its people can give her. Theirs is no enviable task.'

The new kind of critical media scrutiny of the royals' behaviour also extended to a more sensationalist coverage of their private lives. A notable example of this came during Elizabeth and Philip's honeymoon in November 1947, when journalists and camera crews pursued them to their holiday retreat in Hampshire, speculating about the layout of their bedroom and their post-wedding activities. Such an invasion of royal privacy seems mild by today's standards, but at the time it caused public uproar. Many people criticized the media while simultaneously expressing pity for the princess for the way she had been forced to honeymoon 'in a gold-fish bowl'.

This event hastened the emergence of a new idea: that being royal meant losing one's privacy and the ability to enjoy a normal family life. Recognizing how these events had earned the royal couple public sympathy, palace officials made much of Elizabeth and Philip's desire for privacy and their hope to enjoy a normal domestic life, particularly after the births of Prince Charles and Princess Anne in 1948 and 1950. I expand on this theme in Part Three, but for now it suffices to say that this particular PR message, which stresses how the Windsors wish to enjoy fulfilling home lives, is a powerful one. This is because it is anchored in two eternal truths: the first is that private family life is an important part of British culture and the public therefore readily identify with this ideal; the second is that the media exposure faced by the royals can doubtless be tiresome and difficult.

However, the problem with this plea for domestic normality is that what goes on behind closed doors at the palace suggests that the royals' home lives are far from 'ordinary'. As well as the extramarital impropriety that has, since the time of Edward VII, been tolerated (although not necessarily publicly disclosed or condoned), every generation of royalty has left the bulk of their parenting duties to nannies. In the mid-1950s palace officials and a sycophantic section of the media vigorously promoted the narrative that the queen hated being separated from her two young children because of official engagements but nevertheless put her duties ahead of personal fulfilment as was required of her as monarch. But what we now know from those who saw or experienced Queen Elizabeth's parenting style first-hand is that she was an emotionally distant figure. Even when in close proximity to Charles and Anne, she preferred to leave it to nannies to care for them, as was quite common among the upper classes in this period.

Such disingenuousness should not surprise us, given the power of the royal publicity machine and its effectiveness in generating sympathetic coverage of the monarchy. It is significant that today, when there is much greater emphasis placed on 'authenticity' and the idea that parents should be emotionally invested in their family roles, both Prince William and Prince Harry seem to be devoted fathers who are much more involved in the upbringing of their children, possibly inspired by their mother, Diana, who was untypically hands on. However, the princes have, in loudly speaking out against the press, also done much to shore up the idea that their royal lives are unenviable because of constant media exposure, not least when they're with their families.

This emphasis on the loss of privacy which, as we've seen, first emerged in the years after the Second World War, has generated compassion for some members of the House of Windsor and has helped to convince us, the British public, that royal life, despite its wealth, privileges and power, is burdensome. And, in tandem with the public relations message that has, since the reign of George V, highlighted the constant programme of public service undertaken by royalty, the loss of privacy theme has helped to win the Windsors the support of the public while offsetting criticism about the social inequality that underpins Britain's monarchical system.

The case of Princess Margaret, Queen Elizabeth's younger sister, is instructive here. No sooner was the 1953 coronation over than the tabloid press turned their attention to Margaret and the rumour that she had fallen in love with a palace courtier. The man in question was Peter Townsend, who was part of the queen mother's household. He was recently divorced, and he and the princess had begun their clandestine relationship after the death of George VI. Of course, the wider royal family and the queen's private secretary (whom she'd inherited from her father), Tommy Lascelles, thought he was unsuitable for Margaret because of his marital status. Townsend was thus seconded to an airbase in Brussels, where he would serve with the RAF for two years, as he had done during the war; meanwhile, the princess would have the time to make up her mind about whether or not she wanted to marry him.

Townsend's much-anticipated return in 1955 saw public opinion split into two camps, as was the case during the abdication crisis. There were those who believed Margaret should be allowed to marry Townsend and those who opposed the relationship. The press delighted in the drama, a famous *Daily Mirror* front-page headline playfully urging the princess to make up her mind by proclaiming 'Come on Margaret!' She knew that if she married him she would be forced to give up her position in the line of succession. This was to ensure that, in the event some tragedy befell Elizabeth's young family, Margaret could not succeed to the throne and the supreme governorship of the Church of England with a twice-married husband. Faced with the possible loss of status and its accompanying privileges, she decided to give Townsend up. This was an important moment. It generated much sympathy for the princess and crystallized the belief that she put national responsibility and public service ahead of personal fulfilment. But the image of Margaret as dutiful and conscientious would not last, and public compassion for her would, in time, evaporate.

Margaret's much fêted marriage to the dashing celebrity photographer (and commoner) Antony Armstrong-Jones in 1960 was not a happy one. Mutual infidelity meant the relationship broke down as the decade wore on. As it did so, the princess found herself the focus of a more aggressive style of tabloid journalism led by the Sun and News of the World, both of which had come into the ownership of an Australian press baron named Rupert Murdoch. This culminated in a spate of humiliating front-page revelations in 1976 that claimed Margaret was romantically attached to Roddy Llewellyn, a socialite 17 years her junior. These reports stressed that, far from being overburdened by duty, the princess prioritized extra-marital pleasure-seeking in the company of younger boyfriends, often in exotic destinations like the Caribbean.

Such a loss of privacy might have generated sympathy for her in the past, but the fact that she had neglected her role as a royal public servant meant that she seemed to be having her cake (with all of its privileges) and eating it. As one biographer of the queen, Ben Pimlott, recognized, this created difficulties for the monarchy in terms of how it justified Margaret remaining in receipt of civil list payments from the British state to fund her activities as a member of the royal family when her lifestyle mirrored that of the 'dissipated ... idle rich'. Her eventual divorce in 1978 followed by illness brought on, in part, by alcoholism signalled the closure of this especially messy chapter in the story of the House of Windsor, one that witnessed the emergence of a more confrontational relationship between the press and monarchy, as well as the collapse of the idealized image of a harmonious royal family that consistently put the public good ahead of its own interests.

Margaret's fall from grace allowed media audiences to glimpse another side of royal life that had previously been largely concealed from the public – that of individual self-indulgence. Other members of the House of Windsor have since been accused of behaving in ways that have led to a similar fall in public confidence in the monarchy, most notably the queen's second son Andrew and his former wife, Sarah 'Fergie' Ferguson. Shortly after the couple separated, photographs were published by the UK tabloids of Fergie on holiday, having her toes kissed by her financial adviser-turned-lover. This humiliating episode unfolded in 1992, the year famously described by Elizabeth II as her annus horribilis because of the fire that destroyed a large section of Windsor Castle, but also because of the way a critical media had shone light on the scandalous reality of royal private life, with three (out of four) of the queen's children separating or divorcing their spouses following marital breakdown. Most notably, it was the year when Charles and Diana, princess of Wales, confirmed their separation after a spate of press revelations about their extramarital affairs. Their relationship is dealt with in Part Three, but it is important to note here that the disclosures regarding the now king and his then mistress (now wife and queen), Camilla, as well as his emotional neglect of Diana, struck a serious blow to the idea that the British monarchy offered exemplary moral leadership to the nation.

The prince of Wales's adultery suggested that he was unwilling to forgo self-gratification for the greater good – that of his duties as a husband and as the future monarch and supreme governor of the Church of England. Following their fairy-tale wedding, the public had envisaged that the princess of Wales would one day be queen at her husband's side. But the couple's messy separation and divorce shattered this idea and led to a significant increase in public criticism of the crown. Once again it seemed as though the royals were more interested in pursuing pleasure and their own self-interests than in behaving dutifully and honourably, as was once expected of them.

THIRTEEN

A new Jerusalem?

Along with the decline in deference and the rise of a more invasive style of royal press coverage after the war, there was another major change that the monarchy had to adapt to from 1945 onwards. This came in the form of a new type of interventionist government: one that took a much greater interest in the lives of the UK population than ever before.

The war had required the state to mobilize and coordinate the activities of the public on an unprecedented scale, a process that had indirectly uncovered the full extent of the poverty in which large sections of the public were trapped. Clement Attlee's promise to voters that a Labour government would build a 'New Jerusalem' to address the everyday needs of millions of working-class and lower middle-class voters if elected into power saw his party win the July 1945 election by a landslide, removing from power the victorious war leader Winston Churchill.

Attlee's administration set about transforming the country by building homes, creating jobs and transforming the education and health sectors. One of his government's great legacies was a modern welfare state which included the safety net of a national health service that all members of society could access, as well as a comprehensive scheme of national insurance to ensure that the unemployed and elderly could not easily fall into destitution. Labour wanted to ensure that there was no going back to the bad old days of the 1930s.

However, this kind of interventionist government, which took on a central national role in planning and organizing society in order to achieve its aims of greater prosperity and greater egalitarianism, represented a threat to the British monarchy. It directly challenged the crown's historic role as champion of a national voluntary culture which promoted philanthropy as the answer to society's ills. In particular, the royals had carved out a crucial function for themselves in the 50-year period from the late nineteenth century to the early 1940s as the patrons of a patch-work of medical institutions and relief schemes that had, up until this point, helped some of those most desperately in need.

Royal philanthropy thus suffered a big setback in the immediate post-1945 period. The royal aim to be seen 'doing good' for the people of Britain had drawn on the altruism of a family who, like many others of their patrician class, saw charity as a moral necessity. As we've seen, it also provided the monarchy with a purpose in a fast-changing world where suddenly it was required to justify its privileged position, offering the royals a way of engaging generously with a potentially hostile working class in order to win their affection and loyalty.

What quickly emerged after the war was a new 'consensus', with the majority of Labour and Conservative politicians broadly agreeing on the principle that government had an important function to play in caring for the population. Suddenly forced into a back-seat role by a bigger, more ambitious, more socially engaged state, the crown had to work out once again what its place was as part of this new settlement.

It did so in two, knowingly contradictory, ways: first of all, it outwardly supported the new systems and services that emerged out of the reorgani-zation of society in the years from 1945 to the mid-1970s, backing the new popular consensus; second, it carefully identified areas left untouched by the more proactive state and fought a careful rearguard action by cordon-ing these off as royal spheres of influence. And, in response to perceived problems in these areas, the royal family supported new philanthropic schemes and fundraising operations to promote an alternative vision of modern Britain, thus quietly pushing back against the brave new world that emerged out of the Second World War.

We can identify the monarchy's new role, first as supporter of welfare-state-led initiatives, in relation to its shifting attitude to Britain's new National Health Service (NHS), which was founded in 1948. According to one of its principal architects, the minister of health in the Attlee govern-ment, Aneurin Bevan, the NHS would replace the hotchpotch 'patchquilt' of voluntary and charitable medical institutions which had, with signifi-cant royal backing, dominated British healthcare up until this point.

There was a short but distinct period of tension between monarchy and government as the new health service found its feet and the full implications of nationalization, including of voluntary hospitals, became clear. The royal-led medical charity the King's Fund was notably outspoken in its resistance to the NHS, with Queen Elizabeth's uncle the duke of Gloucester leading (as its president) a personal crusade as critic of the new service and defender of the old ways. Nevertheless, an accord was reached between the palace and government whereby the royals were allowed to carry on as symbolic patrons of state-run health facilities, like the hospitals to which they had once given their names as benefactors and fundraisers. This meant the royals could carry on visiting institutions with which they had long-term connections, enabling them to align themselves with the achievements of the NHS as it became a key part of British national life and with the interests of the working-class people who gained most from its existence.

This type of symbolic support for the successes of the welfare state in the first decades of the post-war period was also evident in the thousands of official visits made by members of the royal family to towns and cities up and down the country as they underwent processes of renewal, regeneration and, in some cases, construction from scratch, as with 'new towns' such as Milton Keynes and Telford. Whereas royalty's presence at the opening of provincial buildings in the nineteenth century had signalled their approval for the private philanthropy that usually financed such initiatives, now members of the House of Windsor presided at ceremonies to inaugurate state-led developments like new housing estates, libraries, swimming pools and shopping centres. Thus the monarchy made known its support for government-backed efforts to transform the UK's urban landscape in ways that were designed to benefit the new 'citizen-consumer' of the 1950s and 1960s.

Public engagements such as these imbued the monarchy symbolically with a sense of 'the modern' and conveyed to media audiences that the crown was readily moving with the times. No individual member of the royal family was more crucial to this image of national and royal modernization than Prince Philip, the duke of Edinburgh. Biographers have suggested that his deeply held belief in the value of science, his boundless energy and desire to make something new of his ill-defined position as prince consort, saw him assume an important symbolic role as the public face of British technological and industrial achievement.

From the late 1950s through to the 1970s Philip criss-crossed the UK on board his famous red helicopter (which he often piloted himself as another notable symbol of royal modernity) to celebrate the work of scientists and engineers involved in the development of new kinds of national infrastructure, such as hydroelectric dams, nuclear power stations and sewage works. Royal support for these government-led projects again linked the monarchy to the successes of a far-reaching state which, through until the 1970s, invested heavily in science, technology and new industries (Fig 6).

We can see from the strategic activities of the duke of Edinburgh and other members of the royal family how the crown recognized that Britain's political, social and economic situation was transformed by the war and how, quite sensibly, it aligned itself with this new settlement, thus ensuring that the monarchy continued to exist as a visible national symbol. However, the royals did not simply give up on the older types of philanthropy that had been so crucial to their pre-1939 existence. There was a veritable flourishing of royal-backed charities during the first half of the reign of Elizabeth II, with the House of Windsor devoting special attention to voluntary organizations working at the edges of the welfare state and in areas left largely untouched by new government-backed systems and services.

For example, while post-war Labour and Conservative administrations sought to improve the lives of British children and young people through the provision of new forms of healthcare, education and direct forms of financial support, inevitably some still fell through the safety net and benefited instead from help given by royal-backed charities such as the Save the Children Fund and the NSPCC. In this vein, the then Prince Charles launched the Prince's Trust in 1976 to support disadvantaged young people with training, employment and other work-related opportunities. The historian Frank Prochaska records that between 2006 and 2016 the value of the work of the trust on behalf of society was estimated at being worth £1.4 billion.

However, despite the impressive statistics, the organization's mission statement reads like something written by Prince Albert 175 years ago on the Victorian royal family's Christian duty to those most in need. The Prince's Trust aims 'to promote by all charitable means the mental, spiritual, moral and physical development and improvement of young people, and to provide opportunities for them to develop to their full capacities and enable them to become responsible members of society so that their conditions of life may be improved.'

The sustained royal commitment to these philanthropic organizations suggests that the monarchy has fought a shrewd rearguard action. Although it accepted that times had changed, it did not abandon a voluntary tradition that had served it so well for so long. Furthermore, it is clear that some members of the royal family and their advisers saw Britain's welfare state as a temporary vogue to be grudgingly tolerated but which would, in time, fade away. In terms of the crown's survival, it thus made good strategic sense to keep alive an older voluntary culture that might, one day, make a more fulsome return.

The key figure here again was the duke of Edinburgh. Although this may at first appear counter-intuitive, given his outward support for state-led initiatives during this period, in fact we shouldn't be surprised. He was outspoken, opinionated and believed he should be able to air his ideas in ways that would have been deemed constitutionally problematic for his wife as monarch. Against the backdrop of an economic downturn brought on by the international energy crisis of 1973, Philip publicly aired his long-held concerns about the British welfare state and what he viewed as its suffocating bureaucracy: 'The Welfare State is a protection against failure and exploitation, but a national recovery can only take place if innovators, and men of enterprise and hard work, can prosper.'

This defence of private business interests and what he saw as the individual's freedom to innovate took fuller form in his 1984 book Men, Machines and Sacred Cows. In a TV interview to publicize this pet project, Philip lamented how an overbearing post-war state had given birth to various 'sacred cows', criticism of which, he felt, was taboo. He argued that individual initiative had been stifled by an emphasis on social security, collectivism and the government's control of industry. He also spoke of a failure to develop individual character among Britain's younger generations, which, of course, was something he had long sought to address through the Duke of Edinburgh Award scheme, which he set up in part to nurture self-reliance in young people.

Holding forth in this way, Philip echoed a set of concerns articulated by the Conservative prime minister Margaret Thatcher. The New Right successfully promoted a political narrative of British economic and moral decline which they claimed stemmed from the public's overreliance on the post-war interventionist style of government. According to Thatcher, it was time to liberate the people and their individual initiative. Her answer to the perceived problem was simple: she would create a free-market economy and in the process begin to disassemble what she and her allies consistently presented as a failing welfare state.

Members of the royal family are not meant to express politically partisan views. In Philip we can identify a failure on the part of Elizabeth II and courtiers to rein in restless royals who feel the need to open their mouths when, as figureheads of a constitutional – that is, politically impartial – monarchy, they must avoid doing so. We can also see from the duke of Edinburgh's interventions in public life where it is that his eldest son, Charles, gained inspiration for how to conduct himself. Rather than follow the purse-lipped example set by his mother, the new king, during his tenure as prince of Wales, took after his father as seen from the range of political issues he became involved in as a campaigning figurehead from the late 1960s onwards.

One concern that both father and son used their platforms to address was the protection of the natural world. Advocating that humankind maintain an equilibrium in its relationship with the countryside and environment gained the monarchy support among conservationists and, more recently, climate activists. Philip readily embraced the opportunities afforded him by the conservationist organization the World Wildlife Fund, acting as its international president for 15 years from 1981 to 1996. With the duke's encouragement, the WWF updated its mission statement to emphasize the promotion of biological diversity, sustainable resources and the reduction of pollution and unnecessary consumption – all of which are themes that the prince of Wales subsequently campaigned on in his advocacy roles. Notably, the fact that climate, environment and the natural world are global (as opposed to specifically British) issues has also meant that members of the House of Windsor have enjoyed greater freedom in speaking out about their concerns without appearing overtly party political, while also ensuring they reach an international audience.

More controversially, Charles has also emulated his father's example in advancing causes (often clandestinely as with his infamous 'black spider memos' to political figures) that offer an alternative vision of the UK to that offered by the post-war interventionist state. This has included campaigning for the introduction of homeopathic medicines, which are not on offer through the NHS (because there is no proof that they work). The new king has also used his powerful position to exert pressure on national and local government officials to embrace architectural reform, especially a return to more traditional styles as set out in his controversial

1989 book *A Vision of Britain*, which offered a strong critique of the utilitarian modernism favoured by post-war government planners.

The king has pursued his own personal experiment in urban design through his creation of the town Poundbury on Duchy of Cornwall land, near Dorchester, in southern England. Local planning officials originally hoped that the project would yield significant affordable housing for lower-income groups. As Poundbury's official website makes clear, 35 per cent of all homes that have been built are classed as affordable, with lower-income households able to live alongside wealthier households in order to promote 'social cohesion' and a 'well balanced, mixed income community'.

However, the sociologist Laura Clancy has challenged the social utopianism of the king's model town. She suggests that what he has in fact created is a *faux* Georgian settlement that acts as a tribute to royal patronage (the main square is named after the queen mother while the pub and hotel at the centre of the town is called the Duchess of Cornwall Inn); and, in terms of residential accommodation, Poundbury mainly comprises luxury apartments and villas, most of which are well out of reach of poorer socio-economic groups.

In 1986 Charles also founded a charity called the Prince of Wales's Institute of Architecture, today known as the Prince's Foundation. This organization has educated young people in traditional building design and other related skills, and it has supported the restoration of historic sites such as Dumfries House, a Scottish stately home which became another pet project of the king when he helped to secure its purchase in 2007. Today Dumfries House is open to the public and acts as the operations centre for the Prince's Foundation. Since 2021, however, the charity and mansion have been at the centre of the *Sunday Times* newspaper investigation discussed earlier in this section because of alleged fundraising impropriety, with former valet to the king Michael Fawcett accused of arranging donations from billionaire businessmen to help with the Dumfries House project in return for honours.

While the Windsors can rightly claim that their philanthropy and support for charities have done much to benefit members of the British public – and especially younger people – since 1945, it is crucial that we do not lose sight of the other agendas that are at work here or the bigger consequences of this royal role for the country. Patronage of these schemes and organizations has helped to secure the monarchy's position in a less deferential age by ensuring that its public image is closely associated with 'good causes' aimed at helping those most in need who have often fallen through the gaps in the post-war social safety net. And while, on the one hand, the royal family have outwardly and loudly supported the achievements of the welfare state, they have also staked out the areas beyond its limits as spheres of royal influence. Given central government cuts to areas like health, education and early years care, this has meant there have been increasing opportunities for royal philanthropy to flourish in national life, promoting a 'new normal' where we have come to expect less of the state.

The monarchy has thus helped to keep alive Britain's voluntary traditions but in so doing has used its philanthropy to push back on what it perceives as the excesses of state power and centralized planning. The two most influential figures here have been the duke of Edinburgh and the new king, both men voicing their opinions and championing pet projects in ways that have often proved controversial, particularly for the way they have ignored the constitutional requirements imposed on them as politically impartial representatives of the crown. That the king, following his father's earlier example, has long campaigned to protect the natural world has insulated him from more vociferous criticism. The issue of environmental destruction is extremely important and extends beyond the scope of British politics, commanding significant global attention, especially among younger activists. Indeed, it is with this demographic in mind that Prince William has, more recently, sought to carve out a role as an advocate for action to counter climate change.

Today royal philanthropy is more political than it has ever been, and this poses problems for the monarchy. This is partly due to the international role that the monarchy has embraced in relation to the politics of environmentalism. But it is also due to the opportunistic way it has seized on certain issues in a British context. Since the 1980s, successive Conservative governments have sought to undermine the welfare state. This has led to politicians from both main parties remodelling state institutions through new public–private sector relationships, and through partnerships with the voluntary sector, in order to continue delivering key services to the population. While some changes to public service delivery have doubtlessly improved efficiency, the retreat of the state, particularly under the Tory-led coalition that came to power in 2010, has seen

p.41 Fig 1: Queen Elizabeth II presenting the heir to the throne, Charles, prince of Wales, to his people following his investiture at Caernarfon Castle in 1969. The event met with a mixed public response, and in 2022 we were told there would be no formal investiture for King Charles's heir, William, the new prince of Wales. (© Daily Mirror/Mirrorpix/Getty Images)

p.56 Fig 2: The view from Buckingham Palace's roof following the coronation of King Charles III and Queen Camilla, 6 May 2023. In the 1920s the royal balcony appearance became a powerful symbolic moment designed to convey to the new mass media audience the unity of crown and people. (© Bruce Adams – WPA Pool/ Getty Images)

p.73 Fig 3: The duke and duchess of Cambridge, William and Catherine, in Kingston, Jamaica, March 2022. With its hierarchical – and imperial – overtones, the military parade captured in this image went down badly with sections of the public and media, which claimed the event elevated the royals above the local people as if the island were still an 'infant colony'. (© Pool/Samir Hussein/WireImage/Getty Images)

p.87 Fig 4: Princess Elizabeth in Cape Town, South Africa, in front of the microphone through which she delivered the famous speech 'dedicating' her life to the service of Britain and its empire on 21 April 1947. The speech was crafted by royal aides who understood how the themes of duty and self-sacrifice would evoke a powerful emotional response from listeners across the world. (© Topical Press Agency/ Hulton Archive/Getty Images)

p.113 Fig 5: King George VI, the royal family and Winston Churchill greet the crowds from the balcony of Buckingham Palace on Victory in Europe Day, 8 May 1945. A popular image that is still used in TV documentaries to this day, it has helped to immortalize the royal public relations narrative that, in wartime, the monarchy, parliament and people came together to defend the nation. (© Daily Herald Archive/National Science & Media Museum/SSPL via Getty Images)

p.124 Fig 6: Prince Philip, duke of Edinburgh, descending into a mineshaft during his visit to the Mosley Common Colliery in Lancashire. Philip became particularly closely associated with British industrial and scientific innovation in the 1950s and 1960s. In this period at least, the prince consort was outwardly very supportive of the government's efforts to modernize industry and the economy. (© Staff/Mirrorpix/Getty Images)

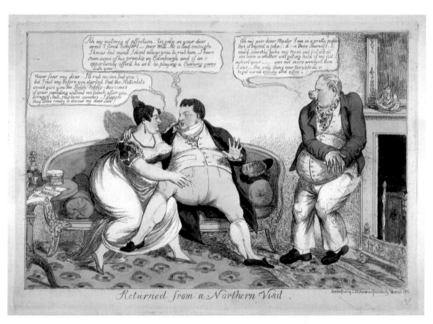

p.157 Fig 7: A satirical cartoon titled 'Returned from a Northern Visit', from 1823, which lampooned King George IV (centre) for his womanizing. On the left we see the monarch's mistress, Lady Elizabeth Conyngham, stroking her royal lover's thigh. The king's dissolute lifestyle did much to undermine public confidence in the British monarchy. (© Guildhall Library & Art Gallery/Heritage Images/Getty Images)

p.158 Fig 8: The Victorian royal family helped to popularize the modern Christmas and, in so doing, presented themselves as exemplars of Christian family values. In 1848 Prince Albert agreed that this illustration of him with Queen Victoria and their children could be reproduced for mass consumption in the leading pictorial newspaper of the day, the *Illustrated London News*. (© Bettmann/Getty Images)

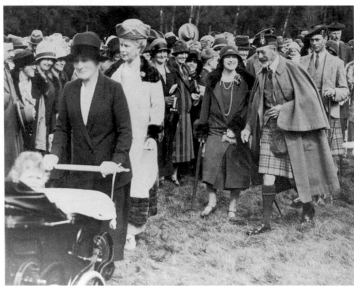

p.164 Fig 9: King George V – seen here in a traditional Scottish tam-o'-shanter and kilt – did more than any royal before him to popularize the idea of the 'family monarchy'. In this picture, taken in 1927 on the Windsors' Balmoral estate, he can be seen alongside his wife and consort, Queen Mary (in the white and black fur coat), his second son, Bertie (walking behind the king in similar dress), and his daughter-in-law, Elizabeth (next to the king). On the far left being pushed in a pram, we can see the future Elizabeth II as a baby. (© Central Press/Getty Images)

p.166 Fig 10: Edward, prince of Wales – later King Edward VIII – was celebrated for his common touch and as a charismatic 'man of the people', which helps explain the huge sense of loss felt by many across Britain and the empire following his abdication in December 1936. Here he can be seen at the FA Cup Final at Wembley Stadium in 1935 shaking hands with the Sheffield Wednesday players. (© Fox Photos/Getty Images)

p.172 Fig 11: The young family of Princess Elizabeth and the duke of Edinburgh were presented as symbolizing the post-war ideal at a time when a new nationwide culture of domesticity was emerging in Britain. Images like this one, from 1951, were made available as mass collectables and were also reproduced in popular souvenir magazines. (© Bettmann/Getty Images)

p.179 Fig 12: Princess Margaret, the younger sister of Queen Elizabeth, became the focus of massive public interest in the 1950s because of her tumultuous love life. One of the first victims of tabloid celebrity journalism, she can be seen here in 1960 at the Badminton horse trials following her engagement to the dashing society photographer (and commoner) Antony Armstrong-Jones. (© Central Press/ Getty Images)

p.185 Fig 13: In the early 1980s, Diana, princess of Wales, injected some much-needed glamour back into the House of Windsor after the difficulties of the preceding decade. And, as a young mother to Princes William and Harry, she simultaneously seemed to represent a more innocent (backward-looking) age, where the Victorian family values espoused by Britain's then prime minister, Margaret Thatcher, prevailed. (© Tim Graham Photo Library via Getty Images)

p.204 Fig 14: A glimpse into Buckingham Palace and what Prince Charles had in mind for his future 'slimmed-down' monarchy while Queen Elizabeth was still on the throne in March 2019. Unfortunately for the new king, such a vision for a smaller, more youthful monarchy – one that focused on him, Queen Camilla, his sons and their wives – has not come to pass because of Harry and Meghan's split from the royal family in 2020 and the bad blood that has built up between him and his older brother, William. (© Dominic Lipinski – WPA Pool/Getty Images)

government neglect crucial areas that have instead been left to a patchwork of voluntary organizations, including royal-sponsored charities, to
deal with.

On the face of it, the return of philanthropy to the front line of politics might at first seem as though it benefits the current generation of
Windsors by giving them new meaningful roles. However, it also leaves
them vulnerable to criticism from those who wish to overhaul what
increasingly appears to be a broken system of government. The last
decade has seen increased political polarization stemming from Brexit
but also from the economic crises that emerged out of the Covid-19
pandemic and the Russian invasion of Ukraine. With public discontent
with the status quo on the rise, the royals could, if they are not careful,
come to be seen as defenders of a malfunctioning socio-political model
that is failing millions.

FOURTEEN

The Queen had no choice

After the British monarchy's reputation was tarnished by the royal family scandals of the early 1990s and the death of Princess Diana in 1997, it was ironic that her sons, Princes William and Harry, would become the key to restoring the crown's fortunes as they grew from grief-stricken boys into outgoing young men. Despite the occasional highly publicized hiccup along the way, the princes appeared to possess the same dutiful qualities that had seen their grandmother, Elizabeth, fêted as the country's leading public servant. Moreover, both seemed to appreciate that the monarchy needed to stay up to date if it was to retain the public's support.

To this end, William and Harry borrowed heavily from their mother's persona, presenting themselves publicly as friendly, familiar figures who, because of the personal trauma they had experienced, could engage on sympathetic and intimate terms with the people they met. This image was enhanced by their tactile behaviour. Like Diana, they hugged and physically engaged with some of the ordinary people they met. And, because they regularly spoke out about their hatred of the tabloid press and the invasive actions of reporters, it became easy to emotionally identify with the brothers as they worked to rehabilitate the idea that being royal is not to be envied.

Meanwhile, both princes' professional lives showcased their dutiful personalities. Harry served in the British army for a decade, touring Afghanistan twice. This option wasn't available to William, who, as second in line to the throne, needed to be kept out of harm's way at all times, but he nevertheless served with the RAF's Search and Rescue Force before joining the Air Ambulance Service, where he flew a number of missions as a pilot. Then, as full-time working members of the royal family, the princes carefully selected the areas on which to focus their philanthropy. Harry's memoir, *Spare*, suggests there was an element of competition between the brothers when it came to deciding who got to do what, which seems to have stemmed from the fact that different types of charity afforded varying levels of public visibility. According to Harry, William was jealous about some of the philanthropy he had been doing because he thought his brother had encroached on one of his areas – the protection of African wildlife.

Between them, the princes ended up focusing their attention on mental health, war veterans, young people and conservation, thus drawing on their past personal experiences, as well as more traditional areas of royal patronage, in order to burnish their reputations as caring individuals in touch with current and older topics of public concern. To further their charitable ambitions, they established the Foundation of Prince William and Prince Harry in 2009 as the fundraising vehicle that would support their projects; this then metamorphosed into the Royal Foundation of the Duke and Duchess of Cambridge and the Duke and Duchess of Sussex after the brothers' marriages to Catherine Middleton and Meghan Markle, both of whom seemed, like the princes, to be likeable personalities who embodied the empathetic, modernizing spirit championed by the new generation of royalty.

But, unfortunately for the House of Windsor, as we all now know, the relationship between William and Harry soured, and it became clear over the course of 2019 that the Sussexes were experimenting with a new concept of royal public service – one that would allow them to strike out on their own innovative ventures separately from William and Catherine. They cut ties with the Royal Foundation in order to assert their independence, but this led to negative press coverage which claimed the couple were frustrated with the way their philanthropic activities were consistently overshadowed by those of the Cambridges.

The Sussexes' break with the royal family is discussed in greater detail in Part Three. But for our purposes here, their desire for independence and, indeed, self-fulfilment through new philanthropic opportunities was presented by the British media as running counter to the idea that royals must put their personal ambitions second to the needs of crown and country. Harry and Meghan seemed to be forgetting that they were first and foremost public servants, as per the tradition started by George V almost 100 years ago. When they announced in January 2020 that they were stepping back from their full-time royal roles in order to pursue lives separately (financially and physically) from the rest of the Windsor family, this was again judged critically by right-wing commentators such as British talk show host Piers Morgan, who painted the couple as irresponsible, selfish and lacking a sense of duty.

The Sussexes' story demonstrates how thinly disguised ambition, with its emphasis on personal gratification, has been interpreted by most in the British media as incompatible with the dominant vision of a monarchy where the self-sacrifice of its protagonists is key. This notion of self-sacrifice involves playing the part expected of you – something Harry's memoir suggests he consistently strove to do – while refraining from doing anything unexpected. It was this that he and Meghan found more difficult. In the figures of the Sussexes the narrative of self-sacrifice slipped as it became clear that they intended to use their platform to suit their own progressive agenda, ranging beyond the issues routinely addressed by other members of the royal family.

The couple's initial suggestion following the announcement that they were departing for North America was that they would juggle their royal duties with new commercial projects. But this was not condoned by the so-called 'men in grey suits' – the backward-looking courtiers advising Elizabeth II – because it flew in the face of an idea of self-sacrifice that was, by this point, accepted as conventional wisdom within the royal household. The most insightful royal commentator currently writing about the House of Windsor is former BBC journalist Peter Hunt. He has argued persuasively that a compromise could have been reached with the Sussexes whereby they were given greater flexibility as part of a new hybrid model that would have seen them effectively half in and half out of the royal family. Such an accommodation might crucially have avoided all of the animosity, allegations and revelations that followed Harry and Meghan's exclusion from the monarchy.

Hunt notes that the one person who might have negotiated such a deal was Christopher Geidt, until 2017 private secretary to Elizabeth II. However, he was ousted in a power struggle because the now king did not agree with his vision for how best to manage the transition from the queen's reign to his own. Before this, Geidt was a renowned unifying figure adept at getting different members of the royal family and their teams to work together, rather than against one another. Unfortunately for Harry and Meghan, he was not present at the so-called 'Sandringham Summit' in January 2020 which decided their ignominious fate for them.

As a result, the Sussexes were hounded out of the UK by a press that cast them in simple terms as the bad guys: they wanted to retain the best aspects of being part of the House of Windsor – the privileges, status and platform – while pursuing their own projects abroad which did not require them to serve the public. The departure was disparagingly referred to as 'Megxit', the implication being that the duchess was the driving force behind their sudden withdrawal from royal life. As we now know, there were other factors at play, not least the rigid stance of the courtiers advising Queen Elizabeth. The *Daily Mail*, which remains the couple's staunchest critic in the UK, has stuck to the line ever since that 'the queen had no choice' but to turn down their idea of a 'half in, half out' formula. In fact, there were alternatives. But the unimaginative, short-sighted, inflexible courtiers who toady up to the throne rejected these ideas out of hand, refusing to recognize how damaging the impact of excluding Harry and Meghan would be for the monarchy.

All of this begs the crucial question of how viable the current model of monarchy is, given the way it continues to require its protagonists, at least publicly, to put service and self-sacrifice ahead of all else. Harry and Meghan revealed how quickly this model can break down, in the process creating havoc for the crown, if individual royals are deeply unhappy with the strictures placed on them. As we've seen in this section, other Windsors – including Prince Philip and the new king during his time as prince of Wales – managed with some success to innovate and discover new outlets for their energies, even if their behaviour wasn't always strictly constitutional. The difference with Harry and Meghan was that they were intent on leaving the UK because of the often poisonous coverage they received in the tabloids: they thus found themselves aligned against the most powerful opinion-shaping force in Britain today, which has continued to snipe at them aggressively ever since they started their new lives.

The current situation is obviously untenable and in need of change. The emphasis on royal self-sacrifice stems from the fact that the House of Windsor has long sought to project a public image where duty comes first, as manifested through forms of service, including philanthropy. But time and time again royals have struggled to live up to this ideal. If the monarchy embraced a different national role, like the one set out in Part Four, then the wider royal family would no longer be required to put on this kind of performance. They could be whoever they wanted to be; and they could choose to do whatever they wanted to do, provided the monarch and heir to the throne conducted themselves in an exemplary non-partisan fashion as part of their new constitutional roles. This would also ensure that, should the prince and princess of Wales's younger children decide they don't want to be public figures, they can live freely as private individuals.

There is another, bigger argument here for a timely downsizing of the number of working royals. Now that the Sussexes have moved on, their old patronages and official roles have been divided up among the remaining members of the House of Windsor. This process has revealed how overstretched and overinvolved the monarchy has become in British national life. Now is the moment for this royal overreach to come to an end. As I've suggested in this section, it is a problem not just for the monarchy but for the country too. In recent years the UK population has had to rely on public services which, stripped of proper funding by central government, are instead supported by philanthropic organizations, including royal-sponsored charities. Despite their good intentions, these organizations are simply unable to offer the level of help required by those in need.

FIFTEEN

It's all part of minding deeply about this country

It is worth briefly recapping the changes that have transformed the nature of the British state over the last 40 years. Government has increasingly sought partnerships that link the public sector to the voluntary and private sectors in order to enable public service delivery. As part of this shift, governments have helped to fund the activities of voluntary bodies, but at the same time most have cut investment in publicly run services, thereby handing over responsibility for the delivery of services to the voluntary and private sectors. This change was particularly stark after 2010, when, as part of a radical – and unnecessary – programme of austerity, the Conservative-led coalition dramatically reduced spending on public services.

It is clear that voluntary sector organizations, such as the initiatives supported by the Royal Foundation and the Prince's Trust, are staffed by hard-working experts who possess knowledge of the challenges they are trying to address. Indeed, government could learn much by engaging more closely with the experts that work for royal-led charities and philanthropic organizations. But sadly, charity has proved to be no substitute for properly funded public services, no matter how good the help offered by these voluntary bodies. Morally speaking, philanthropy absolves the whole of society from taking responsibility for those people who are most vulnerable within it. And at a practical level, because third parties are involved in the delivery of public services, it is more difficult to hold government ministers to account when these services fail.

The British have become used to a new welfare ecosystem of public bodies, charities and other agencies that are today responsible for the delivery of key public services. And the highly publicized royal patronage of organizations within this patchwork has done much to normalize the ecosystem, lending it authority and credibility, while boosting the role that charity plays in place of serious government action.

- - -

We only need look at the activities of the Royal Foundation over the last 13 years to see how it has carved out spheres of influence for itself in British society on issues that successive governments have failed to seriously address. For example, in the early 2010s, Princes William and Harry began to speak publicly about how their mental health had suffered because of the loss of their mother. These conversations led to the creation of new royal charities, such as Heads Together and Mental Health Innovations, which have helped young people and others in need of support. And the princes' openness about their mental well-being also kickstarted a long-overdue discussion about what was once considered a taboo topic.

We must commend William and Harry's activities and readiness to talk about their mental health. However, the failure of government to invest seriously in mental health services across the country has essentially left the door open to the voluntary sector to make this area its own, when what we now need is a proper conversation about how the British state deals with the mental health crisis that has taken hold of the UK since the beginning of the Covid pandemic.

The same can be said of the royals' philanthropy with injured military veterans. This has long been an area of royal interest dating back to the concern shown by Queen Victoria for the men who were wounded during the Crimean War in the mid-1850s. Then, after the First World War, the prince of Wales (the future Edward VIII) set up charitable funds to support the welfare of injured and disabled soldiers, as well as their reintegration into public life. Since the early 2000s, the rehabilitation of veterans has been a cause of particular salience because of British involvement in the Iraq and Afghanistan wars. Until very recently, the public face of wounded servicemen and women was Prince Harry. However, partly because of his royal activities in this area, we have come to see the recovery of our servicepeople as something that can be left to philanthropic organizations to manage.

We know that Britain's Ministry of Defence plays an important role in helping to establish the agenda for veterans' care and in allocating some much-needed state funding to assist with services offered by voluntary charities like the royal-backed Walking With The Wounded. But how is it that we have arrived at a situation where some of those soldiers who have fought on behalf of their country, literally risking everything in the process, return to civilian life and are forced to rely, in the main, on charities to help them recover after combat? In Part One I suggested that we need to rethink how we honour those who have died or been wounded on the battlefield. Is there any better way to honour their service and sacrifice than for the state (and the UK taxpayer) to ensure that, on their return to Britain, all veterans are properly cared for, housed and reintegrated into society?

Perhaps most troubling of all with the UK's 'mixed economy of care' comprising public, private and voluntary bodies is the way children's welfare has increasingly been positioned as an area that is primarily dealt with not by government but by other third-party organizations, including royal philanthropists. Royal activity in this area again seems to be a positive thing at first glance. The princess of Wales has carved out a new role for herself as a leading advocate on early years' development, with a 2021 report from the Royal Foundation's Centre for Early Years finding that an estimated 1.3 million babies and pre-school children in Britain currently live in relative poverty – almost one third of all children of this age group in the UK.

In response to this problem, Catherine has launched the 'Shaping Us' programme, which aims to raise awareness on the importance of the early years to children's development. At the moment it is unclear how, beyond forging relationships with business leaders who might help to fund some of this work, the Shaping Us programme intends to drive forward action on this important topic. The princess's defenders have emphasized the crucial role royals can play in making visible social issues like this one; but detractors of the project (and there are many) have argued that gestures like this run the risk of virtue-signalling if they are not matched with long-term investment and a clear strategy for change.

Crucially, in the last decade more than 1,500 Sure Start early years centres (introduced by the New Labour government in 1999 to promote children's health, care and education) have closed as a result of government cuts. This has contributed to other social problems, including growing pressures on Britain's NHS. Unfortunately for the politically non-partisan monarchy, royal philanthropy on early years development seems to fit hand-in-glove with a Conservative-led austerity programme that has slashed state funding of crucial public services like Sure Start, with politicians deliberately handing over responsibility for social issues to the voluntary and private sectors.

Given what has happened to Britain since 2010, we should not be at all surprised to read that so many children are living in poverty. This period has seen the gap between rich and poor widen. In 2022 the richest 1 per cent of households were worth at least £3.6 million; the poorest 10 per cent meanwhile were worth just £15,400 on average. With inequality rising and the cost of living remaining stubbornly high, more and more families have been forced to turn to charity in order to feed themselves. In 2010 the Trussell Trust (the UK's main organizer of food aid) operated 35 food banks nationally and distributed about 40,000 emergency food parcels; in 2022 it was running more than 1,400 food banks and delivered more than 2 million food parcels. In addition to this, there were over 1,000 other independently-run food banks in Britain in 2022 helping to address food insecurity.

King Charles's first televised Christmas message, on 25 December 2022, celebrated the 'wonderfully kind people who so generously give food or donations' and the work of volunteers involved in 'feeding the hungry'. Then, in January 2023, the prince and princess of Wales were filmed and photographed helping with the packaging of food parcels at a food bank. We can argue that the royals are right to draw attention to this pressing issue and the important work performed by ordinary people to help those in need. But, given what we know about how the House of Windsor has historically searched out opportunities at the edges of the welfare state, notably pushing back on the social role of government where it can, we could be forgiven for viewing these royal interventions cynically as attempts to demonstrate sympathy with the poor at a time when grave socio-economic difficulties could give rise to criticism of the wealthy and privileged, including the Windsors. The same might also be said about the way Prince William has sought to increase the visibility of homelessness in Britain. As the champions of the heir to the throne have reluctantly admitted, there is a real hypocrisy at work when a prince with five residences to his name declares in public that 'everyone deserves a place to call home'.

Some people will judge this cynicism as unfair and will ask what else the royal family could possibly do other than draw our attention to social problems if they want to avoid accusations that they are meddling in politics. They have a point: direct royal criticism of government policy would lead to difficult questions being asked about the political neutrality of the constitutional monarchy. However, as we saw earlier in this section, some of the Windsors – the king and his father included – have historically used their public platforms to speak out about social issues of concern to them, in so doing challenging the role of government in what can be considered a constitutionally improper way, particularly in relation to the purpose of the post-war welfare state.

The other reason why the royal family will not speak out more directly about the failure of government to tackle rising levels of poverty is that for the new activist king it would be self-defeating. Serious government action could deprive the royals of their philanthropic platform. King Charles said in a television interview in 2006 that his philanthropic work was his 'duty' and 'all part of minding deeply about this country'. He continued by saying, 'I think it would be criminally negligent of me to go around this country and not actually want to try to do something about what I find there.' The problem with this kind of approach to social issues is simple: it prioritizes the do-gooding of the individual philanthropist over the social responsibilities of a benevolent interventionist state.

The House of Windsor has consistently promoted voluntary and private sector solutions to social problems. When they draw attention to food banks, they may be motivated by genuine concern but they are also reaffirming the role of charity in a society that no longer has properly functioning public services; and they are also building on a royal public relations campaign that has, since the mid-nineteenth century, emphasized the importance of philanthropy aimed at those members of the public who are suffering the most in the hope that they do not direct their ire at the monarchy.

The reason why royalty's promotion of the philanthropic alleviation of food insecurity is problematic is that it distracts from the urgent need for a government response to this problem (as is also the case with mental health, veterans' care and children's development). For all the incredible work they do, food banks remain a glaring symbol of the UK's broken socio-economic model. Britain's economy is the sixth largest in the world. But, like several other comparable highly developed nations, including Germany, it has allowed for an exponential increase in food banks over the last decade.

Well-meaning Windsors may want to show they care, but their interventions in this area help to normalize the idea of the food bank in a society which, if civilized, wouldn't need them. Access to food in a country as rich as the UK should be a human right, not a privilege. It is past time the royals recognized that reform in this and other areas can only begin when government resumes responsibility for the public's welfare. This will involve rethinking how public services are structured, funded and delivered at a time when social, political and economic challenges are growing ever more complex. And, crucially, it is not simply about pumping more money into the system but about rethinking the system 'from the bottom up', so that the interventionist state is agile, less bureaucratic and more effective at tackling the gravest social issues of our time.

By allying themselves through their voluntary causes to some of the most vulnerable in society, the Windsors make critics of royal philanthropy (like me) seem a bit mean-spirited in comparison. However, as I've tried to suggest here, we need to have a serious conversation about what role we want the monarchy to play in relation to the state. It is within our power to decide whether royal philanthropy continues unchecked or whether the British government takes back control of key social issues. My overriding concern is that if the royals continue to consume the oxygen of publicity on problems like those I've discussed, it could mean that government continues to get away with saying very little about them.

We are at risk of seeing this process play out in relation to climate change. As mentioned already, this has long been an area of royal activity, with Prince Philip, King Charles and, more recently, Prince William all helping to raise awareness of the crisis affecting the environment and natural world. Speaking out about these issues has ensured that the royals have a global platform which has, in turn, helped to boost the profile (and indeed importance) of the crown as an institution with international reach. This was clear before the COP26 climate conference in Glasgow in 2021, where, as head of state, Queen Elizabeth welcomed delegates and spoke of how the aforementioned men in her family had sought to address the challenges of environmental degradation. The new monarch then made one of his impassioned speeches to world leaders in which he emphasized the need for a 'military-style campaign to marshal the strength of the global private sector' in order to deal with climate change.

The problem with this kind of royal grandstanding is that it has the potential to distract from the long-term inactivity of his majesty's government in protecting the natural world (for example, by allowing private water companies to pollute Britain's rivers and waterways); and it has

distracted from the fact that no front-line politician has yet had the cour-
age to explain the big sacrifices required of the public if they are to do
their bit in the global effort to slow climate change. The net zero climate
target that King Charles and Prince William have both publicly championed will require the British to alter their consumption habits drastically,
which will in turn inevitably impact on their material living standards. It is
very easy for the royals to lecture us on climate ambitions, much less easy
to achieve the targets in practice unless politicians are prepared to lead the
public in a new direction while also convincing other, big carbon-emit-
ting countries to pull their weight.

Supported by a group of right-wing journalists, a number of free-market libertarians in the Conservative Party have already begun setting out
their sceptical views about the feasibility and desirability of the net zero
target, pushing back against its aims. One of the most notable sceptics
is former prime minister Liz Truss, whose short tenure as premier was
defined by the mantra of 'economic growth at any cost'. Before this idea
was derailed by her early departure, it seemed likely to involve a cost to
the environment, Truss having asked one her ministers to lead a review
of the 2050 net zero target. It was also Truss's government which advised
the king not to attend the COP27 climate conference in Egypt in 2022, at
which he was due to give a speech. This led to speculation that tensions
had emerged between prime minister and monarch, her vision for a
Britain less committed to climate change targets running counter to the
king's long-term promotion of environmentalism.

If this 'not zero' section of opinion on the political right gains ground,
then it may be that King Charles and Prince William find themselves
ideologically aligned against a vocal faction of politicians on the topic of
climate change, at which point questions will be asked about whether it is
constitutionally proper for non-elected members of the Windsor dynasty
to air their opinions in the first place. Arguably, King Charles's great act
of self-sacrifice as monarch should be to give up his platform on climate
change. Such a move may not win him any supporters among a younger
generation that he is trying desperately to engage with; but if he is to
remain strictly politically impartial as sovereign, then it would be better
for him to step away completely from this and all the other issues on
which he has previously campaigned.

The royal family have long presented themselves as sacrificial figures,
publicly embracing restrictions on their self-fulfilment and self-expression in return for a life of wealth, privilege and power. The new king risks

undermining this equation if he continues to express his ideas and opinions. We already know what he thinks about the environment and – given the political risks involved – there is probably more to lose than to gain from continuing to speak out. Although he and the prince of Wales are currently safe from criticism (there exists a broad consensus of public support for climate action), this could rapidly change as the demands of the net zero target become a reality, especially if we do not have competent democratically elected leaders who can explain why the target merits the sacrifices involved. As I suggest in the final part of this book, there is another important role the monarch and heir to the throne could play in a constitutional democracy – one that would compensate for the loss of their political voices while working to improve the calibre of politician in parliament – which might in turn ensure that the public feel they can approach the topic of climate change more thoughtfully and seriously than ever before.

The final challenge the crown faces in this area is accusations of hypocrisy. For example, the Royal Foundation, which promotes William's environmentalism with the Earthshot Prize, was criticized in 2022 for putting £1.1 million of its funds into JP Morgan Chase, an investment bank that is one of the world's biggest backers of fossil fuel companies. The king, meanwhile, has been accused of double standards because of his extensive use of helicopters and private jets for his busy programme of national and overseas engagements. And back in 2010 the British press uncovered the story that in 2004 one of Queen Elizabeth's aides had secretly appealed to the UK government to see if the queen might receive a special grant to help her pay her fuel bills from a £60 million 'poverty fund' earmarked to help low-income families with rising energy costs, so great had the cost of powering Buckingham Palace and various other royal residences become. Fortunately for the House of Windsor, civil servants had the good sense to point out that this would be a public relations disaster for the monarchy and duly rejected the idea.

It is because of his interests in environmentalism and concerns about the public image of a royal family which has access to, or owns privately, close to 20 residences (ranging from small country estates to Windsor Castle, which has over a thousand rooms) that King Charles has emphasized the need to embrace renewable energy solutions. Today some royal residences are powered and heated by hydroelectric, solar and other energy-saving technologies, while the £369 million renovation of Buckingham Palace has led to a range of eco-friendly solutions being introduced at what was reportedly an extremely energy-inefficient property.

It is because of concerns about the way the monarchy's environmental-ism is perceived by his subjects that the king was also quick to announce in January 2023 that the profits arising from a new offshore wind agreement on the crown estate estimated to be worth £1 billion a year be used for the 'wider public good' rather than as additional funding for the monarchy. Under the rules that have governed the taxpayer-funded sovereign grant since 2011, the king receives 15 per cent of all the crown estate's annual profits to pay for the activities of the royal family, plus an additional 10 per cent for ten years in order to pay for the renovation of Buckingham Palace. What might have thus been a huge boost to the monarchy's coffers will instead be retained by government to use as it sees fit.

This was the right gesture from a king who has, more often than not, demonstrated that he understands the importance of positive public rela-tions. However, he mustn't stop there. If he and the House of Windsor wish to set a good example for the rest of us to follow on climate change, then they should continue to match their words with actions. Dramatically downsizing the number of royals engaged in public service would enable the crown to reduce its carbon footprint. With fewer Windsors working, there would be a much smaller household staff, a reduction in royal trips abroad on private jets, fewer official residences to heat and, with grace and favour homes finally a thing of the past, the royal palaces – with one or two exceptions – could be entrusted to the nation to serve, in the king's own words, the 'wider public good'.

———

The royal family have a tendency to gravitate towards moments of trag-edy in British national life. Aberfan, Grenfell Tower, the murder of Sarah Everard: all of these events witnessed special appearances from members of the House of Windsor. The positive interpretation is that they do so in order to offer leadership and comfort to those affected; but the less charitable view that has gained traction on social media is that in these moments the monarchy acts opportunistically in order to place itself firmly at the heart of the grieving community, conscious of the fact that a royal appearance will receive significant media coverage.

The same analysis can be extended to the royal family's engagement with the NHS during the first six months of the Covid-19 pandemic in 2020. With their usual routine of engagements paused because of lock-down, the Windsors instead sought to take on the symbolic leadership of the country by visibly backing the NHS and its workers through the crisis. Similar to the difficult situation that faced the monarchy of George VI during the Second World War, the palace was clearly fearful that this event could render the House of Windsor invisible, given how it focused on the activities of the essential workers who kept the country running.

In a throwback to the immediate post-war period, the royal family vocally championed the achievements of the NHS as it weathered the pandemic. In a special broadcast Queen Elizabeth thanked 'everyone on the NHS front line as well as care workers and those carrying out essential roles who selflessly continue their day-to-day duties outside the home in support of us all'. On the one hand, royal interventions like the queen's speech rightly valorized the work of medical and support staff at a time when they were under considerable pressure; but it was also the case that she and her kin gained much positive publicity for the way they associated themselves with the health service – which is ironic given how they use private sector providers for their own care.

The Windsors' celebration of health workers during the pandemic may have drawn lots of positive attention to the remarkable work of these people, but it also glossed over the fact that the NHS remains chronically underfunded, with exhausted doctors, nurses and community support staff choosing to leave the sector in droves because of their working conditions. It was with a real sense of pride that I watched events unfold in Britain in 2020 through my television set as the country seemed to rally around the message to protect the health service, with many members of the public even appearing on their doorsteps on Thursday evenings to clap for the UK's carers. Of course, the royals made sure they were also seen to be part of this collective acknowledgement of front-line medical staff.

However, it wasn't long before pride turned to anger and shame as it became clear that, despite Britain weathering the extraordinary circumstances of a pandemic, and the risks taken and personal sacrifices made by health workers, this shared experience was not going to lead to more serious reflection on the shortcomings of the UK's NHS. It will come as no surprise at the end of Part Two that I believe it is time for government to take greater responsibility for the organization and delivery of public services, including healthcare, rather than leaving it to a patchwork of public, private and voluntary bodies to provide support to the British population.

This will require those vested interests, such as the royal family, who gain from the current (inadequate) status quo to step back from the front

line. For too long the House of Windsor has promoted piecemeal philanthropic solutions to deal with extraordinarily complex problems which
require and deserve a more considered holistic approach from government. The positive news is that the pandemic demonstrated that the British
state still possesses some of the tools required to deal with the gravest
challenges. Across the world, governments intervened in their societies,
often radically reorganizing their economies, in order to develop solutions to the most complex global health crisis humankind has ever seen. A
similar kind of state-led response is required now if Britain is to solve its
crisis with public services such as health and social care.

Comparisons with similar highly developed democratic countries are
instructive here. The UK is very generous with the money it raises for
charities, more than doubling what is raised in Germany, and quadru-
pling that raised in France, on the same annual basis. However, public
services, including health and social welfare, rank much more highly in
the continental nations than in Britain. In the European countries, citizens tend to contribute a higher proportion of their monthly salary to
government-backed social insurance schemes which help to fund public
services, including health. Businesses are similarly required to contribute
more to the social security of all of their employees than is the case in the
UK, meaning there is a lot more money in the state's coffers to invest in
services. As a result of policies like these, the gap between rich and poor in
France and Germany is nowhere near as stark as it is in Britain, and there
are far fewer children living in relative poverty than in the UK.

I offer the following solutions simply as food for thought. We need
to begin by rethinking our relationship with the state and the idea of
charity. Specifically, we need to put greater trust back into the state so
that it resumes its role as key public service provider. (As we shall see
in Part Four, the new role that I set out for our constitutional monarchy
as part of our democracy could help lead to a return of trust in government.) Part of this also involves reframing how we see the tax and social
security payments we contribute out of our earnings. To paraphrase US
justice Oliver Wendell Holmes Jr, taxes are a membership fee to live in a
civilized society. And those people with the broadest shoulders, who have
made a lot of money in the UK benefiting from the relative stability of
its economy, its infrastructure and overseas trade links, should be paying
a significantly higher membership fee. The country can only continue
to prosper so long as we care properly for the most vulnerable among
us. We only need look to the USA, where tax rates are significantly lower

than Europe, and where a rapacious private sector fills many of the roles that are performed by government-backed bodies in other countries (for example in healthcare), to see where we in Britain might be heading if we're not careful.

Second, in terms of responding to the climate crisis, the British are in a strong position to commit to the sacrifices that we will all be required to make in order to reduce our carbon footprint. There is an underlying culture of reciprocal social obligation in the UK, perhaps most visible in the country's associational culture, where groups voluntarily come together often with the aim of enriching the life of their communities. It was also visible during the pandemic when citizens made social and economic sacrifices for the well-being of all.

Indeed, Queen Elizabeth's example is instructive here. Throughout her life she emphasized her duty to her people. Of course, we have seen in Part Two how this emphasis was engineered to generate sympathy for the monarch and her family; and we've also seen in the example of Harry and Meghan how the theme of self-sacrifice is unsustainable and unnecessary in the longer term. But the themes of duty and service speak to the kinds of mutual social obligation that we need to embrace fully in order to make the transition to a net zero future – if that is what the public decides it wants. A reorganized royal-backed honours system could continue to celebrate the theme of service while incentivizing at a local level the kinds of behaviour needed to make this transition. However, it is crucial that we do not leave it to the royal family or private sector to lead the defence of the environment and natural world. King Charles was right to highlight at COP26 the crucial role business must play in helping to avert climate catastrophe. Ultimately, though, leadership from democratically elected politicians and from citizens at a local level will be key to building a shared vision of a future where humankind lives in closer harmony with the planet. And only through democratic renewal might we rediscover the confidence and sense of purpose needed to succeed in realizing such a vision.

PART THREE

Family, Celebrity and Scandal

Publicity was part of my heritage, and I was never so naïve as to
suppose that my romance was a tender shoot to be protected
from the prying curiosity of the Press. But what stared at
me from the newspapers that were brought to my room on
Thursday morning really shocked me. Could this be the King
or was I some common felon? The Press creates; the Press
destroys. All my life I had been the passive clay which it had
enthusiastically worked into the hackneyed image of a Prince
Charming. Now it had whirled around, and was bent upon
demolishing the natural man who had been there all the time.

EDWARD, DUKE OF WINDSOR,
A KING'S STORY (LONDON, 1951)

In those first hours and days of November 2016 there was
a new low every few minutes. I was shocked, and scolded
myself for being shocked. And for being unprepared. I'd been
braced for the usual madness, the standard libels, but I hadn't
anticipated this level of unrestrained lying.

Above all, I hadn't been ready for the racism. Both the dog-
whistle racism and the glaring, vulgar, in-your-face racism.

The *Daily Mail* took the lead. Its headline: Harry's girl is
(almost) straight outta Compton. Subhead: Gang-scarred home
of her mother revealed – so will he be dropping in for tea?

Another tabloid jumped into the fray with this jaw-dropper:
Harry to marry into gangster royalty?

My face froze. My blood stopped. I was angry, but more:
ashamed. My Mother Country? Doing this? To her? To us?
Really?

A day or two later the *Mail* weighed in again, this time with an essay by the sister of London's former mayor Boris Johnson, predicting that Meg would ... do something ... genetically ... to the Royal Family. 'If there is issue from her alleged union with Prince Harry, the Windsors will thicken their watery, thin blue blood and Spencer pale skin and ginger hair with some rich and exotic DNA.'

PRINCE HARRY, *SPARE* (LONDON, 2023)

SIXTEEN

The press creates ... the press destroys

Over the last three and a half years many comparisons have been made between the former king turned duke of Windsor, Edward VIII, and Prince Harry, duke of Sussex. Both fell in love with and married divorced American women. Both decided to give up their official roles and royal responsibilities in order to pursue their own ambitions in countries different from that of their birth. Both faced a backlash from sections of the British media because of their actions. And, in their self-imposed exile, both men struggled to redefine their public image, writing highly controversial memoirs to make clear to the public back in the UK their reasons for breaking with the monarchy.

The fact that *Spare* and *A King's Story* gave their protagonists an opportunity to settle old scores while making them lots of money in the process were also clearly motivating factors for Harry and Edward. The duke of Sussex has discovered, much like his great-great-uncle, that life outside the House of Windsor comes with financial challenges if you wish to keep on living like a royal. But one crucial theme less discussed by the media and chattering royal commentariat either at the time of Harry's original split from his family at the beginning of 2020, or following the publication of his memoir at the start of 2023 after a series of high-profile appearances by him and his wife, Meghan, on TV, is the fact that he and Edward are the two clearest examples of the failure of the UK's personality-led monarchy.

By this I mean that, since the nineteenth century, the royal family have been at the centre of our modern culture of celebrity. Partly as a result of wider cultural and social changes, partly by royal design, the monarchy has come to be seen in terms of a set of leading 'actors' whose lives we get to share in through the stories we read in newspapers and via the royal events we watch unfold on the screens – big and small – that today surround us wherever we go.

The problem with this is that a celebrity culture that once celebrated the moral example set by Victorian royalty to the rest of society has, over time, metamorphosed to focus instead on the so-called 'royal soap opera'. This colourful, unrelenting drama began with the abdication of Edward VIII in 1936 and has, since then, routinely punctuated media coverage of the monarchy. By focusing our attention on the personal lives of the royals, journalists have encouraged us to identify with them as individuals whose behaviour and moral choices we are invited to judge. In this respect, the media furore provoked by Harry's recent exploits was nothing new: it was simply the latest instalment in a series of press-generated moments of crisis for a highly dysfunctional royal family, whose private lives have long played out in full view of the public.

The fact that British and international media organizations have consistently failed to ask more serious questions about the nature and durability of the UK's personality-driven model of monarchy is in itself revealing of the major problem that currently exists. It has not been in the interests of the press to question the idea of a personality-led monarchy because it is the media – just as much as the royals – which currently gains most from the status quo. Sex and scandal sell. But royal sex and royal scandal sell even better. So why would journalists and TV producers bother to challenge royal celebrity culture when it is exactly this culture that helps to keep members of the public buying newspapers, glued to their social media feeds and tuning in for more?

The obsession with the monarchy as a celebrity-orientated institution has acted as a distraction from more profound questions regarding the crown's political and social functions. It has also meant the royals have become increasingly reliant on their relationship with the media in trying to ensure that positive publicity – no matter how frivolous or trivial – outweighs negative. The duke of Windsor noted how fickle the media can be. After he had been built up by journalists as a 'Prince Charming' from the earliest moments of his life in the public eye, and become one of the best-known figures in the English-speaking world, many reporters turned on him the moment he suggested he was planning to defy their expectations by marrying a woman whom they deemed to be unsuitable for a king and emperor.

Prince Harry meanwhile was, and continues to be, the focus of a fickle tabloid media. But whereas Edward spent his younger years adulated by the press, rapidly ascending to an almost god-like status before he crashed off the pedestal on which he'd been placed, Harry endured much more mixed coverage from the media from an early age that was in keeping with the far less deferential times. The post-war period witnessed the emergence of a new strain of royal reportage – one that was invasive, irreverent and critical of the actions of the Windsor family – to offset the more traditional strain that was rooted in respect, discretion and reverence.

These two strains of royal coverage together have formed a toxic media culture where a royal can find themselves lauded as a paragon of duty, empathy and moral rectitude one day, but the next their private life and secrets will be splashed across the front pages of the papers and their behaviour – real or alleged – criticized from all angles. Harry and Meghan are a case in point. As the duke of Sussex's words above suggest, his wife didn't really stand a chance with the UK's right-wing tabloids: a mixed-race woman, with well-known progressive social views, marrying into the royal family could have been cause for celebration. But not for tabloid editors wedded to a traditional vision of monarchy, who eagerly waited for the duchess to make minor mistakes which could be spun to readers as major dramas.

I'm not saying that the media was all to blame for the Sussexes' woes, as Harry would have us believe in Spare. It is clear from his autobiography that the prince and his wife live in a world where they want for nothing and where there is a strong, underlying assumption that their ideas and opinions matter. Harry has talked at length about developing an awareness of his past 'unconscious bias'. Judging by the contents of Spare, the prince would also benefit from dwelling at greater length on his sense of entitlement and the privilege that he has enjoyed as a result of his position and platform. As already discussed, the Sussexes also demonstrated a surprising level of ignorance when they thought they could simply break with the House of Windsor in order to pursue new commercial opportunities while continuing to carry out official duties on behalf of the queen. Royal service has historically been equated with personal suffering and sacrifice. Although Harry and Meghan may not have fully realized it at the time, chasing deals with some of the world's biggest digital brands hardly equates to either suffering or sacrifice.

However, while the couple may inhabit a gilded, self-centred echo chamber partly of their own making, I do think they were treated particularly poorly by the British tabloid press. As the above-mentioned quote from *Spare* makes clear, some of the attacks on Meghan were downright racist. And, unfortunately for the Sussexes, the criticism has continued unabated. We saw this with the barrage of negative headlines targeting Harry after his book was released and again in the lead-up to King Charles's coronation, when Meghan was loudly criticized by right-wing newspapers for her non-attendance. I am sure that had she accepted the invitation she would have been just as loudly condemned for 'presumptuously' attending, with her presence also enabling news editors and reporters to fan the flames of the largely exaggerated 'feud' which they've consistently claimed exists between her and her sister-in-law, the princess of Wales.

This is not to say that there haven't been tensions inside the royal family. As Harry makes clear in *Spare*, and as we've heard elsewhere, there is a ruthless dynamic at work inside the House of Windsor. Individual royal 'principals' (as they call themselves) compete for positive coverage often by leaking other – sometimes negative – stories about members of their family to trusted journalists. Each set of principals has their own communications team, and one need only look at reports in *The Times* or *Daily Mail* to see how 'palace sources' – in other words, unnamed members of these teams – use back-channel briefings to keep favoured reporters informed about developments or stories they want published.

At the same time, it is hard to see how Harry's family back in Britain view the Sussexes' fall from grace with anything other than horror. Since the abdication crisis almost nine decades ago, the monarchy has recognized that negative media coverage carries with it an implicit (and sometimes explicit) existential threat. The fact that Harry has gone from the status of hero – his positive opinion poll rating of 81 per cent briefly eclipsed even that of Elizabeth II in 2017, following the announcement of his engagement to Meghan – to not quite zero (it was at 25 per cent in March 2023, two months after *Spare* came out) is a stark reminder to his relatives that, in the words of the duke of Windsor, the press creates, but it also destroys.

Part Three of this book considers how, since the mid-nineteenth century, the monarchy has deliberately embraced new kinds of media coverage, carefully letting in daylight on royal family life, in order to create a public image that is more accessible and human. The public have been able to forge close emotional ties to royalty precisely because of this human element. And these emotional connections have, in turn, helped to ensure the survival of kingship in Britain and the empire-turned-Commonwealth across a 150-year period which has witnessed dramatic political, social and cultural change. However, we must also consider the negative effects of having, in Walter Bagehot's words, 'a family on the throne'.

As we've already seen, there are big problems at the heart of the personality-led family monarchy. Charles III, like his mother before him, seems reluctant to confront these problems in order to change the monarchy so that it is more resistant to the kinds of criticism levelled at it by a British media intent on tearing down 'wayward' members of the House of Windsor who struggle to conform to expectations. The new king has made a slow start with his long-touted 'downsizing' of the royal family, not least because it is impossible for the monarchy to maintain its current level of public engagements if the number of 'working' royals is significantly reduced. Rather, his attempts to streamline the institution have so far only targeted the most wayward of the Windsors, including his younger brother Andrew.

Harry and Meghan have, since leaving the royal family, also made it clear that Charles has done very little to try to curb the excesses of the tabloid media. There has been no significant intervention from the new king regarding the attacks on his second son and daughter-in-law. In part, this reluctance can be explained with reference to Charles's own tortured relationship with the press, which dates back to the first revelations of his extramarital affair in the late 1980s. Having managed, post-Diana, to rehabilitate his public reputation sufficiently so that the media almost unanimously welcomed him into his new position after his accession to the throne, why would he put that approval at risk by publicly criticizing his erstwhile antagonists in the press?

It is this fear of the tabloids that explains why the new king encouraged Harry to agree to a private financial settlement with those newspapers he accuses of hacking his phone, rather than pursue his case in the courts as he has chosen to do. The duke of Sussex appears to have made it his personal mission to draw back the curtain on the invasive actions of journalists and news editors in order to expose the toxic relationship that has developed between the press and the monarchy. He has nothing to lose as someone who is now on the outside of the royal family. His brother and

King Charles, though, have much to lose. They have grudgingly accepted the toxic relationship and have adopted a more accommodating approach with the tabloids – for example, Harry has suggested that Prince William settled his own case against press phone hackers in secret with the newspaper involved. Both the king and the heir to the throne know how crucial the press is to the survival of the crown. Without its support, the monarchy – unless it embraces a new role that does not require it to play the tabloids' game – will disappear.

Speaking out against the press – possibly even to defend Harry and Meghan against the attacks they have endured – would probably jeopardize the king's newfound popularity; but, just as importantly, it would also invite greater scrutiny of the toxic relationship that now exists between the House of Windsor and reporters. As we shall see, it was not always like this despite the fact that, since the age of Queen Victoria, the media has been fundamental to keeping the crown visible and relevant. It is almost literally their lifeblood; and, for their part, the royal family have increasingly sought to court journalists' attention. Harry recently stated how today there exists an 'invisible contract' whereby the palace invites journalists to special events in order to drip-feed them a positive narrative of duty and domestic felicity in order to generate favourable publicity. This suggests that the integrity of both the monarchy and the media has been severely compromised. And, as already noted, it we wanted further evidence of the unholy alliance that connects the crown to the fourth estate, then we need only remind ourselves of the culture of back-channel briefings between royal communications teams and trusted reporters which has worked to ensure royal principals receive positive coverage, often at the expense of others.

A final reason why the royal family want to stick with the status quo is that we, the public, continue to express sympathy for a set of individuals who seem to be harangued and harassed by the press, but who outwardly take the moral high ground by refusing to reply. It is this undercurrent of sympathy for royalty that translates into loyalty and helps us to rationalize the vast privilege they enjoy at the public's expense. Not only this, but we continue to celebrate the 'ordinary' family values espoused by the monarchy when all the evidence at our disposal suggests that the Windsors – with their litany of failed marriages and personal scandals – are far from moral exemplars and definitely not 'just like us'.

When a member of the family breaks cover and reveals that not all is well behind closed doors, it throws the monarchy as an institution into turmoil and raises big questions about the centrality of the crown to British nationhood. The royals have helped to create the toxic media culture that now envelops them, so they must play a leading part in unmaking it. But it is also crucial that we, the public, detach ourselves from the royal drama and sever the emotional ties that we have forged with the present cast of Windsor celebrities. The status quo is having a corrosive effect on public life: it panders to our baser instincts, brings out the worst in the lurid tabloid press and requires the royals to uphold the appearance of domestic harmony when, like everybody else, they are human and fallible. It is past time that we rid ourselves of the soap opera and the fantasy of family monarchy in return for a more sensible, less sensationalist style of kingship that serves a useful purpose as part of our national life.

SEVENTEEN

A family on the throne

We've only been able to 'get to know' the royal family for as long as stories about them have circulated in the media. The new national newspapers of the late eighteenth and nineteenth centuries provided greater visibility to life at court, with leading members of the royal dynasty becoming well-known personalities among the reading public. This benefited the crown when the personalities in question behaved well; when they did not, misbehaviour threatened to bring the monarchy into disrepute and its moral authority into question.

George III was the first modern monarch to take direct action in order to limit the damage created by badly behaved royals. Two of his younger brothers chose as their wives women deemed highly unsuitable by the sovereign: one married a commoner, the other the illegitimate daughter of a leading politician. Marrying below one's social rank in this way was scandalous by the standards of the day. As a result of these unions, the king introduced a new Royal Marriages Act, which was intended to give him oversight and a final say over future marriages involving close family members. Thus George III demonstrated once again a sensitivity to the increased public scrutiny that monarchy was subject to because of new forms of journalism that sought to hold those in power to account. Indeed, he went one step further in trying to generate positive public feeling towards his family by presenting himself as *paterfamilias* of his dynasty. As historian Linda Colley has noted, before his withdrawal from public life owing to mental illness, he was celebrated in newsprint and in court portraiture as a loving family man – an image that journalists would go on to conflate with his role as 'father of his people'.

Low literacy rates and the exclusion of most middle- and working-class people from the world of high art meant that this early imagining of a family monarchy had limited resonance beyond upper-class society.

The king's oldest son and heir also did much to undermine the idea of a family monarchy through his dissolute private life and womanizing, which became the target of satirical writers and cartoonists who boldly challenged royal claims to moral authority (Fig 7). Over time, the prince regent (later George IV) became detested, not least because of his treatment of his estranged wife, Queen Caroline, with whom people identified as a 'wronged woman'. Following her husband's death in 1830, The Times sought to capture the public's mood when it suggested that

> There never was an individual less regretted by his fellow-creatures than this deceased king. What eye has wept for him? What heart has heaved one throb of unmercenary sorrow? ... If he ever had a friend – a devoted friend in any rank of life – we protest that the name of him or her has never reached us.

It was this sense of moral, and indeed royal, decline that Prince Albert sought to reverse when he married Queen Victoria in 1840. Fortunately for the royal couple, unlike many other royal relationships that were solely geopolitical in nature, their union was driven both by dynastic expedience and by true love. Their passionate (and well-documented) sex life resulted in the birth of nine children over 17 years and, in combination with their highly publicized romance, led to a rapid revival in the public image of a happy family monarchy.

We can detect Albert and Victoria's influence in promoting this domestic narrative from the way they specially commissioned artists and, later, photographers to capture scenes of their large family group, dressed as though they were members of the bourgeoisie. Copies of these pictures were exhibited in public galleries but were also available to buy as inexpensive collectibles by ordinary people who might then display them in their homes. Hence the new culture of mass consumerism in the mid-nineteenth century enabled subjects of the crown to purchase pictures of royal personalities onto which they could project fantasies of emotional intimacy and identification. And the fact that people in Britain's overseas colonies were also able to access these images meant the abstract connections that linked the far-flung empire to the 'motherland' were cemented via the family of Queen Victoria – the so-called 'Mother of Empire'.

Albert was also instrumental in using his family to cement the personal bonds that linked the colonies to Britain. The historian Charles Reed has described the prince consort as the 'engineer' of an 'imperial culture centred on the monarchy'. He persuaded his oldest sons to embark on the first royal tours of empire in 1860. The prince of Wales (the future Edward VII) travelled to Canada, while Prince Alfred went to South Africa. The prince consort saw his boys as human links between the motherland and colonies and as promoters of British 'civilization' abroad. Writing to his long-time friend and adviser Baron Stockmar, Albert described 'what a cheering picture is here of the progress and expansion of the British race, and of the useful co-operation of the Royal Family in the civilization which England has developed and advanced'.

The public image of the Victorian family monarchy appealed to the increasingly powerful British middle classes not just because it celebrated a moral vision of empire and the domestic values they so prized; it also celebrated Christian piety. As discussed in Part Two, this was partly to do with charity and the care shown by the royals towards some of the least fortunate within society. However, it was also about the sacred bonds of marriage and kinship as per Christ's teachings. It was, of course, the Victorian royals who helped to popularize the modern family Christmas, with Albert notably agreeing as part of this transformation that scenes of him, the queen and their children gathered around a Christmas tree could be reproduced in Britain's leading illustrated newspaper (Fig 8).

Even the prince consort's premature death in 1861 did not spell the end of the idealized Victorian family monarchy. Now the queen and her children could be seen in souvenir photos gathered in adoration around a marble bust of Albert's head. By the standards of the day, such images conveyed not only the centrality of patriarchal authority to family life but also love and affection towards an absent husband and father.

The appeal of the domestic narrative was not lost on Victoria and Albert's eldest son, the prince of Wales, later King Edward VII. Although he, like his great-uncle George IV, was chronically unfaithful in marriage, he understood the importance of one's public image at the start of a new century marked by the rise of new kinds of human-interest journalism. In terms of his self-presentation, Edward cast himself as the consummate family man. Coming to the throne at the age of 59, he posed for photos (which he knew would be reproduced for public consumption) as a loving grandfather, surrounded by his adult children and a growing brood of grandchildren.

Edward's long-suffering consort, Queen Alexandra, faithfully supported her husband's projection of this domestic image. Despite rumours of his

infidelity being known to the public, the king and queen always maintained an appearance of domestic harmony when out among their
people. The king's reputation as a caring, domestic figure was also notably
enhanced by his well-known love of animals. Coinciding with a massive
growth in dog ownership among middle-class families, journalists paid
special attention to how Edward's canine chums accompanied him on his
travels, knowing full well that these stories appealed to an increasingly
sentimental public.

When Edward and Alexandra were married, on 10 March 1863, it was
presented by newspapers as a day of national rejoicing. The media's claim
that this was an event of national interest was, though, misleading. By
today's standards the 1863 royal wedding was a small, cloistered affair.
But the fact that more was made of it than of any previous royal wedding
reveals how the British press wanted to project the royals as moral exemplars of Christian family life. It was also notable that the royal household
shared information about the wedding with the newspapers in order to
help journalists tell this story of national celebration, which again suggests
that the palace recognized the appeal of the family monarchy narrative.
Significantly, this led to a more serious public conversation about the role
played by the crown in public life.

Writing two years after the royal wedding, the journalist Walter Bagehot
– today widely cited as the progenitor of the ideas behind modern constitutional monarchy – recognized the wide appeal that such royal family
events might have among the public at large. He wrote how 'A princely
marriage is the brilliant edition of a universal fact, and as such it rivets
mankind.' Bagehot was ahead of the curve here: in his manifesto for political change, he advocated that the royal household publicly stage events
such as the prince and princess of Wales's wedding even more elaborately
in order to elevate the family monarchy as the ceremonial (dignified)
centre of national life. He recognized the potential that 'a family on the
throne' had as an emotionally unifying force in society, with the public
encouraged to identify with the lives, loves and losses of a familiar set of
royal personalities.

The family monarchy of Bagehot's formulation took its cues from
the image of Britain's royal dynasty under the stewardship of Prince
Albert. Monarchy was meant to be exemplary: it should project virtuous

Christian domesticity to appeal to middle-class sensibilities and to set a good example to the rest of society and, indeed, the empire. We can argue that, as with his emphasis on the circus of royal pomp and circumstance (Part One), Bagehot's discussion of the exemplary nature of royal family life was about social control, specifically of the British working classes, whose moral sensibilities were alien to him and which he therefore distrusted.

Historian Miles Taylor has added another dimension to our understanding of the purpose of family monarchy. It was also about European dynastic politics. Victoria and Albert were very concerned to link their Anglican monarchy to other, smaller Protestant royal families on the continent. They did this by arranging marriages for their nine children: indeed, the consort of Edward VII, Alexandra, was originally a princess of Denmark, their union strengthening ties between the British and Danish monarchies and the nation states they ruled. The problem with this dynastic matchmaking was that, while it may have enabled closer political bonds to develop in the short term between two countries (especially if they shared a religious denomination), it was no guarantee against family rivalries developing in the longer term.

Victoria became known as the 'Grandmother of Europe' – she had a total of 38 grandchildren and 89 great-grandchildren as a result of the dynastic webs she helped to spin. But one of her grandchildren proved to be a particular menace. Wilhelm II of Germany was a difficult man who was extremely jealous of his British cousins, and he made a great show of attending his grandmother's funeral in London in 1901. With his aggressive foreign policy of *Weltpolitik*, he would do much to undermine the peace-building efforts in Europe made by Edward VII in the first decade of the twentieth century. Ultimately these efforts would, of course, come to nought with the kaiser's ill-fated declaration of war in Europe in 1914. The irony was that the conflict witnessed the toppling of crowned heads of state, including Wilhelm and many other blood relations of Victoria, hence spelling the end of the dynastic royal cosmopolitanism of the pre-1914 period.

George V, who succeeded his father, Edward VII, to the throne in 1910, was the first king to have reportedly studied Bagehot's work on the constitution. He would modernize the monarchy in ways that suggested he had internalized the journalist's ideas on the moral role that royalty must play in society. Those who advised the king on how he should adapt the monarchy to the twentieth century also seem to have been influenced by Bagehot. At the monarch's coronation in 1911, the archbishop of York, Cosmo Lang (later archbishop of Canterbury and close adviser to George), was asked by the king to deliver a sermon in which he spoke of the exemplary moral function of monarchy: he described the sovereign as a 'servant of the people' to emphasize that public duty awaited him (see Part Two); and he described how the king and Queen Mary would together 'uphold before the people the high and happy traditions of a Christian home'.

By this stage the theme of family monarchy had been steadily taking shape (despite a few setbacks) for more than half a century. The palace and its allies had worked with a mostly loyal media to promote the crown's moral authority. The goodwill to George V established among news editors during the First World War helped to ensure that potentially explosive stories involving members of the House of Windsor were kept out of the newspapers.

There was plenty of royal moral transgression going on behind closed doors which, if reported back then, just as today, would have caused a public furore. This included the fact that in the early 1920s both of the king's oldest sons were in relationships with married women. The monarch, who in private displayed a foul temper, often directing his bullying at the prince of Wales (later Edward VIII), managed to convince his second son to give up his illicit affair but could do nothing to stop his heir from carrying on his romance. Then, later on in the decade, George's youngest son, the duke of Kent, had a series of bisexual flings before he became addicted to morphine and cocaine. As I say, this would all be rich pickings for the tabloid hack in the less deferential climate of today. But after the First World War the high esteem in which the crown was held, combined with the culture of discretion and deference that defined the media's relationship with the royal household, meant that all of this remained carefully hushed up.

The king also took proactive measures to maintain the outward appearance of domestic felicity. After the war, he and the queen decided that their adult children would be able to marry partners of their own choosing from among the English and Scottish aristocracy, rather than being required to marry into what remained of the royal cousinhood that extended across Europe, as per the pre-1914 tradition. This was a smart move. The House of Windsor appeared to be putting the personal desires of younger royals ahead of dynastic politics, which appealed to a sentimental public; and it strengthened the 'British' credentials of the monarchy, with the king turning his back on the unpopular, authoritarian Russian and German dynasties which had collapsed as a result of revolution and wartime defeat.

The weddings of the children of George V would, for the first time, be staged as major public events that positioned the monarchy as the emotional rallying point of national life (as per Bagehot's prescription). Mass media was key to this process. The marriages were narrated in close-up detail by the press, newsreels and BBC radio, which all celebrated them as true love matches. The coverage often lasted months, with journalists revelling in romantic betrothals before shifting readers' focus to glittering bridal dresses and star-studded wedding guest lists. Revelatory reports on the young couples' 'feelings' and photographs of them being physically intimate – for example, kissing (on the cheek) – helped to transform the young royal lovers into modern celebrity personalities with whom media audiences could empathize and identify. And, on the day of the weddings, central London was reorganized to create space for huge crowds, the ceremonies unfolding for the first time in more than 500 years in Westminster Abbey, the British nation's spiritual centre, thus reimagining a tradition that has persisted to the present.

The 'national royal weddings' of the 1920s and 1930s played into a mainstream culture of heterosexual romance made classless by the arrival in the 1910s of Hollywood cinema and the growth of popular literary fiction that sensationalized everyday human drama. This was a period when all people, no matter their social background, came to value modern concepts of love and emotional self-fulfilment. The media's intense focus on royal personalities as part of these events therefore enhanced the personal appeal of George V's monarchy. And this was an appeal that the king sought to cultivate beyond British shores in the empire as well.

On Christmas Day 1932 George began what quickly became an annual tradition when he broadcasted a special greeting to his subjects all across the world. His radio messages offered words of encouragement to his listeners at a time of socio-economic difficulty brought on by the Great Depression. But these were also messages that emphasized his sense of duty as king, the importance of international cooperation and the role of the monarch as head of the House of Windsor and as head of an international family of nations. Working with Archbishop Lang as royal speechwriter after 1933, the palace promoted an image of the king as a loving family man to his wife, children and grandchildren but also, just as importantly, as a devoted and benevolent *paterfamilias* to a 'family of peoples ... at peace in itself and united in one desire to be at peace with other nations'.

The idea of the imperial family linked together around the loving monarch quickly stuck. With its personal, caring imagery, this vision of empire appealed to members of the public who were comforted by the emphasis it placed on what one British listener described in a letter to the king as the 'Family Tie and Bond of Union'. The often brutal realities of colonialism were thus carefully disguised behind a veneer of kinship and mutual affection. This symbolism of a family of peoples would also be crucial to the decolonization of empire after 1945. Following her accession, Elizabeth II regularly drew on phrases like 'family of nations' in her speeches and her Christmas broadcasts in order to characterize the new Commonwealth as it emerged out of the remnants of empire. Despite what was often a disorderly and violent withdrawal of British power from the colonies – particularly in places where there were anti-imperial insurgencies, such as Kenya and Malaya – the monarch offered her people back in the UK a reassuring sense of continuity with the past rooted in an identification with her as queen and as head of a global community linked together by personal bonds of friendship and affection.

It is finally worth mentioning that the broadcasts made by George V and the interwar royal weddings also served an important political purpose within a British context. This period witnessed animated discussion among the British elite about the behaviour of the working classes, now endowed with voting power as a result of the Fourth and Fifth Reform Acts of 1918 and 1928. Some of the old monarchies of Europe that had collapsed at the end of the First World War had been replaced by autocratic regimes led by charismatic demagogues who, it seemed, had harnessed the energies of the 'masses' as part of their transformative political projects. The growth of parties on the far left and far right of UK politics, which fed off the misery created by economic depression, increased fears that similar unrest lay in wait for Britain. But set against any such revolutionary impulse was the House of Windsor. For George V, big royal events such as weddings, births, deaths and, indeed, his own silver jubilee in May 1935 were opportunities that could bind the seemingly unpredictable proletariat to the crown through warm feelings of personal affection and loyalty centred on the 'family on the throne'. And, crucially for the monarch, this public relations strategy paid off. He was widely celebrated as a loving father to his people who had popularized the family monarchy as the stabilizing force at the heart of British society and the empire (Fig 9).

EIGHTEEN

The royal soap opera

It is only by understanding the personal appeal of George V and his 'family on the throne' that we can appreciate why the public piled so much expectation on to the shoulders of his eldest son and successor, Edward VIII. On a scale never seen before, George's monarchy had enabled members of the public to forge intimate emotional bonds with royalty and, in particular, with the prince of Wales – the crown's star attraction – who was welcomed by his subjects into his new role on an unprecedented wave of optimism when he succeeded his father as king in January 1936. But within 11 months he was gone, abdicating in order to marry the woman he loved.

We can make sense of the mixed public reaction to the British media's announcement in early December 1936 that Edward was ready to give up his throne if his prime minister insisted that Wallis Simpson could not be his wife, with reference to the enduring power of the 'family monarchy' idea popularized by his father. It is true that many of the monarch's subjects saw his affair with Wallis as a betrayal of his predecessor's values. But as revealed by the historian Frank Mort, for many other people, the new king's star appeal, sympathetic personality and desire for emotional fulfilment meant he should have been able to do as he pleased, irrespective of his government's concerns.

Edward was, by the beginning of the 1930s, one of the best-known personalities in the English-speaking world. Since the war ended, he had distinguished himself (in full view of the cameras) as a forward-thinking man of action: not only did he take to modern leisure pursuits such as flying aeroplanes, driving sports cars and dancing the Charleston; his plain-speaking demeanour and readiness to engage compassionately and directly with the crowds of well-wishers who turned out to meet him and hear him speak as prince of Wales on his tours of Britain and the empire meant media audiences came to see him less as their royal superior than as a symbolic 'man of the people', in touch with their aspirations and fears (Fig 10).

Add to this heady mix Edward's matinee idol good looks and we can begin to understand why he developed a particularly strong following among female 'fans', his celebrity persona coming to rival that of the biggest film stars of the day. One woman who wrote to the king at the time of the abdication crisis – a Mrs McAllister from South Dakota in the USA – enclosed with her letter a

> picture of you … I cut out of a magazine when I was about fourteen, and I think you were the same age. I fell in love with the picture then and have kept it ever since, which is about thirty years … You know and remember perhaps what one goes through at that age.

This source suggests that, as a young man, Edward was a fantasy figure for some of his contemporaries. As with the Hollywood heart-throbs of this period, there was huge speculation among press and public about his romantic life. Again, this type of intrigue set him apart from earlier generations of British royalty. The problem his parents faced was that privately Edward was careless and showed scant regard for the ideal of 'family monarchy' they had promoted. The prince resisted pressure from his father to settle down with 'a suitable, well-born English girl', instead embarking on a string of love affairs, mainly with other men's wives.

While rumours of Edward's moral indiscretions abounded in London high society, the gentlemanly codes of discretion that characterized this world, and the high regard that news editors had for his father and for him (as a public figure), meant that nothing incriminating made it into print. But the problem for the crown was that a disconnect was opening up between the royal family's public image and the scandalous reality. The interwar Windsor weddings and model of Christian home life set by George V and Queen Mary meant that the monarchy came to be seen publicly as head of the nation's morality. However, this idea would be jeopardized the moment the dissolute private life of the heir to the throne was publicly exposed. It is this disjuncture between image and reality that helps to explain the sense of disbelief and, in some quarters, horror when it was finally revealed by Britain's newspapers at the start of December 1936 that, far from a fairy-tale happy ending, Edward was willing to give up the throne he had inherited less than a year before in order to marry a woman judged unfit to be his wife by the country's political and religious elite.

From a purely Christian perspective Wallis was unsuitable to marry a king and emperor who was, simultaneously, supreme governor of the Church of England. The relationship had begun in 1934 and George V, well aware of his son's affair with the American socialite, had reportedly told Prime Minister Stanley Baldwin in 1935 that his son 'would ruin himself within twelve months' of succeeding to the throne because of his behaviour. Another not entirely reliable witness, Alan 'Tommy' Lascelles, private secretary to Edward's successors, also jotted down for posterity that George V had confided in another courtier that he thought his eldest son would abdicate. Whatever the truth of the matter, it is clear that sections of the court were deeply disapproving of Wallis's romance with the king. Divorced once and, by autumn 1936, with another divorce pending so that she would be free to wed again, for those in the know she threatened the very idea of a Christian family monarchy: according to the Church's teachings, she was ineligible to marry the king because both of her former husbands were still living.

However, the fact that many of Edward's subjects – male and female – wrote to him on learning about his relationship with Wallis in order to express support for his decision to marry her and insist that he stay on as king, indicates the way that love, and the monarch's personal charisma, mattered more to some people than religious dogma. For them, a different vision of a family monarchy seemed possible, where King Edward achieved emotional fulfilment with the woman he cared most deeply about. Unfortunately for the monarch, the skilful Baldwin forced him into a position where he had to make a choice between marrying the woman he loved and keeping the throne: he couldn't have his cake and eat it.

The abdication crisis brought into sharp focus two competing forms of personality-led kingship: one was constitutional and rooted in Victorian moral values; the other was dynamic, forward-looking but verged on undemocratic in the way it celebrated the charismatic authority of a celebrity king. The crisis thus serves as a warning to us today about how emotion can very easily trump reason in the way we feel and think about the country's royal rulers.

As we know, Edward chose Wallis and renounced his duty as king, throwing the monarchy into a period of turmoil and instability under the uninspiring but dutiful leadership of his younger brother, George VI, who never managed to achieve the commanding heights of fame and adulation enjoyed by his predecessor. The other notable, though less commented on, outcome of the abdication was that it dispelled – at least temporarily – the hype around the idea of a personality-led monarchy as embodied first by George V and then his eldest son. The editor of the *Manchester Guardian* recognized the changed circumstances when he wrote to one of his reporters that 'we shall in future be saying much more about the Crown and much less about its temporary owner', Edward VIII having failed spectacularly to fulfil 'all the hopes that were being expressed about him'.

The abdication was a lesson to Buckingham Palace that, if it built up the reputations of the royal family too much by helping to turn them into popular celebrities, this could lead to big problems if, for whatever reason, they suddenly revealed human frailties (like Edward), thus falling short of public expectations. Unfortunately for the current set of royals, this is a lesson the monarchy has stubbornly refused to learn. The royal household has worked with the media ever since 1936 to build up individual members of each generation of Windsors so that they become superstars only for them to (perhaps inevitably) put a foot wrong and disappoint – for example, by falling in love with someone unsuitable, or by having an extramarital affair.

The result has been periods of sustained crisis for the crown. And what this points to is a broken formula that no longer works for the monarchy. One of the reasons it is broken is that ever since the abdication crisis the royal household hasn't been able to rely on the discretion of news editors to keep quiet about royal moral impropriety. The abdication released a genie among sections of the British media, which subsequently adopted a much more circumspect – even cynical – position on royal matters. Under George V, the House of Windsor had been treated with kid gloves by a press which loudly proclaimed the king and his family the unifying symbol at the heart of national life, and as the democratic antidote to the kinds of political extremism that emerged in Europe in these years. Now, knowing full well that they had conspired to conceal Edward's affair from the British public by maintaining the veil of secrecy and silence around his relationship with Wallis Simpson, some Fleet Street news editors decided enough was enough: from this point onwards, they would criticize and challenge the monarchy in ways that hadn't been seen since the nineteenth century.

As well as questioning the moral choices made by the ex-king, now known as the duke of Windsor, these voices in the media (notably the left-leaning *Daily Mirror* and the liberal press, including the *News Chronicle* and *Manchester Guardian*) questioned whether the new monarch, George VI, had the resolve and strength of character to perform his job properly. Newspapers also raised concerns about the new king's physical health, reproducing stories that discussed his weakness and speech impediment – concerns that were subsequently echoed by members of the public on the day of his coronation.

The palace public relations machine responded to the loss of confidence in the monarchy after the abdication by projecting the new king as the 'true successor' to his father, George V. As part of this strategy, there was a quick return to an emphasis on the happy family life of the court, notably embodied by the new smiling queen consort, Elizabeth, and her two 'fairy-tale' daughters, Princesses Elizabeth and Margaret Rose. Likewise, duty was once again the order of the day: with the help of compliant media organizations such as *The Times*, the BBC and *British Movietone News*, George VI was projected as a courageous figure who put national responsibility ahead of his personal desire to live a quiet family life with his wife and children.

At a time when private family life was increasingly celebrated by all sections of society as an ideal to which everyone should be able to aspire, the image of the self-sacrificing monarch who put duty ahead of private desire was powerful – not least because it directly challenged the irresponsible kingship of Edward VIII. In the short term, doubts about George VI persisted, as captured by a reporter writing for the *Chronicle* at the time of the new king's coronation: 'there is nothing wonderful (we shall freely admit) about [George VI]. We don't even know him very well ... [But] he is a modest and sensible king.' In the longer term, though, the image of the king as a selfless public servant would win him sympathy and indeed support among his people.

———

Thus Britain's royal democracy was very gradually stabilized around another generation of the family monarchy. Out of the ashes of the abdication rose a new, potent myth of a self-sacrificing monarch who put crown and country first. This myth gained momentum through the war years that followed, during which (according to official propaganda) the House of Windsor shared in the hardship, loss and, ultimately, glory of the conflict. By 1945 Princess Elizabeth, who was now 19 years old, had supplanted her parents as the focal point of the nation's interest and affections. Her brief but highly publicized spell in uniform in the last months of the war had begun the process of turning her into a symbol intended to represent all the young women who had weathered the privations of the Second World War in the hope that it would lead to happier days.

The conflict had seen the royal family deliberately embrace a new public image that made them appear more 'ordinary' (more middle-class) and, therefore, in keeping with the austere times. Given her youth, Elizabeth was described by media commentators as embodying the post-war generation's desire for a return to domesticity after demobilization. There was a great deal of speculation about her romantic life, as there had been with her uncle Edward, during the 1920s and early 1930s. And, like the former prince of Wales, by encouraging the public to take an active interest in the princess as both a dutiful young royal, but also as a human being with an inner emotional life, the royal household and British journalists transformed her into a popular celebrity with whom media audiences could empathize.

Elizabeth's engagement and marriage to Prince Philip of Greece was, despite serious initial concerns, celebrated for the way it seemed to offer the princess a chance of domestic happiness and, equally, for the way it injected a new lease of life into the monarchy. The royal household staged the wedding as a moment of national celebration, thus encouraging the public to emotionally identify with the young couple as they started their new lives together. The duke of Edinburgh, as Philip would subsequently be styled, was, it seemed, only too happy to play the role of picture-perfect husband and father – at least, in public. Historian Tessa Dunlop notes that in private the duke could be an extremely difficult man, sometimes behaving in a bullying and demeaning way towards his wife and future queen. But throughout the late 1940s and 1950s Philip presented himself in public as a model of modern masculinity by, for example, helping his wife push a pram that contained their infant son Prince Charles for the benefit of a newsreel cameraman who filmed this happy family scene for the viewing pleasure of cinemagoers.

The cameraman in question held the official title of 'King's Cameraman' – a special position invented during the Second World War to ensure that all of George VI's wartime activities were recorded on film, which was then released to the public by the main newsreel companies. At the time the king had been worried about Prime Minister Winston Churchill overshadowing him as leader of the war effort and therefore created this 'in-house' role for a cameraman over whom he could exercise direct control in an effort to generate positive publicity. The creation of the King's Cameraman post was symptomatic of a shift in the royal household's approach to the British media after the abdication. Given King George's evident physical shortcomings and the growth in criticism of royalty after the fall from grace of Edward VIII, it was more important than ever to forge new alliances with news providers which could be trusted to produce sympathetic coverage of the monarchy.

The House of Windsor had long counted on the services of The Times, the Daily Telegraph and the BBC in helping to generate positive royal news stories. All three outlets were patriotic and deferential in the extreme. The people that ran them generally maintained good relations with courtiers in the royal household, not least because they moved in the same society circles. As a result, these news organizations often got privileged access to royal family events as part of a mutually beneficial relationship whereby the crown was guaranteed good media exposure (in a way that is not dissimilar to what Prince Harry referred to as the 'invisible contract' used by royalty today to curry favour with certain high-profile journalists).

From the 1940s onwards, Buckingham Palace started to engage the services of a wider range of professionals who could be relied on to burnish the royal family's public image. A new group of trusted photographers took pictures of Princess Elizabeth's family, dressed in everyday middle-class clothing, behaving as a loving domestic group. The public were able to relate to this family narrative because the early post-war period witnessed the popularization of this kind of intimate family photography throughout society. Cheering pictures of the princess with her husband and children served a more urgent purpose too. In the late 1940s the duke of Windsor remained a thorn in the side of the crown, serializing portions of his forthcoming memoir, A King's Story, in one of Britain's leading Sunday newspapers to great acclaim. Given his enduring popularity with sections of the public, the palace thought it was crucial that media audiences remain fixated on George VI and his daughter's family as the respectable, responsible group who were keeping the monarchy going, rather than be distracted by an irresponsible ex-king who had a great story to sell.

The intimate family photographs taken by specially commissioned professionals gave the royal household a way of exercising tighter control over the royal family's media image as well. The images were distributed to the press for reproduction with the explicit aim of discouraging increasingly aggressive tabloid paparazzi from trying to take candid images of the family. Thousands of these royal photographs were also reproduced in colour as part of mass market collectible souvenir magazines, which provided consumers in post-war Britain and around the world with a version of royal life that seemed more informal and accessible than ever before.

The arrival of Princess Anne in 1950 completed the nuclear family of Elizabeth and Philip. Now a family of four, they closely resembled the post-war ideal, symbolizing a national culture of domesticity which celebrated the love that existed between wives and their husbands, and between parents and their children (Fig 11). This was the period when, for all classes of British people, home and family became important sites of emotional enrichment. Reports from the social research organization Mass Observation reveal how many members of the public, while watching the television broadcast of her coronation in June 1953, conversed about the affection that seemed to exist between Queen Elizabeth and her children: her image as a young mother was fundamental to the way people saw her as monarch.

The problem with the idealized public image of the new queen's family life is that it was largely contrived and disguised a reality that was, by the standards of the 1950s, outdated. In public, much was made by the media of the way Elizabeth hated to be separated from her children as a result of having to carry out her public duties as queen. This narrative reworked the theme, first seen with George VI, that a monarch's national and international responsibilities prevented them from enjoying a normal home life and had the intended effect of generating sympathy for the young sovereign.

Much was also made publicly of the 'happy moments' when, after returning home from an overseas tour, Elizabeth was finally reunited with her children, who had stayed in Britain. However, we now know that, behind closed doors, the monarch was an aloof and emotionally distant mother, happily leaving the parenting of her children to nannies and governesses. The new king spoke about this to his biographer, Jonathan Dimbleby (younger son of Richard Dimbleby), in the early 1990s. Charles also characterized his father, Philip, as a bully. As biographer of Elizabeth II, Ben Pimlott, noted, as a result of Charles's candid portrayal of his parents, 'the Monarch and her husband, formerly set in the nation's imagination as the ideal mother and father, became indifferent parents, who caused the marriages of their children to break down by starving them of love'. Others who worked closely with Elizabeth II support this view: a former private secretary said of her that 'if the Queen had taken half as much trouble about the rearing of her children as she did the breeding of her horses, the royal family wouldn't be in such an emotional mess.'

What we can observe here again is the failure of the royal household to learn from the mistake of Edward VIII, where the king's image had disguised the reality of his private life, only for that reality to be made public, throwing the crown into crisis. Fortunately for the queen, her failures as a mother remained secret until the 1990s. However, it is significant that reappraisals of Elizabeth's personal characteristics – particularly in popular fiction such as the series The Crown – have started to chip away at older claims to her moral authority, raising questions about what else might have been concealed from us in terms of the former queen's private behaviour.

By the mid-1950s other, more visible cracks were appearing in the façade of the family monarchy. These also stemmed from the royal determination to promote an idealized family image, despite the fact that some members of the House of Windsor found it difficult to adhere to Christian teachings on marriage. No sooner had Queen Elizabeth been crowned in June 1953 as god's representative on earth, than a new crisis involving another divorced person threatened to undermine the monarchy's public standing. The queen's sister, Princess Margaret, had fallen in love with the courtier Group Captain Peter Townsend, a man whom traditionalists deemed unsuitable because he had previously been married.

However, two decades on from the abdication of Edward VIII, things were very different. In an increasingly secular age, public opinion had hardened against the church's opposition to the remarriage of divorced people, particularly if they were the innocent party, as was the case with Townsend. The Daily Mirror, keener than ever to challenge the moral conservatism of the British establishment, conducted a poll on Margaret's possible marriage to Townsend and found more than 97 per cent of 70,000 respondents supported the relationship.

Despite the outpouring of popular support for the couple, this was still an age where the reactionary forces behind the throne refused to countenance such a marriage. The former private secretary, Tommy Lascelles, Buckingham Palace's press secretary, Richard Colville (also known to journalists as the 'Abominable "No" Man' for his uncompromising stance on media innovation) and the archbishop of Canterbury, Geoffrey Fisher, came down quietly – but firmly – against the lovers. Although Elizabeth reportedly tried to stay neutral in order to leave the final decision to her sister, the involvement of the so-called 'men in grey suits' meant that only one outcome was ever really possible. Hence, modernization was again resisted by the palace in favour of a backward-looking Victorian moral code that held individual members of the royal family to almost impossibly high standards.

The Conservative politician and diarist Harold Nicolson recognized how Margaret's decision to give up Townsend would be interpreted as an act of self-sacrifice – a theme which, as we have seen, has been crucial to generating support for royals who have appeared as victims of their unusual circumstances. Most significantly, though, the Margaret–Townsend episode of 1953–5, like the abdication crisis, accelerated the desacralization of the monarchy. The media storm that accompanied both moments raised big questions about the behaviour of the royal family and encouraged open criticism of a monarchy that had, since the end of the nineteenth century, seemed beyond reproach.

Such criticism flowed from the pens of left-wing journalist Malcolm Muggeridge and the Conservative peer and writer Lord Altrincham. Although they may have seemed like unlikely bedfellows, both thought that Queen Elizabeth was badly advised and that an urgent overhaul of palace personnel was required.

For Muggeridge, writing in *The New Statesman and Nation* (as it was then called), the Margaret–Townsend episode had unleashed an 'orgy of vulgar and sensationalist speculation'. The monarchy had descended into melodrama playing out in full glare of the public. He claimed that the lurid interest in the royals' private lives had been actively fuelled by courtiers through the release of a steady stream of photos of the queen and her young children. (He was right.) In a follow-up piece he also took aim at broadcaster Richard Dimbleby for focusing the public's attention on the romantic, human side of monarchy through his BBC commentary at events like the 1953 coronation.

Muggeridge thought 'the whole show ... utterly out of control' and compared the 1950s media coverage of royalty to the 'fantasy of adulation and sycophancy' that had encircled the former king, Edward VIII, noting how his and the monarchy's fall from grace was all the more spectacular because of the deep personal interest people had been encouraged to take in him as a popular celebrity. Crucially, Muggeridge also believed that the monarchy had an important constitutional role to play, symbolizing national unity and providing a sense of continuity in a changing society. For him, the 'royal soap opera' (a term he coined) trivialized monarchy, thus undermining its more serious purpose.

While Altrincham proposed the same solution as Muggeridge of finding better advisers for the queen, his complaint about the state of the monarchy was different. He argued that the institution and the monarch were hidebound and out of date. He believed that Queen Elizabeth needed to modernize and democratize by making the monarchy more – not less – popular. One other thing that both men's critiques had in common, though, is that they focused on the self-presentation of the royals, remarking on how, because of the modern media, the Windsors were under closer scrutiny than ever before. What their interventions signalled was that from the mid-1950s onwards the royal family were going to be treated with less deference than had previously been the case. This posed a problem because the palace was finding it increasingly difficult to control the narrative spun around the royals by news editors and journalists.

The events of the mid-1950s pointed to the fact that a dissonance had opened between the fantasy of royal domesticity and the reality of life behind closed doors at the palace. The public recognized this incongruity for themselves, and it was what fuelled interest in the private lives of the Windsors, as seen in the success of a series of high-profile publications written by royal insiders and serialized by magazines and newspapers which promised readers glimpses of the reality. This included governess Marion Crawford's The Little Princesses (1950), on the early lives of Elizabeth and Margaret, royal valet John Dean's recollections of life in the service of the duke of Edinburgh and, most significantly, the duke of Windsor's A King's Story (1951).

Marketed as providing the 'inside story' on royal events and personalities, these books were characteristic of a wider culture of revelation in the mid-twentieth century where popular celebrities sold 'confessions' about their personal lives to the highest bidder, which would then be printed for a mass readership. As historian Adrian Bingham has discussed, the royal exposés were further proof if it was needed that courtiers were unable to control those with intimate knowledge of what really went on in the royal family. And such breaches of trust were never forgiven. Crawford, or 'Crawfie', as she was known to the family, was shunned by the royals after writing her book despite the fact that she produced a deeply affectionate portrayal of the queen and Princess Margaret, to whom she had been a surrogate mother figure when they were children.

It was clear that a genie had been let out of a bottle, never to return, when, in mid-1957, the British tabloids circulated the sensational rumour that Queen Elizabeth's marriage was experiencing difficulties – perhaps the most egregious intimation of scandal to be levelled at the royal family since the abdication two decades earlier. The stories of a 'royal rift' gained momentum because the duke of Edinburgh had been on a Commonwealth tour lasting several months and seemed to be in no hurry to return to his wife and young children. The newspapers were even so daring as to question his qualities as a parent (directly challenging his public image as a loving, modern father) and noted his close friendship with Mike Parker, his manservant, who was being sued for divorce by his wife because of his adultery. So serious was the unspoken insinuation that Philip might also have been unfaithful to his wife that the palace broke with protocol and issued an unofficial rebuff to the reports, emphasizing that there was no truth to the rumours.

At a time when public figures were selling popular 'tell-all' exposés which often focused on sex and immorality, media audiences were encouraged to develop a similar prurient interest in the intimate life of their queen. This curiosity stemmed from the fact that people had figured out there were real (fallible) people behind the royal public images. And yet the palace press operation refused to deviate from the fantasy of the idealized family monarchy. Indeed, after the newspaper rumours about Elizabeth and Philip's marriage, the royal household consented to the publication of a new souvenir book titled *The Work of the Queen* (1958), which made clear to readers that the symbolic power of the monarchy partly lay in the example of Christian family life set to the nation by the House of Windsor.

The author of this book, Dermot Morrah, was a long-term and loyal friend to the crown. As a leader writer at The Times he had penned several articles in December 1936 to explain to readers why Baldwin's government was justified in resisting Edward VIII's move to make Wallis Simpson his queen. Then, in 1947, he and George VI's private secretary wrote Elizabeth's 21st birthday broadcast in which she famously dedicated her life to the service of her people. His 1958 book (one of several on a royal topic commissioned by the publisher Pitkin, with the support of Buckingham Palace) focused on the purpose of the modern monarchy and, as with his other contributions, helped to establish the themes through which the public were encouraged to make sense of the royal family's role in society. As well as stressing the crown's constitutional function and the importance of public service, he focused on domesticity: 'if the Queen is to be the embodiment of ordinary English life, she must be seen in ordinary human relationships. Therefore the Royal Family is as indispensable to the representative work of queenship as the Queen herself.'

For Morrah, Queen Elizabeth's authority rested above all in the way her outward commitment to family life mirrored that of the nation. Of course, he was inadvertently helping to turn the queen and her kin into hostages of fortune. By emphasizing that the royals' moral behaviour was fundamental to their public reputation, he was inviting problems by setting an impossibly high standard against which the future conduct of all Windsors would be judged. As one of the 'high priests' of what royal biographer Ben Pimlott has termed the mid-twentieth-century 'cult of monarchy', Morrah was deeply invested in protecting the institution; but, ironically, he was setting it up for failure. The problem for the House of Windsor then (as now) was that the royal household and its allies invited the press and public to see the royals as a fantasy family in order to win the affection and loyalty of the public. But this meant the family's public standing was threatened every time one of them was caught behaving at all improperly.

Unfortunately for the Windsors, an increasingly irreverential press, driven by competition and unimpeded by old codes of deference, was proving readier than ever to leap on any sign of misconduct or hypocrisy in order to challenge the fantasy. But rather than gently dismantle the fiction they had helped to create, lest it degenerate once again into the royal soap opera of Muggeridge's description, the palace carried on much as before, further embellishing the idea that the royals were the model family. In his 1957 article Altrincham had criticized the queen's speech-making style and suggested she televise her Christmas broadcast as a way of reaching out to new audiences. It seems she or someone at the palace was paying close attention to the Tory peer, because that same year the queen delivered her festive greeting to viewers for the first time. But she stuck to the hackneyed theme of her domesticity. Addressing viewers, she described how 'my own family often gather round to watch television, as they are at this moment, and that is how I imagine you now'. The queen's family life and British family life were thus symbolically conflated once more, and the royal merry-go-round began another rotation.

NINETEEN

Killing the monarchy?

The year 1960 brought mixed blessings for the royals and heralded the beginning of a 21-year period during which the monarchy found it harder to maintain enthusiasm among a British public suddenly much more interested in other things. Princess Margaret had fallen in love again, and this time she got to marry her man in a bonanza wedding that was televised in full to the country and world for the first time ever. The groom was the dashing and debonair Welshman Antony Armstrong-Jones – a photographer who spent his professional life at his London studio taking pictures of some of the most famous people on earth, including royalty.

The couple's wedding was portrayed by the press as giving the princess the happy ending she had been denied five years earlier. Much was also made of Armstrong-Jones's commoner status. Though a minor celebrity in his own right, his marriage to Margaret seemed to suggest that the royal family were opening themselves up to wider society. The Snowdons (as they became known, after Armstrong-Jones was ennobled with the title 1st Earl of Snowdon by his new sister-in-law) became one of Britain's most glamorous couples, their lives the focus of intense media interest and, later on, speculation, as it became clear their marriage was ill-fated (Fig 12).

For Queen Elizabeth too 1960 was an important year because she gave birth to her third child, Andrew. This was a happy event in the life of the queen, but it also spelt the end of the public image of the nuclear family monarchy – two parents, two children – as per the post-war ideal of the late 1940s and 1950s. The birth also focused attention on a monarch now in early middle age who, shorn of her youthful beauty, had embraced a notably dowdy style, especially when contrasted to her fashionable younger sister.

Although some members of the public held firm to the idea that the Windsors embodied the family values of the nation, these were values that many of the younger generation seemed to be turning their backs on. The tone of British tabloid news coverage in the 1960s was one of excitement, danger and moral change. Against this backdrop, the ageing family monarchy of Elizabeth II appeared old-fashioned. And the massive public interest the queen and her consort had enjoyed in the years immediately before and after her coronation had started to dissipate, with the focus of the public's attention shifting to new, home-grown (and often working-class) celebrities – perhaps most notably embodied by the pop group The Beatles.

The 'Fab Four' were not, unlike the royals, famous simply for being famous. Their celebrity was rooted in the fact that they were talented songwriters who produced cutting-edge music. Certainly in mainstream popular culture there was a sense that Britain was moving on from a hidebound past where wealth and birthright had determined one's ultimate success in life. Instead, the UK was embracing a future where it seemed as though, if you were gifted enough, you could succeed no matter where you started. The cult of monarchy was being eclipsed by the cult of the self-made star.

On the evening of 21 June 1969, 23 million viewers across Britain (almost half the country's population) gathered in front of their television sets to watch *Royal Family* – a 'fly-on-the-wall' documentary which presented the leading members of the House of Windsor behaving in ways never seen before. For one year, a joint BBC–ITV production crew, led by the director Richard Cawston, had been given unprecedented access to film Queen Elizabeth and her kin up close and personal as they went about their daily activities and engagements. The resulting film included civic visits, garden parties and royal receptions for foreign dignitaries, including the US president, Richard Nixon, who made an appearance towards the end of the programme.

More significant for TV viewers, though, were the scenes of the royals when they were not on official business but instead behaving informally and interacting with one another as though they were just a normal family. For the first time they were seen breakfasting together, chit-chatting and telling one another risqué jokes. Other highlights included a group barbecue next to a loch on the Balmoral estate, the queen and duke of Edinburgh decorating a Christmas tree together with their children at Windsor Castle and three generations of the royal family (plus the corgis) gathered in front of their own TV set in the living quarters of Sandringham House, chuckling along to an episode of *The Morecambe and Wise Show*.

The public response to this experiment in royal reality television was ecstatic. It garnered acclaim for showing the Windsors as more personable, down to earth and human than ever before. As a result of overseas distribution, it was seen by an estimated global audience of 350 million, making it one of the most viewed documentaries of all time. However, not all was well. Although Queen Elizabeth had originally agreed to the project, watching and signing off on the version of the film that was televised, someone at Buckingham Palace was unhappy with the documentary's presentation of the House of Windsor. Despite having been repeated ten times in the intervening eight years, it was withdrawn from circulation in 1977 and broadcasters were asked not to show it again.

Several key figures at the BBC are recorded as having thought *Royal Family* too intrusive. For example, David Attenborough, the Controller of Programmes at BBC2 in 1969, is said to have claimed that it risked 'killing the monarchy' for the way it let in light on the 'mystique' of the institution, undermining the sacred aspects of the queen's public image through its focus on the mundane and trivial. Until recently, with the documentary still officially banned, it was impossible to judge for oneself whether it merited such criticism, unless of course one had seen it when it was originally televised. Then, in January 2021, an unauthorized version of the film was leaked on YouTube, a copy of which was uploaded to the Internet Archive – one of the most helpful online databases for historians of the modern period.

After it resurfaced, some British media commentators were quick to celebrate the film for the way it captured the Windsors behaving in a 'totally unguarded' manner in front of the camera. But such reviews were misleading and failed to recognize what the documentary was trying to achieve. Watching *Royal Family* now, it is clear that the main protagonists were engaged in a carefully staged publicity performance and knew full well that their every action and word were being captured on camera. In this respect, the documentary was another example of the royal household collaborating with trusted allies in the media in order to project a very specific kind of public image to Britain and the world.

The idea behind Royal Family originated in conversations between the palace's new press secretary, William Heseltine, and Lord Brabourne – the film director son-in-law of Lord Louis Mountbatten, known as 'Uncle Dickie' to the Windsors – who was a shrewd media operator. These men believed that such a documentary could have a powerful humanizing effect on royalty at a time when, because of the democratizing social and cultural changes of the 1960s, the monarchy appeared distant, elitist and out of touch. And they were right: this public relations exercise generated hugely positive attention around the House of Windsor by making it seem as though, behind closed doors, the royals were a relatively ordinary family.

However, watching Royal Family again now, it is also clear why the palace had it censored. The film encouraged television audiences to see their royal superiors as complex personalities, possessing positive attributes as well as everyday character flaws. Rather than uphold an image of the royals as the model Christian family of the immediate post-war period, the documentary instead accelerated a trend towards 'desacralization', where journalists have invited media audiences to identify with the strengths and weaknesses of royal individuals. It is Royal Family's inclusion of human frailty that helps to explain why officials had it banned, especially given its focus on the then 20-year-old heir to the throne, Prince Charles, who comes across, in the words of royal biographer Ben Pimlott, as 'gawky and uncomfortable'.

One of the other main aims of the film was to glamourize Charles ahead of his investiture as prince of Wales on 1 July 1969. However, in this respect the film was ultimately unsuccessful. He was not the hyper-modern, charismatic, globe-trotting, good-looking Prince Edward of the 1920s; nor was he a romantic, fairy-tale figure in the mould of his mother or aunt Margaret in the late 1940s and early 1950s. Times had changed. And the documentary's portrayal of the new king as dutiful, sensitive and highly cultured marked him out as different from most other young people in their late teens and early twenties. For many, this was, after all, the age of Top of the Pops, coffee shops, dance halls and looser morals. If we add to this the way the film portrays the prince of Wales and his family as extraordinarily privileged (the opening scenes show a playboy Charles water-skiing and there is emphasis throughout the film on the 'below stairs' activities of the vast train of servants who keep the various royal residences going), we can begin to understand why the documentary was kept hidden from public view for so long.

Royal Family demonstrates how the monarchy has walked a tightrope in attempting to generate favourable publicity through what we might term intimate self-exposure while also trying to avoid revealing too much. The sense that the monarchy's relevance to ordinary people was fading helped to convince the palace that *Royal Family* was a good idea. But this deliberate act of modernization betrayed the royal household's deep anxiety about the relevance of the monarchy to modern Britain and the belief that royalty could be made more meaningful to the public if they were able to glimpse something of the inner workings of the family.

———

In addition to the palace's deliberate attempts to engage the public in 1969, there was another key event in this year – less remarked on at the time – which did even more to accelerate the monarchy's loss of control over its public image. The Australian press baron Rupert Murdoch, took over and then relaunched the popular British tabloid newspaper the *Sun*, having done the same with the Sunday *News of the World* the previous year. Murdoch was an outsider and a republican who thrived on courting controversy and provoking outrage in order to generate sales of his publications. He firmly believed that the royal family should be held up to the same standards and level of scrutiny as other public figures, rejecting once and for all any residual semblance of deference.

The 1970s would prove to be very difficult for the monarchy precisely because Murdoch's press developed an aggressive reporting style which proved so popular with readers that other news titles copied his papers' methods in order to compete for scoops. Exposés followed on Princess Anne's romance with fellow equestrian (and future husband) Mark Phillips. The prince of Wales was similarly linked – though often erroneously – to a string of different girlfriends. But, most notably, Princess Margaret drew huge attention from the tabloids, unfortunately for all the wrong reasons.

One crucial shift ushered in by the Murdoch approach to newsgathering was the way his journalists sought tirelessly to tear the royals off the pedestals that, ironically, Britain's media had created for them in the first place. This happened in 1976, when the *News of the World* published front-page photographs of Margaret on holiday in Mustique in the Caribbean with her much younger boyfriend, the socialite Roddy Llewellyn. Coming at a time when she was still officially married to Lord Snowdon, and set against a grim economic situation back home, these images of the queen's sister cavorting with her lover in an exotic location led journalists to question her priorities and morals. Why was she not carrying out her duties and setting a good example to others, as was required of members of the royal family?

More problematic for Queen Elizabeth was the criticism levelled at the princess by reporters and republican members of parliament that her louche behaviour undermined her claim to the annual civil list payment of £55,000 that she received at direct expense to the UK taxpayer. There was no place for royal self-indulgence in a cash-strapped Britain battered by an energy crisis that had led to uncontrollable inflation and stagnant economic growth. After divorcing Snowdon in 1978 and her subsequent split from Llewellyn, Margaret went into temporary self-imposed exile at the fringes of public life. This brought to an end months of damaging headlines which had, in effect, held up a mirror to the monarchy in order to expose the double standards and dishonesty that undermined its reputation as a family-centred institution.

Growing public concern about the state of the House of Windsor, coupled with the loss of national self-confidence suffered by Britain because of the political and economic shifts of the late 1970s, helped to ensure the news that the heir to the throne, Prince Charles, was engaged to a beautiful but relatively obscure young aristocrat named Diana Spencer was greeted with huge enthusiasm by press and public alike. That the bride-to-be was seemingly well grounded and possessed of a magical 'common touch' that hadn't been seen in the royal family since the days of Edward VIII added to the excitement.

The royal wedding in 1981 was celebrated by the media as a moment of national triumph that not only fixed the House of Windsor by reasserting the Christian moral credentials of the so-called family monarchy but also brought together a country divided by some of the most challenging economic circumstances seen since the war. One year on, Diana was described by a reporter as a 'princess of the people and a princess of our times'. Little did anyone know that within ten years her marriage to the prince of Wales would lie in pieces, shattered by yet more deceit, infidelity and scandal that once again made a mockery of the family on the throne.

TWENTY

Annus horribilis

Despite the outward success of Charles and Diana's wedding, and the arrival in quick succession of an heir and a spare, as the 1980s wore on there was a return of humiliating media exposés and a deep sense of uncertainty about the moral purpose of royalty. Ben Pimlott described how, over the course of a decade, the British monarchy lost 'its previous immunity ... the tinsel adulation that accompanied the 1981 wedding dissolved'. And he noted how 'media hunger' for sensationalist royal stories 'turned the bemused, half resisting, half co-operating, ill equipped dynasty into a circus'.

The main problem was that, once again, the palace refused to learn from past mistakes by sticking to a time-worn public relations narrative of a family monarchy fronted by a new set of popular personalities who simply couldn't live up to the hype and expectation. The princess of Wales injected some much-needed glamour back into the House of Windsor and, as a young mother to Princes William and Harry, she seemed to represent a more innocent age where the Victorian family values espoused by Britain's new prime minister, Margaret Thatcher, prevailed (Fig 13). However, as her popularity grew, so did the risk to the crown should the realities of her unhappy marriage to the prince of Wales be made public. Once again, the monarchy was made vulnerable by the human frailties of its leading personalities.

———

While the Waleses (as Charles and Diana were popularly known) played at happy families in public, other members of the House of Windsor became a source of trouble. Royal biographers have suggested that Queen Elizabeth overcompensated for the lack of love she showed her children when they were young by giving into their every wish and whim later on in life. The problem with this indulgent attitude was that her sons proved to be poor decision-makers and, had the queen adopted a firmer line with them, she might have saved the crown much embarrassment. Indeed, when we look closely at the monarch's behaviour, we can see that her tolerance of her children's often morally wayward actions was a weakness that helped to define the second half of her reign. Furthermore, by the 1980s she was also the head of a bloated royal family which contained various lesser-known royal aunts, uncles and cousins who were not popular with the British public and were regularly labelled by the tabloid press as expensive 'hangers-on'. Had the queen proactively sought to 'downsize' her dynasty, she could have saved herself a lot of trouble and avoided much of the criticism levelled at those members of the extended family when they made the news headlines for the wrong reasons.

One such misstep, which might have been prevented, was the marriage of the queen's second son, Andrew, to the upper-class socialite Sarah Ferguson in 1986. The duchess of York (as she became known) was quite unsuited to the traditional role of a younger Windsor royal. As Pimlott remarked, 'neither beautiful nor talented, she was, to the delight of early observers who discovered a member of the clan it was easy to relate to, outgoing and extremely jolly'. 'Fergie', as the tabloids referred to her, was also celebrated by reporters for her ordinariness (by royal standards). The problem with this was that she had none of the dignity possessed by previous generations of royalty; and, by enjoying herself so much and so publicly (particularly at the many social functions that came with being part of 'the clan'), she put paid to the myth, carefully publicized by the palace since the mid-1930s, that to be royal was to be inexorably burdened by duty and service, which above all, required stoic self-sacrifice.

Another misstep resulted when the queen's youngest son decided he was going to try a career in television. Prince Edward thrust himself into the world of broadcasting by sponsoring a special episode of the game show *It's a Knockout*, managing to persuade several members of his family to participate. The programme was recorded with the consent of Queen Elizabeth and saw Edward, Andrew, the duchess of York and Princess Anne dressed in mock-Tudor outfits leading teams of celebrities over obstacle courses and through challenges, making light of traditional royal ceremonial and court etiquette, all in the name of charity.

While the event was watched by millions and raised about £1 million, it was a royal PR disaster, with TV critics and audiences responding with bewilderment and embarrassment. How had it come to this? Yes, the royals had long sought to demonstrate to their subjects that they were relatable human figures who possessed a sense of humour. But this did not require them to publicly demean themselves, trivializing their station through yet more misguided reality TV.

Thoroughly sick of all the frivolity, the middle-class broadsheet the Sunday Times (which had been a cheerleader of monarchy until this point) began to question the purpose of royalty in late twentieth-century Britain, stressing that the public deserved better. The House of Windsor seemed to be unmoored from reality; the monarchy's sense of self-respect had been abandoned in favour of a cheap celebrity appeal generated mainly by tabloid journalists who poked fun at their royal superiors and who loudly – and sometimes maliciously – challenged the behaviour of the queen's kin. Worst of all, the royals had conspired in their own humiliation with Elizabeth failing to fully appreciate the damaging effect that her adult children's conduct was having on the monarchy.

It didn't help the queen's cause that questions were once again being asked about the personality of her heir and successor, Prince Charles, who was publicly ridiculed following an interview in 1986 in which he admitted to talking to plants in his garden at Highgrove because 'they respond'. His environmentalist credentials – though widely fêted today – were out of step with the times, and his concern for the natural world more often than not derided as that of an eccentric fringe movement. Then, in June 1991, sections of the press expressed criticism of him as a father when he failed to spend the evening at the hospital bedside of his eldest son, William, who had undergone a small operation after being struck in the head with a golf club. Instead, the prince of Wales had chosen to go to the opera. This contrasted with his wife, Diana, who had stayed with her son – journalists making much of the fact that she had cared for and comforted him, therefore implying a striking contrast in the way the princess and her husband undertook their parenting responsibilities.

Coded references like these were used increasingly frequently by the press to indicate to readers that a widening gulf was opening up in Charles and Diana's marriage. Reporters were well aware of the rumours that the couple were essentially living separate lives. But, as in 1936, the problematic reality of the royals' private lives remained largely hidden from public view. News editors were anxious about destroying the fairy tale first woven around the Waleses at the time of their wedding a decade earlier, given how it had seemed to offer new hope to a monarchy and country riddled with self-doubt. However, it was just a matter of time before the floodgates opened again.

Elizabeth II famously described 1992 as her *annus horribilis* – her horrible year. Princess Anne divorced her husband. The duke and duchess of York officially separated after many months of speculation about their marital woes – although this did not mollify prurient media interest as the *Daily Mirror* published embarrassing photos of Fergie having her feet kissed by her financial adviser while on her latest holiday overseas (the newspaper's sales increased by half-a-million overnight). And then a fire destroyed several rooms and prized heirlooms at Windsor Castle, with public sympathy for the monarch replaced by fury when John Major's new government announced that the taxpayer would be footing the £36.5 million repair bill. However, the most damaging episode of all was the publication of *Diana: Her True Story*, by royal reporter turned biographer Andrew Morton. This book contained explosive revelations regarding the Waleses' long-failing marriage and set off a chain reaction of further exposés which shattered, once and for all, the idea that the House of Windsor was a symbol of Britain's happy family life.

Although the press had been hinting at the couple's unhappiness since early 1987, they had done so without hard proof and with a certain trepidation about what full disclosure would mean for the monarchy. Morton's book was based on secret conversations with Diana (which she publicly denied) and her friends, providing a dramatic 'insider's' account of the breakdown of the princess's relationship with the heir-to-the throne and the emotional toll it had had on her. Prince Charles's long-term extramarital affair with Camilla Parker-Bowles was fully exposed for the first time; the princess's struggles with depression, her eating disorder, self-harm and her suicide attempts were all chronicled in detail; but perhaps most damaging of all for Queen Elizabeth and the monarchy was the accusation that Diana had received no sympathy or support from the rest of the Windsors. Diana was cast as the wronged party in an unhappy marriage and as a victim rejected by a cold, unfeeling royal family who had turned their backs on her plight.

Morton's version of events was given authority not just because he was a respected Fleet Street journalist who claimed to have spoken to many of the princess's associates (at this stage Diana's own involvement remained a closely guarded secret); it was also given authority by the fact that the esteemed *Sunday Times* serialized the book, meaning that the revelations couldn't simply be written off as tabloid sensationalism. Ironically, though, it was the tabloids that would really benefit from the exposé. The dam of royal scandal burst open again and now the *Sun*, the *Daily Mirror*, the *Daily Express* and the *Daily Mail* would compete to outdo one another in their attempts to dredge up stories of royal 'sleaze' that would provide readers with glimpses into the moral dysfunction of the prince and princess of Wales's relationship.

For example, the papers got hold of intercepted recordings of private (and very intimate) telephone conversations between both Charles and Camilla and Diana and one of her suspected lovers, James Gilbey, and then released them publicly in what looked like a tit-for-tat exchange, with the Waleses resorting to back-channel briefings against one another. Royal soap opera thus returned with a vengeance. Irreverent, disdainful reports exposed the hypocrisy that had lain at the heart of the Waleses' marriage, egged on by the protagonists themselves. Of course, the royal couple's involvement in shaping the news agenda wasn't known to the public. As far as British media audiences were concerned, it seemed the monarchy had again completely lost control of its image and that there was nothing it could do to reverse its declining fortunes.

Looking back now, we can see how the *annus horribilis* was the result of the short-term shocks of marital disintegration and the fire at Windsor but was also a much longer-term outcome of three challenging decades where the monarchy had increasingly struggled to match a public image of royal domestic bliss with the realities of a royal private life that was more problematic. The 'family monarchy' had always been an ideal – carefully crafted and publicized to appeal to key demographics in British society. Only rarely had it borne a true resemblance to reality behind closed doors. Now, under the harsher scrutiny of a far less deferential press, the disjuncture between image and reality was finally fully exposed, with the resulting damage to the House of Windsor's public standing hard to underestimate.

Some commentators have suggested that the marital breakdown in the royal family in the early 1990s was simply in keeping with wider changes in British family life, given the steady rise in divorces across society through until the millennium. This point of comparison does not bear scrutiny though when we consider the sheer scale of moral impropriety in the royal family in these years, which was by no means representative of the British public at large. What also set the so-called 'War of the Waleses' apart from previous royal rifts was the way both Charles and Diana used the media opportunistically to tell their side of the story in an attempt to generate public sympathy and support. As well as the off-the-record press briefings and leaking of information, the prince and princess openly talked to professional journalists, 'self-exposing' in ways never seen before. The way Diana and Charles used journalists to suit their own purposes was new and a precursor to the situation we find ourselves in today, with royal communications teams secretly briefing their allies in the media to strategically shape the news agenda.

In response to the Morton book and the summer of scandalous stories that it stimulated, Charles engaged the services of the broadcaster and writer Jonathan Dimbleby to prepare an 'authorized' biography. The prince also agreed to a one-on-one on-screen interview in which he admitted for the first time to having a long-term affair with Camilla Parker-Bowles. The TV interview and biography treated Charles sympathetically, acknowledging his wrongdoing but also making it clear to viewers and readers that he was not the only guilty party. However, this was not good enough for the mischievous tabloids, which began questioning Charles's suitability to be king given how he, as future supreme governor of the Church of England, had publicly confessed to adultery – a mortal sin.

That there was open discussion of whether or not Charles should succeed his mother after her death is testament to the fact that royal moral impropriety is serious enough to bring into question the constitutional position of those in the line of succession, echoing the quandary faced by Edward VIII in December 1936. It was once again clear that the behaviour of a leading personality of the House of Windsor had the potential to completely destabilize the monarchy, creating a crisis of confidence that struck at the heart of Britain's royal democracy.

When it looked like things couldn't get any worse for the beleaguered prince of Wales, they did. In November 1995 Princess Diana agreed (under false pretences) to a TV interview with the journalist Martin Bashir, to be aired as part of a BBC *Panorama* special. Watched by an estimated UK audience of 23 million, it was the princess's first major television interview in which she expanded on the allegations first made in Morton's book in 1992 regarding Charles's infidelity. While admitting to her own affair with James Hewitt, an officer in the Household Cavalry, she was asked by her interviewer whether she considered Camilla Parker-Bowles to be a factor in the breakdown of her relationship with the heir to the throne. 'There were three of us in this marriage, so it was a bit crowded,' came her reply, these words immortalizing a narrative of suffering and victimhood at the hands of a callous, unloving husband.

Diana's critics immediately responded to the interview by insisting she was paranoid – embellishing the idea that the princess was mentally unstable, as first articulated in Dimbleby's account. However, there was a significant majority who were deeply moved by her outward emotional candour and sided with her over Charles. Buckingham Palace hadn't known about the interview until the last minute, *Panorama* having kept it a closely guarded secret until the day before it aired. But the response of the queen after the broadcast was quick and decisive: she wrote letters to her son and Diana instructing them to divorce. The letters were knowingly leaked to the press in order to present Queen Elizabeth as the moral arbiter having the final say over the future of the prince and princess. She was belatedly taking control of the situation and, following lengthy and highly publicized legal proceedings, the couple's divorce was finalized in July 1996.

In telling her version of events, Diana attacked her now ex-husband and his family, but she also laid some blame for her ostensible misery at the door of another key actor: the tabloid press. As we saw in Part Two, since the 1930s members of the House of Windsor had made it known publicly how intolerable they found the strains of constant media exposure as part of a wider PR strategy aimed at engendering public sympathy for themselves as 'victims' of the strange new age of mass media. As we've seen in this section, British journalists and paparazzi *did* become more aggressive in their pursuit of royal personalities and compromising stories. Thus there was some truth at the heart of Diana's complaint. However, as Pimlott noted, at no point did the princess of Wales admit her own role in actively engaging the attention of journalists – sometimes openly, sometimes surreptitiously – in order to craft her public image as a victim worthy of people's compassion.

Put simply, the royal family wouldn't exist without the modern media, and yet rarely have they admitted to this fact, preferring instead to present themselves as prey pursued by ravenous reporters. Diana's very deliberate courting of journalists to achieve her own ends, combined with the way she then loudly decried the pressures of media attention that naturally arose out of the scandals she had helped to manufacture, was the logical outcome of what had long been a toxic relationship between the tabloids and royalty.

Perhaps unsurprisingly, this is something that both her sons as adult men have continued to do. They use the media to publicize their public images as happy family men and have, since 2020, used trusted journalists to help tell their side of the story following their own fraternal rift. And yet they regularly complain about the media attention they are subjected to and their loss of privacy despite being complicit in generating much of this attention. Of course, some of William and Harry's complaint is justified and has been backed up with legal action – especially with regard to phone hacking. But, just like their mother, they have also criticized the media in bad faith, with the aim of engendering sympathy and support from us, the media audience.

The key event that crystallized the emerging theme that younger royals are victims of constant, malicious media exposure was Diana's tragic death in August 1997, one year on from her divorce. One of the main figures who gave meaning to this idea was the princess's grieving brother, Charles, Earl Spencer. He publicly said that he 'always believed the press would kill her in the end'. This was a misleading remark. Diana and her boyfriend, Dodi Fayed, were killed in a motor accident in a car driven by a chauffeur who was three times over the legal limit for alcohol consumption. Yes, the couple were pursued by journalists and paparazzi on mopeds along the streets of Paris and into the tunnel where their car crashed; but it was the reckless actions of a drunk driver going at twice the speed limit which killed them.

This fact has also been publicly disregarded by Diana's sons who have suggested that the media were complicit in their mother's death. Most recently, Harry described in his memoir, *Spare*, how

> I'd been told that paps chased Mummy, that they'd hunted her like a pack of wild dogs, but I'd never dared to imagine that, like wild dogs, they'd also feasted on her defenceless body. I hadn't been aware … that the last thing Mummy saw on this earth was a flashbulb.

In this respect, Diana's complicated legacy lives on through her sons, who have kept elements of her memory alive – preferring that other, less comfortable aspects are forgotten, not least her active courting of the media – in order to suit their personal agendas and, in particular, their very public battles for privacy.

TWENTY ONE

Never complain, never explain

Diana's untimely death brought to an end a decade-long period which witnessed a loss of faith among the public in the moral qualities of what would once have been seen as the 'family monarchy'. Even Queen Elizabeth, whose personal poll ratings remained resiliently high throughout these years (in spite of, or perhaps because of, the wayward behaviour of the younger royals) was roundly criticized by voices in the British media for her failure to demonstrate sufficiently publicly and emotionally her sadness that her former daughter-in-law had died. Most disconcerting for the monarchy, though, were the opinion polls which indicated how the sleaze of the 1990s had not just undermined people's confidence in the royal family but also tarnished the crown itself. The number of people who supported a British republic reached 20 per cent at the peak of the War of the Waleses.

However, from 1997 to the start of 2020, Queen Elizabeth, her family and their advisers managed to rehabilitate the reputation of the House of Windsor. They transformed the monarchy into what outwardly appeared to be an institution with widespread appeal, led by a more elderly monarch whose popularity only seemed to increase with age. Improbably, it was through a return to a carefully constructed PR narrative of royal romance and domesticity that this turnaround was achieved. But perhaps most remarkable of all was the failure among courtiers to recognize how quickly this narrative would break apart if it was ever revealed that the reality did not match the public image. Again, the monarchy was failing to heed the lessons of history.

The most impressive turnaround in fortunes concerned the prince of Wales. The 1990s was, in historian Jean Seaton's words, the 'age of feeling' and, in the wake of Diana's death, Charles's reputation underwent a metamorphosis as he suddenly became a loving father to his grieving sons. William and Harry, meanwhile, seemed to grow closer to him, and it was made known that they had accepted his relationship with Camilla, although the public remained much more sceptical.

In his memoir, *Spare*, Harry has pulled back the curtain to reveal how he saw things unfold differently in these years. Although his characterization of his father is generally sympathetic, portraying him as a hard-working and passionate individual, Harry also recalls how Charles used a story brought to him by a newspaper about his second son's recreational drug-taking to his own advantage. Rather than defend Harry, who pleaded innocence, the prince of Wales allowed the story to run as he wanted to 'be presented to the world as the harried single dad coping with a drug-addled child'. Likewise, Harry states that he and William privately pleaded with Charles not to marry Camilla, despite newspaper reports suggesting they fully supported their father's relationship.

The spin doctor responsible for the remaking of Charles's public image (and the person Harry suggests was responsible for throwing him 'under the bus') was communications and PR expert Mark Bolland, who became the prince of Wales's deputy private secretary. Bolland is also credited with orchestrating Charles and Camilla's first appearances together in order to ready the public for the news that the couple intended to marry. The wedding would take place without the usual fuss in 2005, the prince of Wales and duchess of Cornwall (as Camilla would be known) having received the blessing of Queen Elizabeth, although the monarch was not present for the civil ceremony at Windsor Guildhall, because of her position as head of the Church.

The feeling that the new millennium had ushered in a generational shift for the monarchy gained momentum when both the queen's younger sister, Margaret, and her mother died within six weeks of one another in early 2002. Coming in the 50th year of Queen Elizabeth's reign, the deaths of two of her closest family members acted as poignant reminders of her own humanity. As the obituaries made clear, the queen mother's long life (she died at the age of 101) had seen the House of Windsor weather other great moments of difficulty, not least the abdication and the Second World War. Her absence, and Margaret's, during the golden jubilee celebrations in June that year was widely remarked on by journalists, which helped to convey the impression that one chapter in the history of the monarchy had come to a close and another was beginning.

The fact that both the queen mother's funeral and Elizabeth II's golden jubilee met with genuine public interest and, in the latter's case, enthusiasm, suggests that large sections of the British public also wanted to get back to celebrating the monarchy in time-honoured fashion after the horror show of the 1990s. One of the most notable moments of the jubilee weekend was the Buckingham Palace balcony appearance. After the queen and duke of Edinburgh came out on to the balcony with their hands upraised, the prince of Wales emerged accompanied by both of his sons who met with a wild public reaction from the crowds below, the BBC's David Dimbleby, who was commentating live at that moment, notably remarking on the 'screaming' of William and Harry's 'fans'.

Diana's sons had grown into handsome young men, who turned 20 and 18 respectively in 2002. Their good looks enhanced their star status; and public interest in the princes was also heightened by the fact that relatively little was actually known about either of them. After the tell-all exposés of the previous decade, which had given the British public what seemed like unfettered access to the squalid private lives of the royals, there was a marked shift in the way the tabloids reported on the brothers after their mother's death. This was partly by design. St James's Palace (Charles's household) had decided that things needed to change and struck a deal with the press whereby journalists agreed to leave his sons alone so that they could enjoy some semblance of private life in the years after they left school, before they became full-time working royals.

This meant William got to enjoy a university education at St Andrews in Scotland (chosen in part because of its great distance from the London-based paparazzi); meanwhile, Harry went on a gap year touring Australia and Lesotho before returning to Britain to enrol in the army. In return for respecting the princes' privacy, palace officials provided the media with photographs of them and stories about their lives as part of a deal that became known unofficially as the 'pressure cooker agreement'.

This moment of reset between palace and press again saw the royals trying to exercise tighter control over their private lives and public images in ways reminiscent of the 1940s and 1950s. As we've seen, in the years immediately after the Second World War, the House of Windsor engaged the services of trusted photographers to help communicate to media audiences the idea that the royals were the perfect family. Before this a 'rota system' had existed whereby accredited camera operators took it in turns to take still and moving images of the royals, which were then shared among the rest of the media. A similar system exists to this day, which the monarchy uses to control which journalists have access to royal events in order to report on them.

The 2000s also ushered in what Harry has described as the 'invisible contract' between royalty and the media. The monarchy increasingly courted trusted journalists, inviting them to exclusive gatherings with the young Windsors, knowing these reporters could be relied on to produce positive coverage about the royal family. The problem with any deal, though, is that it requires both parties to fulfil their side of the bargain. In 2003 the press accused St James's Palace of failing to do its bit because it hadn't released sufficient information about William in the preceding two years – a criticism that royal officials accepted and addressed.

Hence, through a process of continual negotiation, a new status quo emerged between the British monarchy and media, with the younger generation of royals benefiting from a new set of assumptions. There were, of course, setbacks that raised questions over whether this new model was sustainable. For instance, foreign news organizations were not subject to the same rules, and in 2007 revealed that Harry was fighting as part of Britain's task force in Helmand Province in Afghanistan. This compromised his safety and led to him returning home against his wishes. In contrast, the UK media had agreed to a 'news blackout' – that they wouldn't report on his whereabouts for the duration of the tour. There was also intense speculation about the two young princes' love lives, with gossip columnists devoting much of their time and energy to profiling their rumoured girlfriends. However, despite these challenges, the early 2000s seemed to offer the Windsors the chance of a more peaceful existence in the public eye after the drama of the previous decade.

If the younger royals were to continue to hold on to their privacy, they would have to choose to do things very differently from previous generations. This would have required them to embrace more limited public roles, thus reducing their public visibility and, with it, the media interest in them and their private lives. It is worth recalling that the reason why there had been such intense interest in the personalities of the royal family since 1918 is because members of the House of Windsor embraced new roles as public figures – becoming well-known celebrities in the process – in order to popularize the monarchy by making it meaningful to the new audiences of the mass media.

Withdrawing from the limelight would have been difficult but not impossible. William and Harry would have had to convince senior family members and royal advisers that it was time for the monarchy to embark on a new course that was less celebrity-oriented and which would require them to detach themselves from some of those areas of public life that had been so historically fundamental to their public visibility. But in the end this was too much to ask. A chance was missed. Either the desire was simply not there or other members of the family and courtiers calculated that, if the royals rejected their roles as popular celebrities, it would come at too great a cost to the monarchy's public standing.

As a result of this decision, when they became full-time working royals, William and Harry were required, as had been the case with previous generations of young Windsors, to share a version of their personalities with the public via the media. In choosing to keep the same old show on the road, the brothers opted for publicity, visibility and celebrity, ultimately putting themselves on a collision course with the tabloids, which would now scrutinize their behaviour with the express aim of exposing titillating stories or hints of hypocrisy or deception that could undermine the public images the royals wanted to project.

Far from rejecting visibility, William demonstrated a willing enthusiasm to fulfil the role traditionally expected of him. He married Catherine Middleton in 2011 as part of a fairy-tale wedding that generated huge international interest and closely resembled the nuptials of his mother and father 30 years earlier. The main difference was that the ceremony took place in Westminster Abbey, rather than St Paul's Cathedral. The Christian family monarchy was thus resuscitated once again. And this time it had a distinctive new appeal.

The prince's bride was beautiful but also, most importantly, came from a respectable middle-class family, her bourgeois background carrying strong associations of 'ordinariness' to which members of the public could relate. Through media coverage she had become popularly known as 'Kate', the diminutive form of her name helping to convey a sense of familiarity. The wedding was the climax to a relationship that had developed over more than eight years and which had been the subject of intense speculation. Indeed, various press violations of the couple's privacy saw the palace become increasingly litigious, turning to the royal family's lawyers in order to defend William and Catherine's right to a private life.

This relatively new strategy of using the law to defend the House of Windsor ran counter to an older approach (adopted by the family for most of the twentieth century) captured in the oft-repeated adage, 'Never complain, never explain'. The logic underlying this older strategy was that drawing attention to a problem only made things worse, so it was better simply to ignore signs of trouble. However, this strategy proved entirely inadequate in dealing with the tabloids throughout the 1990s where royal rot was put on public display and left to fester.

The royal family had initially turned to the Press Complaints Commission (established in 1990) in order to try to control unruly reporters, but it turned out to be ineffectual. Engaging in direct litigation therefore seemed to offer the younger Windsors a way of having their cake and eating it: they would be able to embrace public roles as celebrities, but any journalist or photographer who overstepped the mark would be confronted with the full force of the law. Notably, Queen Elizabeth and Prince Charles had experimented with this option before, successfully suing newspapers for breaches of personal privacy. In 2003 the queen took on the *Daily Mirror* after it managed to smuggle an undercover reporter into Buckingham Palace; and the heir to the throne sued the *Mail on Sunday* in 2005 after it printed a quote from his private journal in which he described the Chinese Communist Party officials he met during Britain's handover of Hong Kong as 'appalling old waxworks'.

However, the most dramatic instance where this new strategy for controlling the media was deployed by the House of Windsor was in 2012, when, a year after their wedding, the duke and duchess of Cambridge sued the French edition of *Closer* magazine for publishing gratuitous photographs of Catherine topless while on holiday. This scoop echoed a similar incident in 1982, when a pregnant Princess Diana was photographed in a bikini by long-lens cameramen while on holiday. Back then there had been no consequences for the offending newspapers – except an apology to Buckingham Palace. But now, in the 2010s, the royals took legal action to prevent such incidents from occurring again. The duke and duchess won their case, blocking further publication of the images and with the editor and owner of *Closer* ordered by the French courts to pay significant damages and fines totalling almost €200,000.

For the most part, William and Catherine benefited from very positive news coverage generated by a media enamoured with the couple's seemingly true love story. The fact that the duchess refrained from expressing any strong opinions in public on any subject meant that, as the writer and novelist Hilary Mantel noted, she quickly became a kind of cipher – or blank canvas – on to which members of the public could project their hopes for the future of the monarchy. And very soon the Cambridges were fulfilling some of these hopes: the births of their three children – George, Charlotte and Louis – in quick succession were presented by the monarchy and media as important events that demonstrated once more the blossoming of an idealized royal family life.

From the moment of their children's births onwards, William and Catherine knowingly invited the public to share in the life of their young family. In keeping with a wider royal public relations strategy, the Cambridge children, like their parents, tend to be dressed in middle-class garments from affordable brands so that other parents can aspire to the model of family life set by the royals by purchasing the same clothes for their children. Meanwhile, control has been exercised over the family's public image through the creation of official social media accounts which are regularly updated with photographs of the five at home together, some of which are supposedly taken by Catherine. Images such as these have given the now prince and princess of Wales the power to carefully curate their family's reputation, while providing media audiences with what seem like more intimate and authentic glimpses of the couple's idyllic domestic life than ever before.

The return of happy home life embodied by William and Catherine has been central to a resurgence in the monarchy's popularity, not least because it is more broadly representative of a return to domesticity at a national level among the millennial generation of which they are part. Studies note that millennials are getting married and *staying* married in contrast to their baby-boomer parents, whose generation experienced a significant increase in divorce and separation. As sociologist Laura Clancy notes, rumours of marital unhappiness have recently attached themselves to William and Catherine, creating doubts in some quarters (particularly online) about the vision of idealized family life that they have otherwise managed to project. Needless to say, if these stories were ever proved true, it could do irreparable damage to the couple's image and, as with other royal moral crises, undermine confidence in the crown. But such is the risk that comes with projecting an idealized royal domesticity in the twenty-first century.

TWENTY TWO

Don't make my final years a misery

Prince Harry opens *Spare* with a description of a meeting that took place between him, his brother and his father in the gardens of Frogmore, Windsor, immediately after the funeral of Prince Philip, duke of Edinburgh, in April 2021. At this point the royal family was still very much in crisis mode. Harry and his wife, Meghan, had left the UK more than a year before to begin their new lives in California. Once settled, they had used the world's media – most famously an interview with the television host Oprah Winfrey – to explain their split with the rest of the House of Windsor.

According to Harry's recollections, the then Prince Charles and Prince William simply couldn't understand why it was that he and the duchess of Sussex had moved away and then aired the family's dirty laundry in public. Harry recalls that during one of the heated arguments he had with his brother that afternoon, Charles suddenly interjected: 'Enough! Please, boys – don't make my final years a misery.'

But such pleading from the new king has failed to stop his younger son from lashing out at those individuals and organizations he holds responsible for his and Meghan's suffering. As well as revealing how strained Harry's relationships with his family back in Britain have become, *Spare* paints a picture of a Windsor dynasty that is dysfunctional and which has descended into competition for positive publicity as a result of the corrupting influence of the tabloids. One of Harry's main arguments is that his family refused to take seriously his concerns about his and Meghan's privacy and coverage in the newspapers. He also suggests that, because he's not in the direct line of succession, the media have always treated him less respectfully and as inferior to his brother, William, the future king. Perhaps most damaging of all is Harry's allegation that, as the 'spare', he has been the 'fall guy' – a convenient distraction to be picked on by hostile reporters to save the blushes of other members of his family.

It is certainly the case that from the mid-2000s onwards a series of exposés that targeted Harry presented to the world a young man who, deeply troubled by the death of his mother, sought refuge in late-night drinking sessions with friends and girlfriends. The public image of the 'party prince' that was constructed by the tabloids was one of youthful irresponsibility, and contrasted with the persona of his older brother, who was viewed as serious and dutiful. Here there is a historical comparison that can be drawn to Princess Margaret in the 1950s and 1970s. Whereas reporters were cautious in how they reported on Queen Elizabeth's personal life, the newspapers felt they had a freer hand to question the behaviour of her younger sister, the 'spare', particularly after she was no longer in the direct line of succession.

Like his brother and sister-in-law, Harry has resorted to the law to protect himself and his family against invasions of their privacy. However, he has done so, he claims, against the express wishes of his wider family who have consistently sought to discourage him from taking on the press. According to the duke, this is because Charles and William, despite their own legal battles with newspapers, want to stay on good terms with the tabloids in question, rather than have Harry complicate relations between the monarchy and one of the most influential sections of Britain's media.

What this points to is a situation replete with hypocrisy that seems unsustainable and in need of change. Without the backing of his family, Harry has so far led this campaign for change on his own. Indeed, he and Meghan have embodied a modernizing agenda ever since their highly publicized wedding in May 2018. Morally and culturally speaking, this was a key moment for the British monarchy. A celebrity actress who had African American heritage and had been married once before, was joined in matrimony to a 'prince of the blood' in St George's Chapel, Windsor, in what represented a dramatic leap forward for a royal family and Anglican Church that before the 1990s had adopted an uncompromising stance on divorce. And, at a time when researchers were predicting that by the end of the current century the UK could be 30 per cent mixed-race, the House of Windsor seemed to be moving with the times.

It was this sense of royal modernity that gained the duke and duchess of Sussex a huge following among younger media audiences. This generation has tended to be more alert to the progressive causes the couple have championed, as well as their personal plight at the hands of an aggressive press. The story of their split from the House of Windsor at the start of 2020 has been retold *ad nauseam*, so I'm not going to repeat it at length. As I noted in Part Two, the Sussexes' desire to pursue their own ambitions beyond the usual remit of what we have come to expect of young royals was ultimately incompatible with an institution that, at least publicly, emphasizes duty and self-sacrifice above all else. For our purposes here, it is simply worth mentioning that their experience in leaving their royal lives behind is instructive in three ways.

First of all, Harry and Meghan's example is clear evidence, yet again, that by investing its future in the personalities that front the 'family monarchy', the House of Windsor's popularity is only secure so long as those person-alities do as they're told and behave in the ways expected of them. The loss of the Sussexes has been a blow to an institution that has been looking for new ways to connect with the younger generation. Indeed, their continuing popularity with younger people is a problem for the remaining royals and, in particular, for the future king and queen, William and Catherine.

According to *Spare*, the now prince of Wales was unsympathetic to the challenges that Meghan faced on joining the royal family, and he was unsupportive of Harry and his wife when they were struggling with negative headlines. This has cast the heir to the throne in a colder light. Moreover, the memoir has, once and for all, shattered the public image of Harry and William as close confidants, united in both their grief follow-ing the death of their mother and in the shared project of stabilizing the crown after the moral turbulence of the 1990s.

Second, the Sussexes' actions suggest that there are other ways of doing things and that the rest of the royal family could take note of such innova-tion. Without official royal duties to perform, the couple have reinvented themselves as full-time advocates of progressive social causes and as lifestyle 'influencers', emphasizing the importance of 'personal well-being'. Huge partnership deals with organizations such as Netflix, Spotify and Random House have ensured that the couple are more than financially secure and that they have large public platforms to speak out about the things that matter to them. I'm not suggesting for one moment that Charles III or his eldest son should launch their own podcasts or publish 'tell-all' autobiog-raphies. Rather, my observation is simply that *things can be done differently* – that in the age of digital media there are new roles the royal family can perform which do not require them to pander to the tabloid press.

Third, and finally, in breaking the royal mould Harry and Meghan have also demonstrated a resolute determination to protect the privacy of their children – something that runs directly counter to the way William and Catherine have publicized the lives of their children in order to project an idealized vision of family life in which media audiences are encouraged to share. The Sussexes' desire to protect the privacy of their children infuriated tabloid newspapers that staunchly claim to defend on behalf of the public the 'we pay, you pose' concept of monarchy. But actually, Harry and Meghan's approach is arguably much kinder to the children in question, given how it protects their right to a private life. On reaching adulthood they may choose to be public figures like their parents. It only seems fair that they should at least have this choice in the first place.

Rather than trying to glue his fractured family back together, the question we should be asking ourselves is, how might the new king transform the broken model of the 'family monarchy' to ensure that the House of Windsor is future-proof and that we never get to see a repeat of the periodic moral crises that have done so much to undermine the crown since 1936?

To begin with, it is important to note that no other European constitutional monarchy has a celebrity family monarchy on the scale of the UK's House of Windsor. The closest example to the British royal family is the Dutch dynasty. King Willem-Alexander and his queen consort are well-known public figures in the Netherlands, where there exists a culture of monarchism that centres on the couple and their daughters. Much like the Windsors, the Dutch tabloids take an interest in the private lives of their royals. This relationship is also carefully managed by a professional royal PR operation designed to emphasize certain themes – royal glamour, family intimacy, ordinariness – distracting from other less palatable issues, such as the royals' privileged lives or personal scandals involving the family.

However, outside the Netherlands, apart from royal devotees, no one knows who these personalities are; and it is the same with the Scandinavian royals: they are not global stars, nor are they the focus of the world's media in the way members of the House of Windsor are. What this tells us is that, the bigger a monarchy becomes in terms of the stardom of its lead cast of performers, the bigger problems will be when things go wrong. What could be a conversation restricted to the national media about concerns regarding a moral decision taken by a member of the royal family instead takes on an international dimension, with a global audience invited to take an interest in the media story, meaning any problems arising are potentially much more difficult to resolve.

In Norway and Denmark there have been recent efforts to 'downsize' the royal families. This 'slimming down' has cut out minor royals so that the public's attention is instead focused on a core set of betterknown personalities who will carry the monarchy forward. Minor royals are also, of course, often subject to the criticism that they are expensive 'hangers-on', enjoying the perks that come with being connected to the dynasty without having to perform the duties and public roles. We know that King Charles originally aimed to slim down the House of Windsor when he became monarch. But this was a process he was forced to begin early when, in 2019, his younger brother, Andrew, gave a deeply humiliating interview to the BBC's Emily Maitlis, in which he failed to apologize for, or fully recognize the consequences of, his friendships with the sex offenders Jeffrey Epstein and Ghislaine Maxwell. After the interview was broadcast, Andrew was reportedly told in no uncertain terms by Charles that there would be no return to life as a working royal for him: Maitlis's exposé had again revealed the morally wayward nature of the duke of York, and this time there was no coming back.

The king's plans for a slimmed-down monarchy were scuppered by Harry and Meghan's departure. It was originally intended that they would be two of the leading royals carrying out activities on behalf of the sovereign, alongside Queen Camilla and the prince and princess of Wales (Fig 14). Instead, Charles has had to draw on the services of his sister, Princess Anne (ever the dutiful workhorse), and his youngest brother and sister-in-law, Edward and Sophie, the new duke and duchess of Edinburgh, in order to fulfil a busy schedule of events. As I suggested in Part Two, there is one easy way to slim down the House of Windsor and that is by dramatically reducing the programme of public service and engagements undertaken by working members of the royal family. The monarchy has created this work for itself so that its royal personalities appear 'useful' and 'worth it'. But that doesn't mean that royal-sponsored philanthropy, civic visits and honours investiture ceremonies are, as they currently exist, having a positive long-term impact on modern Britain.

King Charles could help to protect his dynasty against further family scandal by disassociating himself from minor royal figures on the fringes of the House of Windsor who might become liabilities for the monarchy as a result of bad behaviour – for example, by exploiting their royal connections for their own professional purposes. A major slimming down would free up the 'grace and favour' accommodations once lent by Queen Elizabeth to the various cousins, aunts, uncles, nephews and nieces in royal residences such as Kensington Palace. In aid of cost-cutting, a streamlined dynasty would also need significantly less security, which, as we saw at the time of the king's coronation, is by far the most expensive element of having a celebrity family on the throne. And, of course, all of this would have the positive upshot of focusing greater attention on a core group of royals – the monarch and, in particular, the heir to the throne – as they go about promoting a programme to strengthen Britain's democratic political culture as per my suggestions in Part Four.

The next step is for the monarchy to stop courting the interest of the tabloid press in the way it has done since the end of the First World War. As we saw with George V, he put on show the family life of his dynasty through weddings and other big events that generated huge press coverage in order to try to popularize his monarchy with the audiences of mass media. The problem was that, in promoting his family as an idealized domestic group, the king left his crown very vulnerable to criticism when a new, irreverent form of human-interest journalism revealed what life behind palace doors was really like. Put simply, image has rarely matched reality with the Windsors, and this has in turn helped to fuel tabloid interest in their private lives. But it is past time that a monarch said enough is enough. And, given his own chequered history as a husband and father, Charles III is in an unusually powerful position to acknowledge that human frailties affect us all and, in so doing, call time on the family monarchy narrative.

In practical terms it would mean that the king would need to put an end to a royal public relations strategy which has seen the Windsors carefully project a version of their family life to the people of the UK and world in order to encourage us to empathize with them. Instead, we would have to become accustomed to much smaller royal weddings and funerals, and a new approach to the media whereby royals no longer feel obliged to parade themselves and their families in front of the cameras. I've hinted already at how such a move could mean royal children getting to enjoy private lives as they grow up. But, just as importantly, such a move would weaken the hold of the tabloids over the monarchy, as journalists would no longer be looking to punch holes in the idealized family image. We might instead come to accept that the country's royal rulers are fallible and that they will almost certainly make mistakes in their private lives. Crucially, though, provided they took their new *public* roles seriously at the centre of national politics, this shouldn't matter as they would be performing an important purpose.

Of course, if the king were to *unmake* the toxic relationship that currently exists between the monarchy and the media – a relationship he and his predecessors helped to create – it would lead in the short term to a loss of visibility and dignity and a likely increase in criticism from tabloid news editors and journalists intent on maintaining the royal soap opera that has been so crucial to keeping them paid. If they're courageous enough and braced for this initial storm of protest, then the House of Windsor have all they need at their fingertips to make clear publicly why the move away from the family monarchy narrative is necessary. Social media provides the royals with a direct channel to the media audience they have, for so long, sought to keep on side. And as Harry's recent exploits demonstrate, younger members of the public, in particular, appreciate candour and honesty. The long-term gain of ending the royal pantomime by refusing, once and for all, to play to the tune of the tabloids, is surely worth the initial setbacks and sacrifices.

With the end of the royal soap opera, it is possible that public life in Britain might become a bit calmer, with the media no longer beholden to the latest trivial development in the ongoing drama of the House of Windsor. This could in turn lead to a more sober reappraisal of who we are as a people and what we want from our leading public figures. It is certainly time that we judged the royal family on their public actions, as opposed to their private behaviour. But such a shift in approach is only possible if we, the media audience, demand better of our royal rulers. We need to decouple ourselves from the false fantasy of the family monarchy, forgetting the frivolity and scandal, in order to create a new national culture no longer overshadowed by the whims and weaknesses of a dynasty who have routinely demonstrated over almost a hundred years that they are far from moral exemplars.

PART FOUR

Nation, Democracy and the Constitution

Why has 'chapocracy' failed us? It may be that changed
circumstances, in particular the Brexit turbulence, have made
it difficult for those who wish to behave properly to ascertain
correct courses of action. Much of the present difficulties
might reflect a Prime Minister who, for all his gifts, is tone
deaf on the melodies of the constitution. Perhaps, more
widely, the current political environment has tended to elevate
'chaps' who are less inclined to be 'good'. The supply of well-
intentioned candidates might have diminished, as could the
general level of respect accorded to previously understood
rules, possibly in society as a whole. It could, moreover, be that
the 'good chap' system was always flawed, that it was neither
desirable nor as effective as was imagined, and that any success
that it appeared to attain owes much to a measure of fortune,
that has now expired, exposing its fragility.

ANDREW BLICK AND PETER HENNESSY,
GOOD CHAPS NO MORE? SAFEGUARDING THE CONSTITUTION
IN STRESSFUL TIMES (LONDON, 2019)

While in practice constitutional power has shifted from
monarchs to their responsible ministers, in legal form much
constitutional power remains exercisable by the monarch,
and in extreme circumstances could validly be exercised by
the monarch against the advice and wishes of the monarch's
ministers. The mere existence of such reserve powers and the
possibility of their use is usually enough to cause ministers to
moderate their behaviour or alter it to accord to the monarch's
preferences, without the monarch having to exercise hard
power at all. Its effectiveness is enhanced by the fact that the

exercise of this soft power is cloaked from public view by both convention and, in more recent times, rigorously enforced laws of secrecy.

ANNE TWOMEY,

THE EXERCISE OF SOFT POWER BY FEMALE

MONARCHS IN THE UNITED KINGDOM

(WINCHESTER, 2020)

TWENTY THREE

No more good chaps

In late August 2019, the UK's then prime minister, Boris Johnson, advised Queen Elizabeth to 'prorogue' parliament in an act now seen as humiliating for the sovereign and royal household. The queen, as head of state and supposed defender of the nation's democratic institutions, was made to look naïve and powerless in the face of a dishonest premier who, a little over one month into his new job, misled the aged monarch in order to get her to pause all parliamentary business through prorogation so that other politicians would be unable properly to scrutinize and challenge his Brexit plans in the lead-up to the UK's departure from the European Union.

Johnson's actions were contested by lawyers and were ultimately found to be constitutionally improper by the Supreme Court of the United Kingdom. It ruled that his 'advice to Her Majesty [to suspend parliament] was unlawful, void and of no effect'. Officially, then, parliament had never been prorogued in the first place. But after two weeks of legal wrangling, during which parliament had been closed and politicians unable to debate, the damage had already been done. Johnson – who was never one to play by the (in this case unwritten) rules – had tested the limits of his constitutional powers and in so doing made a mockery of the queen's position as the safeguard against prime ministerial abuses of power.

So alarmed were palace courtiers by the behaviour of a gung-ho PM who evidently cared little for constitutional propriety and even less for the way British politics had conventionally been conducted that special contingency plans were put in place to ensure the reputation of the queen could never be put at risk again by his oversized ambitions. Almost three years on, in the dying days of Johnson's premiership, and with his parliamentary colleagues now rapidly abandoning him like rats fleeing a sinking ship, the concern was raised that he might try to hold on to power by asking the queen for a dissolution of parliament and a snap general election.

This was something that Johnson's own Conservative MPs vehemently opposed, fearing political annihilation by popular vote after a prolonged period of government mismanagement and scandal. But some people in government believed Johnson was so convinced of his own personal popularity – having secured a significant mandate from the public to lead the country in the 2019 general election – that he thought he could go directly to the British people again in order to get their backing via the ballot box to carry on in post.

In Britain's representative democracy, when a prime minister loses the support of his or her parliamentary colleagues, he or she is required to resign and step aside if it is clear there is someone else in their political party who can carry the confidence of MPs and, therefore, form a working government. However, the premier who has lost the confidence of their party must first accept their fate, something Boris Johnson was unwilling to do – at least to begin with.

This notion that a PM will accept when their time is up adheres to the 'good chaps' theory of government, which constitutional historian Lord Peter Hennessy has long argued was central to the relatively smooth functioning of British democracy. But no more. In a recent article Hennessy and his co-author, Andrew Blick, suggested the 'good chaps' system is broken. This is because the theory required that all key political figures behave as 'good chaps' (whether male or female), playing by a set of commonly accepted rules with a high sense of duty, selflessness and professional integrity. As became clear in Johnson's case, these qualities were entirely lacking. And as prime minister he *could have* insisted on requesting a dissolution of parliament, putting Queen Elizabeth in another very difficult position.

If this had happened, the queen would have been forced to face Johnson down because another Conservative leader (who could command the support of the party) could have been found to replace him. But she would thus have been drawn directly into party politics, which would have compromised her impartiality as monarch, thereby causing embarrassment to the throne and risking a constitutional crisis if Johnson then refused to resign, determining instead that he would get his election via a dissolution.

This is where things get a bit complicated. According to Britain's unwritten constitution, the monarch is the only person who can decide whether to grant a prime minister a dissolution of parliament. Usually this is a formality as the monarch must, ultimately, always adhere to the 'advice' given to them by their PM – in other words, if Johnson had insisted on ending the parliamentary session and calling a general election, then, according to precedent, the queen would have had to comply with her premier's wishes. And yet, at the same time, another set of constitutional guidelines – known as the 'Lascelles Principles' – assert that the queen would have been within her rights to refuse such a request. She would have drawn on her so-called 'reserve powers', the simple existence of which constitutional lawyer Anne Twomey suggests is usually enough to 'moderate' the behaviour of ministers.

However, to prevent such a constitutional showdown arising between the monarch and prime minister, Elizabeth's private secretary, Sir Edward Young, the Cabinet Secretary, Simon Case, and Graham Brady, the Conservative MP who oversees leadership contests within the party, held crisis talks on how to respond if Johnson insisted on a general election. Their plan was simple: the premier would be denied an audience with the monarch. If he called the palace to ask the queen for a dissolution, he was to be told she was unable to come to the telephone. Then, having success-fully delayed the PM, Brady would, if necessary, orchestrate an immediate vote of no confidence in Johnson's leadership of the Conservative Party, thus making it clear to him that he had to quit.

These were secretive machinations of the highest order designed to outflank what Lord Hennessy described as a 'rogue Prime Minister'. In the end these measures were not required as Johnson backed down and announced his resignation – almost certainly in the knowledge that this conspiracy had been hatched against him in order to thwart any last-gasp attempt to cling on to office. But what this chain of events once again demonstrated is the way the UK's unwritten constitution has a deeply problematic discretionary quality, not least because it lacks a clear set of codified rules. Some of the most influential figures in British politics, including individuals close to the sovereign, had to engage in opaque, almost farcical improvisation in order to protect Queen Elizabeth's repu-tation and keep the business of government going.

This begs two key questions: should we not expect greater transparency in a modern democracy? And why haven't the uncodified constitutional powers exercised by the crown that are, more often than not, determined by precedent, been articulated more clearly in writing in order to lay down the rules of politics once and for all?

Queen Elizabeth's celebrated function as safeguard of the UK's democracy was undermined by Johnson's unlawful prorogation of parliament in 2019 and she could have been drawn into a second damaging controversy had the shadowy troika of Young, Case and Brady not acted to outmanoeuvre the prime minister by determining that the queen would be kept away from her telephone. Surely a more robust system of checks and balances could be introduced to constrain the behaviour of unruly ministers? And with the public's trust in government and UK political institutions at an all-time low, hasn't the time come to rethink how British democracy works and what role a twenty-first-century monarchy might fruitfully play in strengthening the country's democratic values?

Part Four examines how Britain's version of democracy has been implicitly tied to the evolution of the monarchy over the last three centuries, with the crown giving constitutional politics a façade of respectability and continuity. But this façade is now crumbling. Countries that once looked to the 'Westminster model' as a shining example of parliamentary democracy are bewildered by what British politics has become.

This is not simply because of the emergence, since 2016, of more embittered and caustic political debate; nor is it simply due to a few 'bad eggs', who have risen to the top and got hold of the levers of power (although both Johnson's chaotic premiership and that of his successor, Liz Truss, which was shorter but similarly tumultuous, were the result of structural problems in the current party system). Rather, there is a deficit of democracy in the unwritten constitution and the fabric of the UK's political culture. By this I mean there are fundamental problems in the way government and politics work, not least because of a corrosive elite influence that has weakened many of the ideals championed by modern, progressive democracies.

The vagaries of the UK's current unwritten constitution have enabled political abuses of power and what has been termed 'democratic backsliding'. For example, political scientists have noted a regression from parliamentary democracy towards a more autocratic mode of government by the 'executive', where political power is concentrated in the hands of the incumbent prime minister and the cabinet, with the House of Commons struggling to properly scrutinize government policies. As part of a wider effort to resist such 'backsliding', I think there are roles the monarchy could play – some rooted in tradition that have fallen into abeyance, others new, that would require imagination – which could lead to political renewal and a strengthening of Britain's democracy in the short and long term.

To be clear: the vision for constitutional monarchy set out here does not challenge the central tenet that the king or queen only acts on ministerial advice in matters of significance. The monarch must always adhere to the instruction of his or her ministers, unless the minister in question is trying to subvert the rules – written or unwritten – of the constitution in order to seize power undemocratically, in which case the royal reserve powers may come in to play. The sacrosanct idea that the monarch adheres to the advice of elected ministers has evolved over more than 300 years and reflects a balance of power that favours the elected (members of parliament) over the unelected (monarchical) elements of the constitution – key in a modern democracy. But as Twomey has noted, the fact that Britain does not have a written constitution that specifies the crown's functions has given the sovereign considerable discretion to exercise 'soft power' behind the scenes, hidden from public view and, more recently, by laws of secrecy. Although this is problematic, there is also an opportunity here. Because of his ill-defined constitutional role, Queen Elizabeth's grandfather, George V, was able to offer what the historian Frank Mort has described as 'fresh interpretations' of how he as king might involve himself in public affairs. I firmly believe we are overdue such a 'fresh interpretation'. Here is why.

TWENTY FOUR

Democratic monarchy

This chapter sets out a new programme for constitutional monarchy in the twenty-first century in order to contribute to the ongoing conversation about how the House of Windsor responds to some of the major political challenges of the present. There needs to be greater discussion of the UK's constitution and the place of King Charles within the current political system. For the last seven decades, the influence Queen Elizabeth exercised in government 'behind the scenes' was shrouded in secrecy. This limited public discussion of her influence, especially given how the British media and political elite have, for the most part, kowtowed to her public image as the impeccable non-partisan constitutional monarch who was above reproach. Yet, when we *have* glimpsed the queen's influence – in indiscreet comments made by former ministers or in government files that have made it past the censors and into the public realm – we can see a monarch who clearly had opinions and expressed them to politicians.

The assumptions that underpin the programme for democratic and constitutional change that I set out here are threefold. First, that democracy's journey in the UK is far from complete and, second, that the House of Windsor could play an important role in the country's ongoing political evolution. As the middle chapters of this section show, the monarchy has undergone a significant political transformation since the reign of the first Hanoverian monarch, George I. By the nineteenth century it had become a 'parliamentary monarchy'. And by the start of the twentieth century it was maturing into a 'constitutional monarchy'.

There have been periods of dramatic change in the political functions of the crown, often in response to a wider set of grave social or political problems such as we are facing today, as was also the case when George V came to the throne in 1910. My argument is that the next logical step is for the crown to become a truly 'democratic monarchy' by playing an active role as constitutional guarantor of the health of democracy, ensuring its continuity while working to counteract the backsliding and complacency that has set into British politics in recent years.

This brings me to my third assumption. In order to achieve such a change in the role of monarchy there would need to be a significant updating of British law via an Act of Parliament. As academics have previously suggested, this update could be embodied in a 'Monarchy Act' that clearly codified in writing the new role of the crown in constitutional politics. This would replace the current set of conventions and traditions, which articulate the powers that the sovereign continues to exercise and which exist partly in writing and partly in the institutional memory of those who work in the main departments of state, including the royal household. The Monarchy Act would define the position of the crown in politics and in British society more broadly, setting out comprehensively the powers belonging to the reigning king or queen, as well as the roles he or she may and – just as importantly – may not play in national life.

I am not advocating the idea that the UK necessarily embrace a full written constitution. Although the Monarchy Act could be introduced as part of a much wider codification of the constitution if there was support for it, it could just as easily exist as part of the hybrid constitution (partly written, partly unwritten) that currently exists in Britain, where some parts of government have their function articulated clearly in writing. There is recent precedent for this: for example, in the Cabinet Manual compiled under the then cabinet secretary, Gus O'Donnell, between 2010 and 2011. Likewise, if we look to one of the most successful democracies in the world that is also a constitutional monarchy, then Sweden (which has consistently ranked more highly than the UK in league tables measuring the vitality of its democracy) can offer inspiration. In 1974 it carefully redefined the role of its monarchy in politics and society through a new 'Instrument of Government', which today forms one of four key 'Basic Laws' that make up its constitution.

For a Monarchy Act to be implemented, one of the UK's two (as it stands) leading political parties would either have to propose and win a referendum on constitutional change or have to be elected with a significant majority (for the avoidance of doubt) to enact a manifesto that put constitutional change unambiguously at the heart of their policy agenda. Again, other successful European democracies offer examples that Britain might emulate: notably Denmark, which used a referendum to make changes to the functioning of its constitutional monarchy in 2008.

Although codification altering the British monarchy's position could fold on to the kind of constitutional changes currently being explored by the UK's main centre-left party, Labour, a process of consultation and debate on the proposed Monarchy Act would need to take place in public, given how it would lead to a profound redefinition of the crown's national role.

I discuss the constitutional 'roadmap' by which a Monarchy Act might become law in much greater detail in the Conclusion of this book. Here, though, I will sketch out how a Monarchy Act might work in practice once it is on the statute book.

A Monarchy Act could reinvigorate and give new meaning to the monarchy's role as safeguard of Britain's democratic system – a role that has been ascribed to it by political commentators since the late nineteenth century. Republican critics of monarchy have long argued that kingship, with its emphasis on elite power, wealth and hierarchy, is antithetical to democracy. But as the Scandinavian constitutional monarchies (Denmark, Norway and Sweden) demonstrate, kingship need not be mutually incompatible with democracy: the Economist Intelligence Unit's 2021 Democracy Index ranked all three in the top six strongest democracies in the world; the UK, meanwhile, was placed 18th.

As I've made clear already in this book, a monarchy that is fit for the twenty-first century is a monarchy that is de-personalized – less about the kind of problematic and distracting royal celebrities discussed in Part Three and more about the roles the crown can usefully perform to bene-fit the nation at large. The formula for kingship as reimagined here, far from further decoupling the monarchy from the business of government as per the trend of the last 300 years, would instead reassert the monarchy's powers of oversight in order to strengthen checks and balances on elected politicians. Such powers of oversight would simultaneously work to embed the seven Nolan principles – first set out by the UK government in 1995 – as defining features of Britain's political culture. One major reason why large swathes of the public have lost confidence in politicians is that too many have failed to uphold these principles – selflessness, integrity, objectivity, openness, accountability, honesty and leadership – over the last four decades. In addition, the crown's new function would extend to promoting democratic education and brokering new political relationships, with the aim of facilitating conciliation and compromise as

part of a new politics that addressed long-term challenges, in order to coun-
terbalance the often hurried, haphazard policy-making of governments
that are caught up in the short-term electoral cycle.

The king or queen would, of course, exercise no direct formal power,
thus guaranteeing that their political neutrality remained beyond doubt at
all times. And, as already stated, they would continue to defer to ministerial advice as per constitutional convention. Rather, working in the name
of the monarch, a 'Crown Committee' of elected parliamentarians from
across the political spectrum, supported by a team of civil servants, would
be given the power to ensure British democracy was strengthened in the
following five ways:

1. By drafting a new ministerial code of ethics, which, following
   parliamentary assent, the Crown Committee would then defend
   by holding to account any elected politician deemed to have
   breached it through misconduct;
2. by holding to account the executive (the prime minister and
   cabinet) by requiring that all ministers communicate only through
   officially sanctioned channels that are open to the scrutiny of
   members of the Crown Committee;
3. by countering mis/disinformation in public life through a new
   fact-checking system and by holding to account any political official deemed to have knowingly misled the public;
4. by promoting a new democratic education to the adolescent and
   adult population through school/college-wide initiatives and
   community engagement that: a) encourages critical thinking;
   b) deepens the public's knowledge of the workings of the UK's
   constitutional democracy; and c) enables national participation
   in politics;
5. by encouraging 'deliberative', long-term policymaking through
   cross-party initiatives and innovative engagement with citizens'
   assemblies that address key areas of governance (health, housing,
   energy and industrial strategy, environment, agriculture, education, artificial intelligence).

These are hardly radical proposals. Much good work along similar lines is
already being carried out by the various select committees of the House
of Commons, which are widely seen as one of the most positive and
important innovations in British politics of the last 30 years. However,

select committees lack bite and the ability to formally penalize wayward politicians. Likewise, the fact that we now have an official ethics adviser in government who is responsible for investigating and reporting on breaches of the current ministerial code by politicians seems, on the face of it, to be a good thing. However, the ethics adviser is not a fully independent role. He or she has, first, to seek permission from the incumbent prime minister before starting an investigation, making it easy for a rogue PM to evade scrutiny if they have behaved improperly. It is also the case that any sanctions for wayward ministers recommended by the ethics adviser can only be implemented with the backing of the premier, who thus has ultimate say over the enforcement of ethical standards in public life.

The fact that there has been so little discussion about the weaknesses of the current 'checks and balances' that exist within Britain's constitution is testament to the fact they lack visibility and publicity – something that the Crown Committee as set out here would not want for, since it would be working expressly in the name of the monarch to defend and strengthen the UK's democracy. The monarch and heir to the throne could support the work of the Crown Committee by publicly championing its activities, acting as symbolic leaders of a national project designed to strengthen Britain's democratic political culture. However, for the monarchy mean-ingfully to embrace its role as the safeguard of British democracy, it too would have to accept the need for greater transparency, accountability and integrity in all its dealings. For example, it would be impossible to continue to maintain the kind of silence that has until now existed around the behind-the-scenes role the monarch and palace have played in national politics. The wealth of the Windsor family would similarly need demys-tifying, particularly given the grey area over what constitutes private, as opposed to public, property. Finally, the culture of secrecy that prevents researchers from accessing important archival files that document that monarchy's historic interactions with the British and Commonwealth governments would need to come to an end in the interests of openness.

Needless to say, such a transformation of the monarchy's constitutional function would see the reinvigoration of the crown and its wearer as potent symbols of democratic values. The sovereign would remain above party politics as conciliator, symbolic protector (and promoter) of consti-tutional norms and enforcer of ethics in public life – a triumvirate of roles that would surely be worthy of celebration on national occasions. Whereas other parliamentary bodies and institutions have consistently struggled to prevent abuses of power by those in high office, the monarchy currently

commands sufficient respect and visibility for a Crown Committee working on its behalf – if given the authority and power – to be able, in full
view of the public, to root out corrupt practices, disciplining those individuals who fall short of the high standards that should always be expected
in public life.

As this section makes clear, the Monarchy Act would, in effect, be a
British answer to a British problem. It would necessitate change to the
monarchy's position that would draw on precedent, taking inspiration
from the crown's past constitutional roles while also embracing cautious,
but deliberate, modernization. It would ensure the monarchy's continuation as part of a new constitutional settlement – just as was the case under
George V a hundred years ago. And it would give the crown an important
role to play in helping to deal with some of the biggest political challenges
of the mid-twenty-first century, including the negative effects that ministerial misconduct, deceit, secrecy and short-termism are having on public
confidence in democracy.

The programme for political renewal envisaged here is long overdue. The complacency that tended to characterize how Queen Elizabeth
approached the idea of change was matched by the media's consistent
failure to engage in serious discussion about how the monarchy's constitutional function might be adapted so as to respond better to the needs
of today. It is past time that the most effective elements of the crown's
historic constitutional role were brought to the fore as part of a new effort
to strengthen the UK's democratic institutions and restore public trust in
politics.

TWENTY FIVE

One who reigns but does not rule?

Immigrants and asylum seekers who wish to obtain British citizenship are first required to pass the 'Life in the UK' test in order to demonstrate their knowledge of what life is like in modern Britain. They respond to a series of 24 questions (chosen at random from several hundred) on British culture, society, politics, geography and history. My wife, now a UK citizen but originally a French national, prepared for this test in 2018. While helping her to revise, I was struck by the uncomplicated, airbrushed version of the nation's political history that new arrivals to the UK are expected to internalize as conventional wisdom.

The monarchy is presented as the 'anchor' that has underpinned the evolution over time of England-cum-Great-Britain-cum-the-United Kingdom of Great Britain and Northern Ireland. The crown is a constant presence that gradually and willingly ceded the political power that it once exclusively enjoyed to elected politicians representing a growing number of 'the people'. According to this narrative, the monarchy gained in return a new set of attenuated powers, most notably as a unifying force in British national life and as the politically neutral symbol of the public's democratic freedoms.

This historical interpretation, which, let us not forget, is the officially sanctioned version of events, makes clear that the crown has played a central role in the development of Britain's political freedoms and the continued success of its democracy. It is a story that begins with the signing of Magna Carta in 1215 by King John of England and ends in the present day. The 11-year interregnum that resulted from the English Civil War and execution of Charles I for abusing his royal powers – during which the country was led by Oliver Cromwell and then his son as 'Lord Protector', before Charles II was installed as king in 1660 – is presented as a fleeting aberration from an otherwise unbroken story of royal-led advancement and continuity.

But those in line to become UK citizens learn nothing of how, in the modern era that followed the restoration of the monarchy, Britain's kings and queens have, far from willingly letting go of their political power, sought to continue to influence government decision-making while actively resisting attempts by elected politicians to curb royal interference in politics. Nor are prospective Britons encouraged to learn about how members of the current Windsor dynasty have 'meddled' in affairs of state, by lobbying government ministers and civil servants via secretive back channels on issues that are of personal importance to them, as was the case with the new king's famous 'black spider memos' – uncovered as part of a *Guardian* newspaper investigation.

The partial and incomplete version of the UK's recent past that new arrivals to Britain are encouraged to learn provides a reassuring fantasy of steady democratic progress and of passive constitutional monarchy. It also aligns with the semi-fiction first articulated by Walter Bagehot that the British monarch is one who 'reigns but does not rule'. Idealized pronouncements on Britain's burgeoning democratic polity like this one were typical of a class of intellectuals who interpreted the nation's history through the 'Whig' lens of exceptional, unbroken progress.

However, as we've already seen, Bagehot, far from describing the realities of the mid-nineteenth-century constitution, was actually setting out a vision for *future* political success. Writing in the 1860s, he believed the constitution's and nation's fortunes hinged on elected politicians being able to exercise real (what he termed 'efficient') power in governing Britain, while the monarchy acted as a pleasing distraction – a 'dignified' symbol that appealed not to the head but to the heart. This symbolic monarchy could unite the country (at a time of growing social tension) while simultaneously acting as a conduit for the passions of a politically restless proletariat who wanted the democratic right to vote (but would not be given it in full for more than 50 years).

Bagehot's vision of constitutional politics exercised a disproportionate influence over the way the monarchy publicly presented itself throughout the twentieth and early twenty-first centuries, ever mindful of the need at least to *appear* non-partisan and above party politics. In part this was because Bagehot's ideas were taken up and refined in other treatises by writers such as William Anson, a constitutional lawyer who similarly sought to define the crown's role in politics in the last years of the nineteenth century. This helps to explain why Bagehot has continued to exercise significant influence over today's constitutional theorists and historians. Most have sought to explain the monarchy's current role in relation to government and British society by drawing on Bagehot's themes and concepts. For example, focusing on the so-called 'three rights' that Bagehot invented and ascribed to Queen Victoria in her dealings with ministers – the right to be consulted, to encourage and to warn – academics such as Vernon Bogdanor have written books assessing how judiciously subsequent monarchs have exercised these circumscribed powers.

The problem is that it is impossible to know exactly what political influence monarchs have wielded over ministers in the last 150 years because of the culture of royal secrecy which haunts the historical record. Throughout this period, the sovereign themselves, their private secretaries and, notably, prime ministers have been at pains to conceal the behind-the-scenes 'meddling' of the monarch and royal family in affairs of state. Most disconcertingly of all, this culture of royal secrecy persists to the present day.

There are, of course, a clear set of political and constitutional functions that have become part of the monarch's public routine of duties and engagements. These include the monarch's speech at the state opening of parliament, in which he or she reads out the government's plans for the new parliamentary session; and the provision of 'royal assent' (essentially the monarch signing off) on all new laws passed by both the House of Commons (the 'lower' chamber, where elected politicians debate and vote on new laws) and the House of Lords (the unelected 'upper' chamber, made up of peers of the realm whose job today essentially consists of reviewing laws passed by the Commons before they are presented to the sovereign).

However, the secretive influence that royal rulers have brought to bear on government officials are, more often than not, shielded from public view, partly by codes of discretion that – as we have already seen – connect the royal household to government, but also through the processes of official record-keeping. As noted in the introduction to this book, written records documenting the overtly political activities or opinions of the British monarch are hard to come by, with key individuals such as the sovereign's private secretary and the cabinet secretary – the chief civil servant at the heart of government business – acting as buffers and filters between crown and politicians. These individuals work to deliberately obscure traces of royal influence, mindful that part of their job is to maintain the image of royal impartiality.

Interactions between monarch and ministers are often not documented at all. This is the case with the sovereign's weekly private audience with the prime minister, which has been a tradition since 1945. The contents of the monarch's 'audience' with the PM are not minuted and remain entirely confidential. It is only because of indiscreet remarks made by former prime ministers that we have gained some insight into the nature of these meetings, and the way Queen Elizabeth fastidiously exercised her right to be consulted, to encourage and to warn.

Unfortunately, where written evidence does exist documenting the political activities of the monarch, it is often held back from the prying eyes of historians or, worse still, deliberately destroyed. At his personal instruction, much of Edward VII's correspondence with government officials was burned after his death. And, sadly, there have been repeat episodes of royal archival arson ever since. This is above all to maintain the idea – as embodied most recently by the late queen – that the monarch is inviolable and above party politics.

Vernon Bogdanor even admitted as much when he emphasized that secrecy is crucial to maintaining the outward appearance of the monarch's neutrality: a 'fundamental condition of royal interference is that it remains private'. A similar assessment came from the Labour (and republican) politician Tony Benn, who suggested that the crown's behind-the-scenes role in constitutional politics was like a 'state-within-a-state, surrounded by barbed wire and covered in secrecy'. And constitutional lawyer Anne Twomey has said of Elizabeth II that 'if and when the records in Windsor Castle (the site of the Royal Archives) are eventually opened, it is likely that we will see a Queen who was more politically engaged and interventionist than the public ever imagined'.

But thanks to the detective work of historians like Peter Hennessy and, more recently, Frank Mort, Heather Jones and Andrew Lownie, we have begun to gain new insights into the inner workings of the constitution and the often central political role played by the monarchy at crucial moments in Britain's recent past.

In order to understand the uneven evolution of the crown's constitutional and political powers, we need again to cast our minds back to a time when the sovereign reigned *and* ruled. In the modern period, the Hanoverians of the eighteenth and early nineteenth centuries exercised significant influence over ministers and political decision-making. This was despite the fact that a stronger parliamentary system emerged out of the Wars of the Three Kingdoms in the mid-seventeenth century which dramatically limited the powers of the sovereign.

With the Hanoverian succession in 1714, it was clear that a king or queen could now only rule with the consent of politicians. George I was the second dynast in 25 years to have been nominated to the throne by parliament. The first was William III, the Dutch prince of the House of Orange, who was placed on the English throne with his consort, Queen Mary, as co-ruler following the Glorious Revolution of 1688. The autocratic ('absolute') powers wielded by monarchs prior to this quickly became a distant memory, with the new balance of power between crown and parliament enshrined in the 1689 Bill of Rights.

With the ascendancy of parliament as the country's lawmaking body, it was clear that monarchs could be made and unmade as politicians saw fit. Now kings and queens were invited to rule and, on accepting this invitation, entered into a contract whereby they owed obligations to their people. These obligations included defence of the Anglican faith – as set out in a new coronation oath. If a monarch did not take their responsibilities seriously, then their influence could be reduced, and they might even be removed from power altogether. The last time this happened was in 1936, with Edward VIII.

Thus, by the time England entered a formal political union with Scotland in 1707, creating the kingdom of Great Britain, the monarch had a set of constraints imposed on them, including that laws could only be passed with the 'threefold consent' of the (after 1708) elected House of Commons, the unelected Lords and the sovereign. Nevertheless, this new 'parliamentary monarchy' – led by five Hanoverian kings between 1714 and 1837 – remained in a position to influence the course of British politics provided it worked broadly with the grain of change.

The most notable 'prerogative powers' that remained in the possession of the sovereign pertained to the dissolution of parliament (bringing to an end a government's time in power in order to hold a new election) and the dismissal and appointment of key ministers. It remained in the gift of the monarch to decide when a new parliament was to be formed and which men would lead the government. Indeed, this was the period in which the office of 'prime minister' emerged, with the king delegating power to his premier as key decision-maker in parliament.

The king inevitably had his favourites to whom he would turn to lead the country, even when the politicians in question did not always command significant support in the Commons. George III was also notorious for paying bribes to voters so that he could retain the services of favoured ministers by manipulating the outcome of elections. But this did not lead to any major outcry, and the king usually got his way: the first three Hanoverian monarchs were, broadly speaking, popular and their opinions respected by a political class that continued to exhibit extreme deference towards the throne.

Britain was thus far from a modern democracy in the eighteenth century. The members of parliament who sat in the Commons were elected by a small voting public comprising a wealthy propertied elite. But government was changing in ways that would further constrain the political influence exercised by the crown. The state's bureaucracy was professionalizing and growing, limiting some of the informal influence wielded by the royal court. Further afield, a new class of wealthy businessmen, who were making money in commerce in Britain's growing empire and as part of the industrial revolution in the nation's expanding towns and cities, were increasingly the focus of political discussion. The monarchy found that it had to respect this group's interests if it was to avoid accusations that it was too closely aligned with the old and decadent aristocracy. This was a charge levelled at George IV, whose extravagant, debauched lifestyle led to both an outpouring of criticism against 'Old Corruption' and increased scrutiny of the power wielded by the crown in politics.

George's successor, William IV, was celebrated as a cautious reformer and greeted with renewed enthusiasm for the way he seemed more attuned to the atmosphere of political change. However, this did not prevent him from falling foul of the most important constitutional development in more than a hundred years. The 1832 Reform Act severely constrained the monarch's ability to appoint a prime minister of his or her choosing. It was a landmark piece of legislation. By reorganizing the constituency system and by enfranchising a larger number of voters from a wider cross-section of society, the political parties vying for power were now competing for the political legitimacy to run Britain as conferred on them by 'the public', not the monarch. The Reform Act signalled a shift towards a fuller democracy, and the king would be expected to respect his people's wishes as articulated to him by those politicians who sat in the elected House of Commons.

It followed that a prime minister now had to be able to command the confidence of the House of Commons (control a majority of seats and have the support required to pass laws) in order to stay in post. If he lost support and was unable to pass laws, he would be expected to resign and, if necessary, a general election would ensue in order to make clear which party had a mandate to govern from the public. However, in 1834, unhappy with his prime minister, Lord Melbourne, William dismissed him and his government and gave his Tory rival, Sir Robert Peel, an opportunity to form a government. However, in the resulting general election, Melbourne's Whig party held on to their majority in the Commons, meaning the king had no option but to invite him back as prime minister to form a new administration.

This moment revealed how the balance of power in British politics had shifted. With the voting public having spoken, including many of those 'new men' who had made their money in imperial commerce and industry, the king had no choice but to heed the views expressed by his subjects and move with the times. It was politicians who now wielded decision-making power as bestowed on them directly by the electorate; and this was the last time a monarch would ever sack a prime minister.

TWENTY SIX

To be invisible is to be forgotten

On coming to the throne aged just 18 in 1837, Queen Victoria made several high-profile mistakes, perhaps to be expected of someone so young and inexperienced. Her early favourite was the same man her uncle William had tried, unsuccessfully, to get rid of – Lord Melbourne. This led to her backing him to stay on as prime minister when the rules of Britain's nascent democracy demanded that she appoint Peel as premier. However, with her marriage to Prince Albert in 1840, Victoria gained a formidable adviser. The prince consort was 'democratically minded' and understood the implications of the post-1832 constitutional settlement for the monarchy. With Albert's help, Victoria would become a diligent and canny political operator.

Albert saw how, with the rise of Britain's bourgeois democracy, the crown risked serious unpopularity if it became associated with controversial policies or was seen to be too close to one or other of the two main political parties. Better that it be seen – at least publicly – as a non-partisan force above the political fray which could work with politicians of all stripes. This would ensure that the monarchy could continue to exercise some influence over the direction of the affairs of the nation and empire, no matter which party was in government.

Albert and Victoria thus sought to court the Whigs (later the Liberal Party) and the Tories (who became the Conservatives), as well as smaller parties. The prince consort, with his usual drive and energy, forged excellent relationships with many of Britain's leading statesmen and, in the words of one prime minister, became 'an informal but potent member of all Cabinets'. During the two decades from 1840 to 1861 where he and the queen effectively reigned together as 'joint sovereigns', they were particularly 'potent' when it came to foreign policy, often working through their extensive networks of relations and contacts in Europe and the empire to try to achieve their aims.

However, while the royal couple could often find themselves at odds with ministers over international affairs, they were careful not to overstep constitutional boundaries, particularly in domestic politics, recognizing that their room for manoeuvre was limited. The period up to the prince consort's death in 1861 witnessed the professionalization of cabinet government as the source of executive decision-making power. This in turn encouraged the emergence of 'constitutional monarchy' where, with its political authority in retreat, the crown looked for new sources of power in society – not only as an institution that stood symbolically above party but also in the realms of philanthropy and as promoter of Britain's middle-class family values.

This is not to say that the evolution of constitutional monarchy was complete. Far from it. With Albert's sudden passing Victoria returned to being a much more overtly partisan figure. This partisanship would define her later reign, particularly the influence she sought to exercise over ministerial and ecclesiastical appointments. She bore a special grudge against the Liberal prime minister William Ewart Gladstone, because she found him uncooperative and his politics too progressive. Indeed, she actively worked to frustrate his plans not only by fiercely opposing him in their meetings but also by surreptitiously engaging with his rivals in a bid to undermine him. Meanwhile, she lavished praise and attention on a new set of favourites, including one of Gladstone's great adversaries, the Tory premier Benjamin Disraeli, who was (quite naturally) a staunch defender of his queen's political assertiveness.

To his credit, Gladstone kept his monarch's indiscreet behaviour secret as he was keenly invested in maintaining the outward appearance of an impartial monarchy that was part of a balanced constitution. Like many other Liberals at the time, he saw the reduction of the crown's powers as indicative of the success of a political system that had seen significant democratic progress – even if he couldn't prevent the interference of an anti-democratic queen. Indeed, after the voting franchise was extended to new sections of the public in 1867 and 1884 with the Second and Third Reform Acts, elected politicians could claim a legitimacy to govern society as conferred on them by a growing number of 'the people' in ways that an unelected monarch simply couldn't. And despite Victoria's efforts to control events, the overwhelming demand for the democratization of political power, especially among those groups still excluded from the franchise (such as Britain's women), meant this was a battle the queen was never going to win.

It was the pervasive sense that Britain had achieved a level of unequalled political maturity by the late nineteenth century that helped to render the crown a non-controversial symbol of national greatness. As the historian Jon Parry has noted, ordered liberty, stability and fairness were catchwords that became positively associated with constitutional monarchy, not least because those societies where such values did not seem to be deeply embedded – notably France and the USA, which had succumbed to political revolution and civil war respectively – had rejected monarchy in favour of republicanism.

Of course, this lauding of British exceptionalism ignored inconvenient realities. As we've seen, an imperious queen meddled behind the scenes. And her prolonged mourning for Albert damaged the throne's reputation. Bagehot addressed this point in an article in The Economist in 1871: 'The queen has done almost as much to injure the popularity of the monarchy by her long retirement from public life as the most unworthy of her predecessors [George IV] did by his profligacy and frivolity.' He would return to this theme a few years later with his warning to the monarch that 'to be invisible is to be forgotten ... To be a symbol, and an effective symbol, you must be vividly and often seen.'

As far as Bagehot was concerned, then, Victoria was failing to play her part properly. In 1867 he had published his treatise on the constitution, which made the compelling case for a monarchy that was visible and ornamental. He had put pen to paper in order to celebrate what he saw as the peculiar successes of Britain's model of government, and to sketch out more fully a symbolic role for the monarchy which would simultaneously allow politicians to get on with ruling the country. Though a progressive-minded liberal by the standards of the day, his essays on the constitution envisioned the monarchy working as an essentially anti-democratic distraction from the everyday business of politics. The 'family on the throne' could appeal to the hearts of the British masses, channelling their passions away from politics and integrating them firmly into the nation, at a time when they were demanding a louder say in how the country was run.

It is revealing that Victoria was horrified by what she saw as the radicalism of Bagehot's proposals. She knew full well that his prescription did not match the reality and would require her to give up those remaining political powers she enjoyed informally wielding. The queen's successor,

Edward VII, also paid little heed to Bagehot's ideas. Like his mother, he saw politics in terms of personalities in need of shaping. This was one of the reasons why he managed to carve out a central role for himself as Britain's chief royal diplomat aiming through the force of his own larger-than-life character to strengthen his country's ties to its European allies as a way of nurturing peace on the continent.

Notably, Edward also engaged in backroom conspiracies with leading Liberal politicians in order to try to ensure the smooth transition of power from an ailing prime minister to a new man who had his personal backing. Eventually, though, the new king would come unstuck in 1909 in his dealings with the Liberals. Under the leadership of Prime Minister Herbert Asquith and his chancellor of the exchequer, David Lloyd George, the party aimed to reduce poverty through a financial bill that would introduce a welfare state, paid for by increasing taxes on the landed aristocracy, most of whom sat in the unelected House of Lords.

Just as turkeys don't vote for Christmas, so the Lords were unprepared to accept a bill passed by the elected House of Commons that would introduce new levies on their personal wealth. Thus, in 1910, the first in a series of constitutional crises and major political disputes that required direct action from the monarchy shattered the popular notion that government in Britain had evolved organically to create a perfectly balanced system where power was evenly distributed across the main institutions of state.

It is worth dwelling on these crises and disputes as they led to dramatic changes in the way the crown exercised political power and brought into much sharper focus the formal ways the sovereign could intervene in politics. These moments established more firmly in the minds of politicians and public alike what it was that constitutional monarchy stood for as part of the country's increasingly dynamic – and representative – system of democracy. And, without a clear blueprint to follow, Buckingham Palace would increasingly cling to the prescient ideas of that harbinger of change, Bagehot, who claimed that the monarch had key rights and reserve powers which could and should be exercised in moments like these. Notably, it is to this period of innovation that we can also look for ideas of what King Charles may do in the future.

TWENTY SEVEN

The spirit of generous compromise

David Lloyd George's 'People's Budget' (as his finance bill was popularly known) was eventually passed into law in April 1910 by the House of Lords. But not before his party had won a hard-fought general election held to prove to the peers, once and for all, that voters supported the imposition of new taxes on the landed gentry in order to pay for the Liberal welfare schemes. However, the fact the unelected Lords had initially tried to thwart the plans of a democratically elected government had led to growing calls for reform of the Conservative-dominated upper chamber. Especially vocal in their criticism of the power of the peers were the left-wing Labour Party (which, following its founding in 1900, had gained a firm foothold in parliament) and Irish nationalists, who had seen plans for Irish home rule derailed by the Lords in 1893. Meanwhile, Prime Minister Asquith gave an indication of his feelings on the matter when he described the Lords' behaviour as constituting 'a breach of the Constitution and a usurpation of the rights of the Commons'.

Labour and the Irish nationalists backed the Liberals' passage of the People's Budget on the condition that they would together turn their attention to limiting the powers of the Lords. It bears repeating: turkeys don't vote for Christmas, and the unelected Lords refused to approve a new Parliament Bill which aimed to curb their power of veto over legislation passed by MPs in the democratically elected Commons. So, once again, British politics entered deadlock with one constitutional crisis evolving into another much bigger crisis, which would require action from a king who, it was well known, was good friends with many of the aristocrats who sat in the upper chamber.

Edward VII's desire to protect the rights of the House of Lords put him squarely at odds with a prime minister who was bent on reducing the powers they exercised. Asquith was prepared to advise the king that he should create

300 new Liberal peers (a prerogative power retained by the monarch) so that the upper chamber was flooded with men loyal to the prime minister, who would then ensure the bill to limit the powers of the Lords made it on to the statute book, becoming law. As Edward's private secretary explained to the prime minister's private secretary, the king regarded 'the policy of the Government as tantamount to the destruction of the House of Lords'. The monarch went on to make clear to his premier that he would only countenance the creation of so many peers if Asquith fought and won a *second* general election, specifically on the issue of House of Lords reform.

As royal biographer Jane Ridley has noted, some commentators have criticized the king for 'stretching his constitutional role' – code for behaving unconstitutionally. If the monarch was following Bagehot's formula, then he should have simply accepted Asquith's advice that he create the new peers in order to ensure the passage of the bill, thus resolving the deadlock. But as far as Edward was concerned, his premier's insistence that he, as king, formally pledge to create the peers if the Liberals won a general election was deeply insulting: such a pledge would commit the monarch to a specific course of action, putting him on a constitutional collision course with the Lords. Hence his hesitancy. The feeling in the royal household was that an unprincipled prime minister was undermining the political neutrality of the king, and Edward described how he could 'no more be on friendly terms with [the Liberals]. They are not only ruining the country but maltreat me personally and I can neither forgive nor forget it.'

What the short-sighted monarch failed to see was that the lack of a clear legal pathway forward which might resolve the impasse between Commons and Lords meant that Asquith, as an elected prime minister, had to look for an unconventional, circuitous route through which to end the stranglehold that the unelected, undemocratic peers exercised over the final passage of new laws. That route involved significant improvisation, with the king called on to play a role in trying to break the deadlock. But – typical of a man who saw politics in terms of personalities – Edward instead interpreted the Liberals' solution as an attack on both his prerogative powers and on a vested interest, the aristocratic Lords, with whom he was personally closely aligned.

In the event, Edward died before a general election could be held on the matter. He was succeeded in May 1910 by his eldest surviving son, George V. The new king insisted on commemorating his father as a politically impartial head of state, despite the fact that the latter had taken against, and proven obstructive of, the Liberals' policies over the preceding year. As far as George was concerned, Edward had acted as conciliator in trying to resolve the division between the aristocratic and democratic elements of the political system. To this end, he staged a special lying-in-state where his father's body was transported to the beating heart of the British political nation, the Palace of Westminster. It was received by both the Houses of Commons and Lords, and then put on display in Westminster Hall for three days, during which an estimated 350,000 members of the public visited in order to pay their respects to the dead king.

Let us be in no doubt: Edward, though less active and interfering in domestic politics than his mother, Victoria, was not the flawless constitutional monarch he was made out to be after his death. As we've seen, his interests ran counter to the democratizing spirit of a progressive Liberal Party. Nevertheless, the idea that the modern monarch could act as an impartial actor for mediation and agreement clearly resonated with members of the new king's court. George would adopt this position more forcefully than this father, and he viewed his task as monarch unambiguously as one that centred on what he perceived as the 'national interest'. Through his interventions in politics he aimed to bring stability to his country by, wherever possible, promoting compromise as a way of slowing down change, especially given the rise of organized Labour and the unpredictable energies of a restless proletariat, both of which he deemed a threat to the established social order and crown.

The crisis over reform of the House of Lords was finally resolved with the passage of the 1911 Parliament Act. It brought to an end the peers' right of veto over new legislation passed by the Commons, replacing it with the right of delay, which continues to this day. Following the accession of George V in 1910, the Liberals and Conservatives initially agreed to come together as part of a special 'Constitutional Conference' in order to try to find a route through the constitutional impasse without involving the new king, as it had his beleaguered father. However, it failed to reach an agreement. Believing that he now had no other option, George acceded to Asquith's request that, provided the Liberals won an election on the issue of Lords' reform, he would, if required, create sufficient peers to ensure the change in law made it onto the statue books. In the end this was unnecessary. The Liberals won their general election and the Conservative-dominated Lords caved in, finally approving the Parliament Act in the knowledge that it would irreversibly reduce their powers in government.

George, like his father, Edward, felt that this episode had tarnished the crown's outward reputation for neutrality and made a mockery of the monarch's prerogative power to create peers. The historian Frank Mort has emphasized how the king's sense of frustration and injustice led him to adopt a new approach to constitutional politics. From now on, he would refuse to let the crown be overtly politicized by statesmen like Asquith. Instead, he and his courtiers would champion more loudly than ever before the idea that the throne was 'above party' and that it would actively promote conciliation and social cohesion between different interest groups in order to resolve political crises.

In private, George V was far from politically neutral. Both he and his consort, Queen Mary, were dyed-in-the-wool Conservatives, and for some contemporaries the king's views were too much to stomach. While still chancellor, Lloyd George wrote to his wife from the monarch's Balmoral residence where he was staying describing how 'the whole atmosphere reeks with Toryism ... The King is hostile to the bone to all who are working to lift the workman out of the mire. So is the queen.'

The monarch was in fact more concerned with the lives of his working-class subjects than Lloyd George gave him credit for. Yes, the king feared what he saw as the potentially explosive political energies of a proletariat about whom he knew relatively little and which he therefore distrusted: for example, he opposed the idea that all working men be given the right to vote, believing this would empower a progressive Labour Party which he viewed as a threat to the royal status quo in these years. But he also sought to demonstrate to his lowliest subjects that he was interested in their welfare. He did so by embarking with the queen in 1912 on the first in a series of 'good will' tours of working-class communities in poverty-blighted parts of industrial Britain that had experienced significant social strife.

The royals hoped that these interactions between the monarchs and 'the masses' would help to offset the rise of any anti-royalist feeling among those subjects of the king who, because of their living and working conditions, were predisposed to support a Labour movement which promised change. At the same time, though, the tours drew on a tradition of royal philanthropy, whereby well-meaning members of the royal dynasty sought to engage with sections of the public in order to do good and – just as importantly in the age of mass media – to be seen doing good. As we have seen, this kind of PR charm offensive was also used effectively during the First World War to counter the sudden return of anti-monarchism to

British shores in 1917, and, most importantly, it is something that continues to this day.

The spirit of royal conciliation between classes and factions was also on display during the industrial unrest of 1911 and 1912. A massive wave of coal and transport strikes brought Britain to a halt and, in a series of surprising behind-the-scenes interventions, George V urged government ministers and business owners to look for an agreement with the trade unions. Once the strike action was over, the king publicly commended the compromise that had been reached. This, then, was the king as constitutional conciliator par excellence, even if in private the monarch revealed a more reactionary side: he was notably damning of the striking workers and critical of the New Industrial Council formed to give voice to their concerns.

As historians have noted, the king's views on Irish home rule were also far from impartial. He was a staunch unionist and initially opposed the devolution of political power to what would become a self-governing Ireland. He thus found himself aligned, once more, with the Tory Party (full name the Conservative and Unionist Party). With the Lords veto finally gone with the passage of the 1911 Parliament Act, the Liberal government revived its plans for Irish home rule in 1912. But this led to another political crisis in 1913–14. The people of Ireland (and their elected representatives) were bitterly split between those who wanted home rule from Dublin and Ulster unionists from the northern Irish counties who wanted to see their country continue to be governed from Westminster. The sectarian dimensions that mapped on to this political divide between Catholic home-rulers and Ulster protestants served only to enflame tensions and, in the summer of 1914, it looked as though Ireland was on the brink of civil war.

The king's answer to this political crisis was, once again, conciliation. He had initially toyed with the idea of refusing royal assent to any home rule bill that would, in effect, divide up his kingdom. However, in the end he proposed a formal conference at Buckingham Palace that took place in July 1914. Involving all sides, George V hoped that such a meeting might result in a peaceable solution acceptable to all. In his opening speech to the delegates he encouraged them to cooperate in a 'spirit of generous compromise' in order to avoid 'fratricidal strife'.

Unfortunately for the monarchy, the conference failed to resolve the key sticking points, including the demands of the anti-devolution Unionists. Thus, the contentious Home Rule Bill – what became the 'Government of

Ireland Act' – was subsequently passed by parliament and grudgingly given royal assent by George V in September 1914. However, a month prior to this, Britain had declared war on Imperial Germany and its allies, and it was thus agreed by the British government that Irish self-government would not come into effect until the European conflict (the First World War) had come to an end. This did not prevent Irish nationalists from trying to throw off the shackles of British control through armed insurrection in 1916, in what became known as the Easter Rising. The violence that characterized this episode was a taste of what was to come in Ireland, which descended into full-on war in January 1919, with nationalists and unionists taking up arms against one another in pursuit of their respective political aims.

The Irish War of Independence ended in summer 1921 with the signing of the Anglo-Irish Treaty, which confirmed the partition of Ireland through the creation of the Irish Free State (later the Republic of Ireland) and Northern Ireland, which would remain part of the UK. The plans for partition had been drawn up a year before as part of the Government of Ireland Act and now, in June 1921, in another act of attempted mediation, the king travelled to Belfast to open the new Northern Irish parliament. The monarch's widely acclaimed speech played an important part in helping to bring the War of Independence to an end: the king appealed 'to all Irishmen to pause, to stretch out the hand of forbearance and conciliation, to forgive and forget, and to join in making for the land which they love a new era of peace, contentment and good will'.

Although the violence in Ireland did not stop there, the king's Belfast speech represented what was perhaps his most significant intervention in politics in a decade during which he, as a constitutional sovereign, had sought to perform a new arbitrating role in affairs of state. Though a full-blooded unionist, the king's views on Irish home rule softened over time and he had never borne a grudge against those of his subjects, mainly in the south of the country and mainly Catholic, who were the loudest supporters of devolution. Indeed, he had gone out of his way in the past in trying to appeal to Catholic opinion, recognizing that as monarch of a diverse, multifaith nation he needed to demonstrate personal concern for all of his people, no matter their creed, even if as supreme governor of the Church of England he was defender of the faith.

The historian Heather Jones has noted how King George was particularly opposed to the role that violence played in Irish politics, and he sought out a role as royal peacemaker, despite the fact that this contradicted the more hostile, uncompromising stance of his then prime minister, Lloyd George. The political problems in Ireland would continue well beyond the reign of George V, but so would the monarchy's emphasis on conciliation. Elizabeth II and Charles III promoted rapprochement in Ireland in the late twentieth and early twenty-first centuries, even though royal family members who were close to both the queen and the then prince of Wales were assassinated by the Irish Republican Army in 1979.

It is also in relation to this long-term emphasis on royal peacemaking in Ireland that we should interpret the new king's tacit support of British Prime Minister Rishi Sunak's 'Windsor Framework'. This policy has sought to resolve the main political and economic problems that have affected Northern Ireland since the UK left the European Union – problems that, if left unaddressed, might have led to a return of civil strife in the region.

Before Sunak announced his new deal, Buckingham Palace would have been consulted on what it might be called. Because of the culture of secrecy, which obscures our understanding of interactions between monarch and prime minister, we don't know what happened or where the inspiration came from to name it after the king's dynasty and ancestral home. But King Charles would never have let his premier use the Windsor name as part of a political project which he opposed, or thought might fail and damage his own personal brand. Rather, his involvement in this crisis and his implicit support for his government's policy as conveyed through the name the Windsor Framework, was intended to promote a solution to a crisis that could otherwise lead to a return of violence and national instability in Northern Ireland.

Why does all of this matter? Well, what we can see from 1911 to 1921 is how a new king and his advisers reinterpreted the role that a constitutional sovereign could play in politics and across wider society. The remodelling of monarchy as a force for conciliation came about as a result of a series of crises and disputes in national life, propelled by new democratic forces that demanded the redistribution of power in Britain, whether it be to elected parliamentarians, workers and their trade union representatives, or to the supporters of Irish home rule.

Looked at now, we can see how the actions of George V were carefully calculated to slow the winds of change. Presenting himself publicly as a champion of moderation, the king aimed, first and foremost, to preserve what he could of the status quo. In private he was less diplomatic, often expressing the kind of reactionary, anti-democratic views that had also characterized his father's outlook, and which had led to constitutional deadlock in 1909–12. George recognized, though, that change was inevitable: better that, when it came, it unfolded in ways agreeable to the crown that would not undermine the monarchy's position at the apex of British society.

What we can learn from King George's example is that because the monarchy's role remains uncodified there is leeway for reimagining the political function of the crown in public life. And what we can take from this period of tension, conflict and bloodshed, and apply to the present, is the idea that the crown can act as a force for mediation between different interest groups. Charles III must avoid expressing any opinion or promoting any course of action that could be viewed as overtly politically partisan. Nor must he seek out roles that deliberately work against the winds of change – as his great-grandfather was so adept at doing. Nevertheless, there is an opportunity for the new king here.

Given the fragile state of Britain's democracy today, there is once again room to reinvent the monarchy's function as promoter of conciliation and compromise. A 'Crown Committee', working in the king's name, could aim to foster cross-party consensus on key political issues as part of a broader effort to develop long-term strategies that address some of the big challenges with which British politics – in its current short-termist state – is so ill equipped to deal. Indeed, the aforementioned problems in Northern Ireland that arose post-Brexit might very well have been avoided in the first place if previous governments had been more far-sighted.

If the crown adopted a new, progressive role as a force for mediation between political parties and interest groups, with the ambition of embedding long-term policymaking in our democratic culture, it would be working to reduce the corrosive polarization of political debate, which could lead to a much more deliberative – thoughtful – style of democracy, particularly if it was coupled with a national educational programme specifically designed to enhance our critical thinking skills and deepen our understanding of our democratic political institutions.

Such a redefinition of the constitutional role of the monarchy would be based on historic precedent but informed by innovation. Instructive comparisons can again be made with how the monarchy of George V evolved through the 1920s and first half of the 1930s, during which the king's new constitutional role came into sharper focus. Crucially, it was during this period that the crown came to be widely seen as the moral defender of Britain's new mass democracy – a role Charles III could revive in order to suit the needs of today. However, behind the veneer of what seemed to be a well-functioning royal democracy, King George's covert actions often verged on the unconstitutional, and highlight the problematic role played by a monarchy in politics when a sovereign conflates his or her personal views with the 'national good'. There are other important lessons here for the new king as well.

TWENTY EIGHT

The good of the country

Just as our democracy today is menaced by forces inside and outside the UK, so Britain's interwar democracy seemed to be under threat, notably from new kinds of populist extremism. Far-left communism and far-right fascism both took root in parts of Britain in these years. The fact that these ideologies had also taken hold of European nations in the chaotic aftermath of the First World War, notably leading to the creation of aggressive authoritarian dictatorships in Italy and the USSR, also served to highlight the fragility of the old order. Against this back-drop of political upheaval, George V's crown would increasingly be seen as the resilient symbol of Britain's gentler democratic system and the bulwark against autocracy.

The king's political activities in these years gave substance to this demo-cratic dimension of constitutional monarchy. The 1918 Representation of the People Act (the Fourth Reform Act) enfranchised all adult men over the age of 21 and women over the age of 30. The king had long feared such a change, but the Lloyd George government forged ahead with its plans for a mass extension of the vote, partly in acknowledgement of the service performed by working-class people on behalf of their country during the First World War.

Now the proletariat could exercise their political voice it was not long before they elected a left-wing government. In 1924 Ramsay MacDonald was invited to Buckingham Palace to be installed by the king as Britain's first ever Labour prime minister. Since the early 1900s George and his father had fretted over the rise of socialism in British politics, conflat-ing it (incorrectly) with republicanism and viewing it as a destabilizing influence in national life. This royal fear of the left mainly sprang from the monarchy's concerns about one key individual, nicknamed 'that beast' by a younger George V. The man in question was James Keir Hardie, the

Scottish trade unionist and former Labour leader, who was virulently anti-monarchist in his views.

However, in 1924 the king publicly demonstrated exemplary impartiality by welcoming MacDonald and his Labour colleagues into office – just as he would any other party – even if, in private, he still expressed an innate distrust of socialists. The historian Frank Prochaska has suggested that the king's deliberate courting of Labour and the trade union movement in this period was designed to reconcile socialism to the monarchy (many trade union leaders were among the first people to receive the new civilian honour, the OBE, when it was instituted in 1917). The king's charm offensive seems to have paid off. At its 1923 annual conference, Labour had debated the motion 'Is republicanism the policy of the Labour Party?' – and the republican caucus was defeated resoundingly by a vote of 3,694,000 to 386,000.

It seemed, then, that Britain's version of socialism *was* believed to be compatible with kingship. By the time they found themselves in government for the first time, the vast majority of Labour politicians had abandoned all thoughts of republicanism. Many on the left valued the more socially engaged type of monarchy embodied by George V. And, in a pragmatic sense, they recognized that Labour's political advancement required them to embrace the status quo and play by the accepted rules of the constitution. To adopt an anti-monarchy stance would be counterproductive, both tarnishing the party in the eyes of a mainly royalist electorate and damaging the prospects of the millions of working people who stood to gain from a left-wing government.

It was also the case that MacDonald and his parliamentary colleagues found themselves moved by King George's ostensible friendliness and generosity of spirit in 1924, interpreting the king's ready acceptance of them as the ultimate mark of their own success and legitimacy. Of course, the king had his own designs. Not only was this about burnishing his public image as an outwardly impartial constitutional monarch; he also needed the Labour leader to weaken the more radical elements on the left: as King George's most recent biographer, Jane Ridley, notes, MacDonald could 'contain the deferential, respectable working class within a moderate Labour Party and split them from the Bolsheviks [communists] and Red Clydesiders'.

The king's democratic approach to politics was also on display in his interactions with the Tory Party – the other main party of government between the two world wars. When Prime Minister Andrew Bonar

Law resigned from office in 1923, he did not advise the palace on who should succeed him. Normally the king would adhere to the guidance of the outgoing premier and invite their nominated successor to form a government. But Bonar Law was dying and was unprepared to offer a recommendation to his sovereign, precipitating a small but nevertheless significant crisis.

The king and his advisers were forced to take secret soundings from senior Conservatives about who was best placed to succeed Bonar Law. Two candidates stood out from the pack: the long-serving and seasoned foreign secretary, Lord Curzon, and a man very much his junior, but who had risen with aplomb to the office of chancellor, Stanley Baldwin. To the surprise of many, George V called on the latter to take over the running of the government, his decision informed by the fact that Baldwin, as a democratically elected member of the House of Commons, was better placed to lead Britain; Curzon, on the other hand, owed his parliamentary position to his aristocratic lineage and inheritance of his family's seat in the House of Lords. In the post-1918 age of mass politics where the lower chamber ruled on behalf of an expanded electorate, the king had gone with the safest – and most democratic – option.

Although he played the role of good constitutional monarch in public, King George's opinions in private often remained deeply reactionary. In the spring of 1926 he was worried about the industrial unrest incited by miners whose wages were at risk of being cut by employers. In the talks that followed, the Trades Union Congress declared it would call a general strike if the demands of the miners were not met. In a letter to the queen, the king wrote despairingly of the miners: 'What hopeless people they are. It [a general strike] will throw everything back just when they [sic] were beginning to improve, will cost the country many millions & cause a lot of bad blood & give pleasure to our communists & the Russian Soviet.'

The king's position was far from neutral. And at the start of May, when the threatened general strike began, he was, as ever, active behind the scenes, this time throwing his support behind the Baldwin government's uncompromising position against the picketing workers. He also notably put pressure on ministers to deal directly with the more radical elements involved in the industrial action, advocating the detention of communist agitators.

It is clear, then, that there were limits to King George's belief in conciliation. As far as he was concerned, the general strike went against the interests of the country, and he viewed its failure after nine days of unrest as cause for relief. As the majority of miners traipsed back to work for longer hours and lower wages, the king celebrated what he saw as a uniquely British desire for order, noting in his diary 'what wonderful people we are'.

Throughout this turbulent period George was motivated by what he interpreted as the 'national good' – something he would later describe in his first Christmas broadcast in 1932 as a desire for 'reasoned tranquillity within our borders'. But as the events of 1926 proved, the king's understanding of the collective good prioritized stability and the interests of business and government over the needs of his poorest subjects, who were always the ones to suffer most through pre-Keynesian cycles of economic downturn.

The king's interpretation of the 'national good' would also inform his reaction to the most severe economic crisis in Britain's recent history. In mid-1930 what would later become known as the Great Depression began. It was a massive global recession triggered by the collapse of the US banking sector following the Wall Street Crash in October 1929. With credit frozen and loans called in, businesses both sides of the Atlantic began rapidly shedding employees in an effort to stay afloat. Even then, many went bust. And suddenly, the British Labour government – the second led by Ramsay MacDonald – found that, like other governments across Europe, it had to spend huge amounts of taxpayers' money on unemployment relief (known as 'the dole') in order to support the families of mainly working-class men who had lost their jobs.

MacDonald's administration struggled to control events and, with the situation spiralling out of control, was faced with a difficult choice: maintain the level of dole payments to workers or reduce the payments in an attempt to avert likely economic catastrophe. However, with the prime minister unable to persuade a sufficient number of his Labour colleagues to vote through such a reduction, he prepared instead to tender his and his cabinet's resignation to the king.

At this point the monarch intervened decisively, believing that if the government fell it would cause more uncertainty and lead to the collapse of Britain's currency, the pound sterling. When MacDonald tried to tender his resignation, the king insisted that he stay on and head a cross-party 'coalition of individuals', convincing him that it was his duty to deal with the crisis. And, having gained the backing of the other party chiefs (Baldwin from the Conservatives and Herbert Samuel of the Liberals) for the idea of an emergency coalition, the monarch arranged a meeting with all three politicians and instructed them to form what would become known as a 'National Government' under MacDonald's leadership.

If we accept that Bagehot's three rights (the right to be consulted, to encourage and to warn) determine how British monarchs can legitimately exert influence over ministers, then the formation of the 1931 National Government was the single most controversial (and arguably unconstitutional) intervention made by any sovereign since Queen Victoria. All pretence that the king accepted the advice of his prime minister was abandoned when George refused to agree to MacDonald's resignation (offered on three separate occasions, no less). Historians disagree over whether the king was 'instigator' or 'facilitator' of a coalition arrangement, which had already long been under discussion in party circles. What is clear, though, is that the king saw an opportunity to stabilize the country by creating a working government and that he covertly cornered his prime minister into pursuing a specific course of action to that effect.

Given the dire economic situation facing Britain, the king may – morally speaking – have been right to act as he did. The economic crisis did begin to lift. And, at the general election that was held shortly afterwards to give MacDonald and his National Government the popular mandate they needed to steer the country out of the doldrums, they were returned to power with an overwhelming majority – vindication, perhaps, of the new palace-backed arrangement.

But even if the king's actions can be justified on moral grounds, they were hardly prudent politically. The creation of the National Government indirectly led to the decapitation of Labour and the strengthening of Baldwin's Conservatives. Most of MacDonald's socialist colleagues refused to follow him into the new coalition and he was expelled from his own party for what was seen as his great 'betrayal'. George V recognized the significance of his actions when he wrote to one confidant noting how 'MacDonald has burnt his boats and can never be Labour Prime Minister again but he has acted in the only right and strong way by [sic] the good of the Country.' It is worth re-emphasizing: MacDonald had 'burnt his boats' at the express wishes of his monarch.

The remnants of Labour that were left after the humbling election defeat to the National Government complained bitterly of the way MacDonald's behaviour had split the party, while some of its more left-wing adherents took direct aim at the monarchy, suspecting (quite rightly, as it happens) that the crown had played an instrumental role in shaping events. The socialist intellectual Harold Laski talked of a 'Palace Revolution', while the

Labour MP Stafford Cripps warned of the need to deal with the malign influence of 'Buckingham Palace' the next time a majority Labour government won power. Unfortunately for Cripps, this would have to wait. The Tory Party would hold on to power, taking over the National Government after MacDonald retired as prime minister in 1935 and then governing essentially alone until the end of the decade, when the arrival of another world war led to the formation of a second emergency coalition.

The controversial intervention made by George V in 1931 teaches us three important lessons that we can still apply in the twenty-first century. First of all, this moment again perfectly captures the problem of having an uncodified constitution where the influence of the monarch is not specified. The sovereign was able to exercise significant discretion, improvising in highly unconventional ways in order to achieve his own aims.

Second, despite having made a positive name for himself as a force for conciliation, the king overplayed his hand (in constitutional terms) by clandestinely orchestrating the creation of a coalition government which, in his personal opinion, was best placed to deal with a crisis. Throughout the negotiations, there was a firm emphasis on the 'national good' as the king and his advisers understood it. But George's definition of 'the good of the country' (his words) was not shared by most of the Labour Party or, for that matter, the millions of unemployed workers who stood to lose from cuts to the dole. The king's behaviour therefore put him directly at odds not just with elected members of parliament but also with a significant number of his subjects.

Third, although it is unlikely that a monarch could act either as discreetly or as decisively today as the king did in 1931, it is significant that a similar culture of secrecy continues to distort our understanding of royal interactions with government. Indeed, King George's crucial role in the creation of the National Government would remain a closely guarded secret until his official biographer was given permission to lift the lid on the extent of the king's involvement 16 years after the latter's death. It is perplexing that, more than 90 years on, a similar level of secrecy continues to obscure our understanding of how George's successors have engaged with elected officials in the intervening period.

In this respect, we can see why a king who has opinions on what constitutes the 'national good' and makes them felt in secret represents a threat to democracy. It does not even matter if the monarch's interpretation of the 'national good' aligns with that of a significant majority of the public. Here the proactive environmentalism of Charles III comes to mind. Unfortunately for the monarch, there will always be groups that hold oppositional views to him on topics like this one, particularly as we learn more about the many sacrifices people will be required to make in order to slow the climate crisis. And when the UK's modern democracy is, first and foremost, about citizens being able to exercise their political voice by voting for politicians who speak for them, it follows that if the monarch is truly to become the defender of democratic values, then he or she must exercise no political voice whatsoever. The past teaches us that those thrones which are least secure are those where the crowned head of state has become linked to a big political issue that has become increasingly fraught and contentious. And, though there may currently exist a broad consensus that we need to live in closer harmony with the natural world, political opinion is already bitterly split on how we might achieve such a goal.

The good news for the new king is that the survival of Britain's democracy, while explicitly political, is an uncontroversial issue, particularly when we consider the alternatives. And there is thus an opportunity for the monarchy to ensure that democracy endures and thrives partly by making sure that the British public are properly informed about key political issues, such as the environment and climate change, so that they can make evidence-based decisions about which political party is best placed to deal with the big challenges of today. A Crown Committee that has a remit that encompasses fact-checking in public life could establish a national centre modelled on the UK NGO 'Full Fact', which has done much to counter mis- and disinformation in politics. Equally, the committee could exercise the powers needed to hold politicians and public figures to account when they pollute our public discourse with lies and falsehoods.

———

There is a strange irony in the fact that the main reason there wasn't a greater outcry from the left about King George's actions in 1931 was that he was held in high esteem by a majority of Labour politicians, who saw him as the embodiment of democratic and constitutional progress. These were defining themes of the king's last years on the throne. A monarch who had become more vocal – harnessing the power of radio to communicate with a mass media audience in ways not dissimilar to the European dictators – explained the meaning of kingship and its centrality to Britain's national stability, its political freedoms and success.

These ideas, irrespective of whether or not they matched reality, were propagated with such fervour by a chorus of voices across the political spectrum that they became conventional wisdom. With the worst of the recession having faded from view in Britain by late 1933, George V became the symbol of a political culture which seemed gentler, more orderly and more peaceable than those nations on the continent – notably France, Italy and Germany – that were still recovering from the shock of the economic downturn.

It is precisely because the king was publicly seen as a kindly, paternalistic 'democrat', who had led the country through such dark chapters as the First World War and Great Depression, that there was real sadness when he died at the age of 70 in January 1936. His legacy is still felt today. During his 26 years on the throne he irreversibly transformed how people understood constitutional monarchy. In a reign marked by profound social, political and economic upheaval, the king had ensured the meaningful survival of the monarchy by adopting new roles, including as political conciliator and mediator, in order to make kingship compatible with Britain's mass democracy.

And such change is instructive. Far from the kind of gradual change that the monarchy had undergone during the previous two hundred years, when George V came to the throne in 1910, he embarked on a major programme of royal modernization that aimed to engender national stability and was motivated, above all, by a desire to save his crown.

TWENTY NINE

The perfect constitutional monarch?

George V's other great legacy was his granddaughter Elizabeth II. The old king was recorded as saying (in what was probably an apocryphal story designed to smooth over the aberration of his first son's reign) that he hoped 'nothing [would] come between Bertie [his second son] & Lilibet [Elizabeth II] and the throne'. Succeeding to the throne 16 years after her grandfather's death, Elizabeth inherited an institution that had continued to change. As before, the nature of this change was partly determined by the personality of the reigning monarch. While George V had recognized the need for modernization, Elizabeth's father, George VI, was a more conservative figure (in the 'small C' sense of the word). He was suspicious of innovation and his intellectual limitations meant he tended to do what he was told by his often equally rigid advisers.

However, we also need to explain George VI's resistance to change with reference to the events that made him king. His conservatism was partly designed to push back on the short-lived modernizing streak of his older brother. During his brief, unceremonious reign Edward VIII had tried (unsuccessfully) to revolutionize the monarchy in ways that threatened the model of constitutional kingship established by his father.

In some respects, Edward's version of monarchy was closer to that of George V than historians have cared to admit. As a dutiful lieutenant to his father throughout the 1920s and early 1930s, he too embodied the spirit of royal conciliation. He readily engaged with working-class communities and their political representatives in new ways, publicly supporting their interests in order to create an inclusive vision of Britain that valued labour and capital. And, as a celebrated war veteran, Edward was extraordinarily popular among ex-servicemen, whose welfare and reintegration into society he publicly championed at a time when many felt they had been let down by government.

Edward also invoked his father's spirit of conciliation in order to promote Anglo-German rapprochement, sponsoring a number of schemes designed to bring veterans from the two countries together. The old king was privately supportive of his eldest son's efforts, although, unlike his father, Edward lacked discretion and displayed a worrying tendency to openly voice his opinions. He continued to do this on becoming king, which put him at odds with elected politicians. Most famously, while touring mining districts in the South Wales valleys in autumn 1936, he declared 'something must be done' about unemployment in the region, and these careless comments were used by the press to attack the record of the Conservative-led National Government.

Most troubling was Edward's desire to appease Adolf Hitler – albeit that his conciliatory stance was broadly representative of the rest of the royal family and many other members of the British elite at this time. The new king is reported as having privately threatened his prime minister, Stanley Baldwin, that he would abdicate if the British government dared to resist the Nazis' remilitarization of the Rhineland on the Franco-German border in March 1936. One can therefore make the argument that Edward was temperamentally unsuited to be monarch, given the constitutional constraints that were meant to limit what he said either in public or in private to his ministers. That he felt he was within his rights to air his concerns so defiantly is testament, in its own way, to his desire to emulate the more outspoken European dictators, for whom he'd expressed admiration in private.

Edward's abdication in December 1936 was the most dramatic demonstration of the way he had, through his modernizing impulses, strayed too far from the blueprint of constitutional kingship established by his father. One of George V's successes was that, publicly at least, he had turned his dynasty into the much fêted idealized 'family monarchy' (see Part Three). But Edward's unwillingness to marry a suitable spouse as part of a conventional Christian union threatened the very foundations of family monarchy. And, in determining that he would marry a woman who would shortly be divorced for a second time (with both ex-husbands still living), the new king's actions represented a direct challenge to accepted religious doctrine and undermined his own constitutional position as supreme governor of the Church of England.

The historian Philip Williamson has discussed how, from the start of his reign in 1910, George V had promoted the teachings of the Anglican church while also encouraging conciliation with other denominations

– notably Catholicism, nonconformism and Judaism. He thus put the monarchy at the heart of an inclusive national culture of religion. Edward's initial plans to make Wallis Simpson his wife *and* hold on to his crown came unstuck when he was confronted by his premier, the quietly courageous Baldwin, who admired the Christian moral values of the monarchy of George V. On realizing that the prime minister had the support of the conservative political, religious and media establishments, Edward knew he had little choice but to renounce the throne in order to marry the woman he loved.

The abdication witnessed the reassertion of prime ministerial authority against a rogue king and acted as an important reminder to contemporaries of where real power lay in Britain's political system. However, the crisis also dramatically demonstrated how fragile the country's personality-driven constitutional monarchy really was. In just over a quarter of a century the UK's political settlement had come to hinge on the character traits of one key individual. In the figure of George V the crown was both virtuous *and* popular – and the constitution therefore safe. Edward – though he lacked his predecessor's moral virtues – was even more loved than his father, in part because he seemed to be Britain's answer to the kind of charismatic leader that had taken hold of Nazi Germany and fascist Italy. And, contrary to the arguments of most historians, it is clear he continued to command huge levels of popular support and affection, especially among the working classes, during and after his abdication.

That the loss of Edward's dynamic kingship was keenly felt by sections of the public was evident in the muted response to his successor – the stammering George VI. The new king was widely seen as lacking the qualities of his older brother. He was an uninspiring if dutiful substitute. British journalists even commented on George's 'unremarkable' personality in the lead-up to his coronation in May 1937, in what was a clear sign of how the abdication had dented the culture of deference that had previously surrounded the throne.

However, following the abdication, most political and media commentators did not focus on the personality of George VI (knowing full well he was a pale imitation of his predecessors) but instead emphasized that both the continuation of the monarchy and the coronation of the new king symbolized the remarkable resilience of Britain's constitutional democracy. This was, after all, a country where the monarch was expected to behave in a certain way and uphold certain values; when a king or queen was found wanting, elected politicians could replace him or her with someone more suitable.

Thus, the crown as a symbol of the balanced constitution – where a monarch reigned but ministers ruled – suddenly became much bigger than its wearer. This was a convenient theme, given how the new monarch was a charisma vacuum. In this way, George VI's very absence of personality created space for a triumphal celebration of Britain's parliamentary system, which contrasted in the late 1930s with the aggressive, personality-driven dictatorships of Europe. Echoing the comments of the nineteenth-century Liberal thinker Earl Cowper, the crown was once again characterized as the 'chief bulwark ... of [Britain's] liberty' and defender of the country and constitution against continental 'Caesarism'.

The events of 1936–7 were key to hastening the emergence of a monarchy where the sovereign would, through a combination of circumstance and choice, have less to say publicly and privately about affairs of state than ever before. David Cannadine has noted how George VI 'unlike his older brother [and father] ... harboured no desire to assert himself in matters of high policy'. Because of his evident shortcomings, he found himself 'on the edge of events', either unable or unwilling to take a more decisive role.

As an 'emasculated' monarch, whose principal aim was to stabilize the crown in the wake of the extreme turbulence caused by the abdication, George was generally resolved to passivity and to opting for the least controversial solution when faced with difficulty. Thus he threw his weight behind Prime Minister Neville Chamberlain's (controversial) appeasement of Hitler. He even allowed the ill-fated premier to appear alongside him and the rest of the royal family on Buckingham Palace's balcony to rapturous cheering in order to signal that the crown endorsed the prime minister's signing of the Munich Agreement on 30 September 1938 in an effort to secure peace in Europe. And when that agreement failed to stop Nazi expansion, the king, although initially suspicious of the anti-appeaser Winston Churchill and disinclined to see him as prime minister, bowed to the pressure of events and invited the latter to form a new coalition government on 10 May 1940.

Far from the heroic figure portrayed by the Oscar-winning actor Colin Firth in the film The King's Speech, George VI found himself cowed by his new premier, who quickly eclipsed the sovereign as the symbolic focal point of the British empire's war effort. Courtiers went to great lengths to try to generate favourable publicity around George in order to offset what they saw as Churchill's worrying tendency of 'push[ing] the crown under the bed'.

Although George's symbolic authority was ultimately enhanced by his wartime role – not least when he agreed to share the palace's balcony for a second time with a prime minister, in this instance the victorious war leader Churchill in May 1945 – the king's political power was further diminished by the time the conflict ended. The emergency of total war had led to a consolidation of executive power in the War Cabinet of the coalition government headed by Churchill and his deputy prime minister, Labour's Clement Attlee.

When Attlee and Labour won an unexpected landslide victory at the general election of July 1945 with their promise of a radical political programme that would transform Britain from a society dominated by corporate and private interests to one where central government and new public bodies would play a more active role in reducing poverty and social inequalities, King George (a thoroughbred Tory in the mould of his parents) could do very little except worry and throw explosive tantrums, known inside the palace as his 'gnashes'.

The king was no supporter of the Labour government's plans for nationalization and state-led redistribution. He privately opposed the implementation of Britain's NHS for the way it encroached on the royals' traditional charitable activities in this area of public life (see Part Two). However, he could do nothing to slow the winds of change that were once again blowing through politics and society. Instead, the king was reduced to carping from the sidelines – although occasionally such carping did pay off.

Attlee, who was perhaps trying to protect his monarch from accusations of interference, later claimed that at no point did George's views have any effect on the Labour government's policies. But some have speculated that his opposition to the prime minister's proposed appointment of Hugh Dalton (whom the monarch despised) as foreign secretary in the 1945 government did give Attlee pause for thought, and helped to sway him towards one of the king's firm favourites instead, the former trade unionist, Ernest Bevin.

Although the monarch cared little for the socialist policies of his new Labour government, it seems that he took his responsibilities as a non-partisan constitutional head of state seriously – even if at times he exercised liberally his Bagehotian right 'to warn' his ministers. Indeed, he rubbed along with them as individuals, as suggested by his fondness for what one royal biographer has described as Bevin's 'bulldog English views and earthy sense of humour'. The king also developed a good working relationship with Attlee, who, according to the journalist and future Labour leader Michael Foot, was very moved when George died prematurely, at the age of just 56, in February 1952.

A 25-year-old Elizabeth II thus came to the throne at a time when the power the British monarch exercised as part of constitutional politics was in retreat. And, in her youth and innocence, she would pick up where her father left off, notably inheriting the same inflexible, unimaginative advisers. However, in a more interesting turn of events, she would also inherit the prime minister who had done so much to eclipse her father during the Second World War.

Churchill had returned to power at the head of a Conservative government in 1951. After the Elizabethan succession, he took it upon himself to use his weekly audiences with the queen to tutor her in the nature of politics and the constitutional role of monarchy, as he understood it. Although he found the new sovereign to be a charming and serious student, it was clear that she was both inexperienced and politically ill informed – a view widely shared by other politicians who met her in these early years.

Writing more than seven decades on, at the time of the death of Elizabeth II, journalists and commentators celebrated the queen as the 'perfect constitutional monarch' – not only for the way she'd accumulated significant political experience over her long reign but also for the way she had unhesitatingly welcomed into office 15 different prime ministers from across the political spectrum, irrespective of her own political beliefs. As already discussed, it is only if or when we are finally given access to official sources that document in fine detail the queen's interactions with government officials that a serious assessment of her successes and failures as a constitutional sovereign can begin. Nevertheless, at risk of seeming premature, one can offer an initial interpretation based on the limited amount of information currently available, including the anecdotal testimony of those who worked with the queen.

That Elizabeth helped to maintain the union linking England to the three Celtic nations – Wales, Scotland and Northern Ireland – is evidence of a successful policy of royal-backed political integration. The queen felt she was able to speak about the union in positive terms, given her constitutional role as head of the British state. The monarchy is historically bound up with the union – a fact that escaped the Scottish nationalists, who criticized the queen for what they saw as her unconstitutional celebration of the 'benefits which union has conferred' in her 1977 Silver Jubilee speech to the Houses of Parliament.

More controversially, Elizabeth issued a gentle warning to her Scottish subjects that they should 'think very carefully about the future' before voting in the 2014 independence referendum. It later emerged that the queen intervened at the behest of her prime minister, David Cameron, who thought, having agreed to the referendum, that he might then lose it to the nationalists. Elizabeth's words did provoke the ire of the independence campaign at the time, despite the fact that her careful phrasing ensured she avoided accusations of overt partisanship.

The queen displayed a deep affection for Scotland, its people and culture throughout her reign. This helped to maintain her popularity there, in turn strengthening unionist sentiment. For some years it had been rumoured that she wished to die at Balmoral – a desire motivated by her love of the royal family's ancestral Scottish home (bought by Prince Albert in 1852) but also, surely, by the understanding that her death north of the border would resonate publicly and set the scene for an elaborate ceremonial send-off. In the event, her mortal remains were transported from Balmoral back to the political centre of the British nation, London, before being transferred to Windsor for burial – a journey that captured symbolically the intimate and constitutional aspects of her monarchical identity.

Since his accession, the new king has been actively engaging with the people of Scotland, prompted by the same worries about the fragility of the union that inspired his mother. A recent poll conducted by the news website Unherd revealed that Charles III has 'a Scotland problem' in that he and his monarchy are significantly less popular north of the border than anywhere else in the UK; hence the urgency with which he's set about trying to endear himself to the Scottish people as their new king. He has had plenty of practice in this kind of PR offensive. During his long tenure as prince of Wales, he supported his mother in preserving the union with the three Celtic nations. Despite having endured what was, in hindsight, an absurd piece of invented pageantry for his investiture at Caernarfon Castle in 1969, he developed a serious interest in Cymru, which in turn gained him a popular following among sections of the Welsh public.

The late queen's other success as constitutional sovereign has to be her public record as impartial arbiter of British politics. According to royal biographers and journalistic anecdote, she enjoyed good relations with almost all of her prime ministers – not just those on the right, such as Churchill, who shared her aristocratic heritage and with whom she had much more in common culturally. The best book on the monarch's reign remains, by some margin, Ben Pimlott's The Queen – the last printed edition of which was published to coincide with Elizabeth's golden jubilee in 2002. Pimlott was a historian who specialized in the post-1945 period and wrote various acclaimed biographies of Labour Party grandees. He goes into some detail when chronicling the queen's relationship with another of his favourite subjects – two-time Labour prime minister Harold Wilson. Sovereign and premier delighted in one another's company: the queen was intrigued by the refreshingly ordinary, plain-speaking north-countryman; the prime minister meanwhile took the monarch into his confidence, used her as a confidential sounding board for his ideas and interpreted his ready accep- tance at court as the ultimate mark of his own success (like various other left-wing politicians before him).

The queen's reputation as a non-partisan figure, who engaged fairly with politicians of all stripes, persisted through until the end of her reign. This ensured that the monarchy lent British politics a semblance of decency and dignity (notably enhanced by the queen's longevity) even when certain prime ministers were doing their utmost to wreck the shop. For some, Elizabeth inspired a sense of confidence in the constitution through her consistent example of detached, but not disinterested, polit- ical neutrality. Indeed, it was this reputation for non-partisanship that critics of monarchy such as the political theorist Tom Nairn identified as a key reason for the failure of republicanism in twentieth-century Britain. By avoiding political controversy, politicians and people of all persuasions could collectively identify with the queen as an even-handed head of state.

However, Pimlott offered an important corrective to the triumphalist narrative of royal neutrality and detachment. He pointed to a failure of political imagination on the part of the queen and those who advised her, particularly during her first 'bountiful years' on the throne, which he argued she wasted, missing an opportunity to modernize the monarchy so that it better fitted the social democratic spirit that was emerging in Britain after the war. Instead, an inexperienced queen was prompted by the same backward-looking courtiers who had advised her father to seek the easiest and least controversial solutions when problems arose, opting for passivity as her default public position in constitutional politics. In turn, Elizabeth was happy to accept the comfortable status quo, compla- cent though it may have been.

The problem with such passivity was that it did not always have the desired effect of protecting the queen's reputation for political impartiality. Before 1965, when the Conservative Party finally introduced an internal election process to select a new leader (and prime minister while in government), it relied instead on the monarch to appoint its leader. The king or queen would usually do this by following the recommendation of the outgoing premier or, when such advice was not forthcoming (as in 1923), the monarch's advisers would take soundings from the party in order to ascertain who it wanted as leader.

But when there was no one clear candidate there was trouble. As we've seen, George V opted for the politician best placed to lead democratic Britain when he invited Baldwin to take over from Bonar Law. Faced with similar Tory indecision in 1957 and 1963, Elizabeth II and her advisers decided – as per their policy of passivity – to leave it to senior Conservatives to take (and interpret) soundings from within the party, rather than implement a process by which the opinion of all parliamentary members might be canvassed transparently and fairly.

As might have been anticipated, the senior Conservatives tasked with taking the party's temperature gravitated towards their own preferred candidates, who would, in both instances, end up being invited by the monarch to form governments. However, the selection of Harold Macmillan (in 1957) and Alec Douglas-Home (in 1963) as prime ministers did not pass without criticism of the role played by the crown. Both soundings appeared to disadvantage R. A. Butler, arguably the most able and certainly one of the most forward-thinking figures in the party. It seemed as though he had twice been ignored by an 'aristocratic cabal' intent on installing more patrician figures as prime minister; Pimlott notably judged the queen's appointment of Douglas-Home as 'the biggest political misjudgement' she ever made.

THIRTY

Queen's consent

Elizabeth's complacency in the first decades of her reign can, in part, be attributed to the wider circumstances in which she found herself. Britain had entered a relative golden age of peace, prosperity and what historians have termed 'political consensus', centred on the government's support for the new welfare state and a belief, shared by both parties, in social aspiration. According to Peter Hennessy, the queen favoured the relatively easy-going mood of this period and all it was doing for her people. One of the queen's failures, then, which ranks alongside her policy of passivity, was her reluctance to adapt constitutional monarchy in these good years, in order to anticipate the political challenges that would arise when, under growing social and economic pressures, the post-war consensus began to break down.

The 1970s and 1980s witnessed the emergence of regional social, economic and cultural divides in Britain that have, in many cases, persisted to the present day. Some of these divisions were exacerbated (and even encouraged) by the policies of Margaret Thatcher's Conservative government. In search of quick fixes to increasingly complex economic problems brought on by globalization, her administration implemented a set of radical reforms which, while in the short term extremely effective, were ultimately deeply polarizing and short-sighted.

Queen Elizabeth is reported as having viewed the destabilizing influence of Thatcherism with apprehension and as a threat to the social democratic fabric of the post-war years. Not only were the New Right's economic and anti-welfare policies antagonistic to large sections of the public (particularly in the once great industrial centres of the country and in inner-city working-class communities), but they also fuelled social conflict and tension. Given how social cohesion was key to the survival of monarchy for most of the twentieth century, the queen was, from a purely self-interested perspective, correct to view her prime minister's reforms with concern.

It was also the case that the Thatcher government's foreign policy paid scant regard to the ambitions of the Commonwealth (led by Queen Elizabeth), which included in this period the aim to bring about the end of the racist apartheid system in South Africa. As the historian Philip Murphy has shown, the UK government often found itself adopting oppositional positions to the Commonwealth on international issues in these years. This raised profound questions over the divided loyalties of the British monarch, who had a constitutional responsibility to the UK as its head of state and the impartial arbiter of national politics, while simultaneously holding the role of head of the Commonwealth and promoting its goals abroad.

So concerned was Queen Elizabeth about the actions of Thatcher's government in Britain and in relation to the Commonwealth, that she expressed serious disapproval to her premier in their weekly audiences. But in mid-1986, in an unprecedented breach of the queen's consti-tutional neutrality, the Sunday Times reported that it had been briefed by her advisers to the effect that she found her government's policies to be 'uncaring, confrontational and socially divisive'.

Although the palace subsequently tried to play down the significance of her intervention, Queen Elizabeth was, in effect, speaking out to let her people know that she was worried about the impact of Thatcherism. It is likely the queen's comments were also designed to make clear to her prime minister how frustrated the monarchy was with what it viewed as the damaging radicalism of the government's policies and reforms. Some historians have speculated that the queen's words had the desired effect of curbing the excesses of the prime minister's more extreme ideas. Thatcher was later heard telling civil servants how 'the Queen wouldn't like that, so we can't do it'. This comment supports Anne Twomey's anal-ysis that Elizabeth secretly brought to bear forms of informal pressure on her ministers, which dissuaded them from adopting certain positions with which they thought their monarch might take issue.

What the queen was arguably doing was improvising (in an unconstitu-tional way) in order to rebalance a weakness that had been exposed in the UK's constitution. Her Majesty's Most Loyal Opposition was at the time divided, with the larger Labour Party led by the hapless socialist Michael Foot. This had helped to put Thatcher's Conservatives in what seemed like an unassailable position. Britain's majoritarian (winner-takes-all) electoral system – also known as 'First Past the Post' – means that a popular prime minister who commands a large majority of seats in the House of Commons can, in effect, repeal old laws and introduce new ones, no matter how radical, provided their own side agrees with the policies and votes them through.

Some commentators would argue that Thatcherism was democracy at work, the prime minister and her policies embodying the will of the British people. However, an alternative view is that what emerged in these years was, in the words of another contemporary politician, an 'elective dictatorship'. Thatcher's Conservatives never won an outright majority of the public vote. The most they achieved was 43.9 per cent in 1979. And, although the main opposition parties shared significantly more of the popular vote between them, because of the UK's majoritarian electoral system they found themselves with far fewer seats in the Commons and no say in lawmaking. The impotence of the opposition meant that, during Thatcher's 11 years as prime minister, power became centralized in a seemingly invincible figure who wielded her authority in a more autocratic manner than any of her predecessors.

The centralization of power did not end with Thatcher. As political scientists have noted, the trend continued under New Labour's Tony Blair, whose style of 'sofa government' saw him consolidate decision-making power in 10 Downing Street and surround himself with a large entourage of unelected advisers, thus blurring the lines of political accountability. The UK's unwritten constitution has enabled such innovation, particularly when the government of the day goes unchallenged because it has a significant majority in the Commons. One cannot help but draw the conclusion that some of the UK's most recent prime ministers – including Boris Johnson – have felt able to act with impunity precisely because of this consolidation of power in a 'core executive' which lacks transparency and is not subject to sufficient parliamentary oversight.

Writing in the 1990s, Hennessy found that the four officials responsible for interpreting constitutional conventions (the monarch's private secretary, the prime minister's private secretary, the cabinet secretary and the Commons clerk) agreed that 'if you have an unwritten constitution, you make it up as you go along'. This is not very reassuring. But it gives us some insight into the way ministers and governments have been able to reinterpret their constitutional roles to suit their own ends. As far as we can tell based on the available evidence, the queen – the so-called defender of democracy and figure ultimately responsible for upholding the constitution – did little (apart from publicly and privately reprimanding Thatcher) to ensure that checks and balances remained in place so that parliament could continue to scrutinize and, where necessary, challenge the activities of government.

Queen Elizabeth's reluctance to adopt a more proactive approach to constitutional change was in keeping with her long-term policy of political passivity. Her failure to do more to oversee the evolution of the constitution has to be partly attributed to the people who advised her, most notably senior aides such as her private secretaries. Courtiers tend to be ex-military figures or civil servants, whose loyalty to the throne is beyond question. However, they are often selected based on their elite backgrounds, where a certain (conservative) view of the world prevails. As with all organizations that lack diversity, the royal household has often been slow to embrace change. In 2021 an important *Guardian* exposé revealed how the royal household had in the 1960s secured secret exemptions from race and sex equality laws, meaning it could continue to employ senior staff exclusively from a limited talented pool comprising mainly elite white men, without facing external criticism.

The files unearthed by the *Guardian* are important for two reasons. First of all, they reveal an institution that actively resisted embracing new perspectives. If Queen Elizabeth had had other people advising her from a wider cross-section of society, then this could have led to new ideas and fresh thinking about how constitutional politics was evolving. Most of the blame for the failure to diversify her household rests, unfortunately, with the queen. She could have insisted that the palace recruit much more widely in order to ensure all types of opinion were part of discussions at court, so that she was therefore regularly listening to a more representative chorus of voices from around her kingdom.

Second (and more disconcerting), the *Guardian* investigation exposed how the House of Windsor has historically gained from the lack of transparency that is embedded in the British constitution. In its startling series of revelations about the monarchy, the paper uncovered how the sovereign and her heir had, unbeknown to the public, been exercising powers whereby they could vet and amend proposed laws that affected the monarchy's powers and interests. The 1960s opt-outs on equality legislation were just the tip of an iceberg of exclusions and legal changes that benefited the royals and which were made possible by an opaque constitutional procedure known as the 'Queen's Consent' (now the 'King's Consent' under Charles III).

More than a thousand laws were specially submitted by government to the palace for vetting as part of this procedure, stretching back to the start of the queen's reign in 1952. The monarch was able to insist on changes to draft legislation where the crown's rights, revenues, personal property, estates and other interests were affected. The palace refused to say on how many occasions Elizabeth requested changes to draft legislation. But we know that her interventions helped to change transparency laws in order to conceal her private wealth from the public; and we know that she obtained exclusions from green energy laws that would have required her to allow for the construction of pipelines across her Scottish estate in order to heat homes and businesses using renewable energy.

As the constitutional expert Adam Tucker wrote at the time of the revelations: 'the anti-democratic potential of the consent process is obvious: it gives the Queen a possible veto, to be exercised in secret, over proposed laws.' And as another specialist in constitutional law at Oxford University, Thomas Adams, put it, the consent process gives the monarch 'the kind of influence over legislation that lobbyists would only dream of', providing cover for the crown secretly to exert influence over the shape of legislation as it makes its way through the Houses of Parliament.

Clearly, if we want a revival of democratic values in Britain with the monarchy taking the lead in promoting integrity, transparency and accountability, then the crown needs to come clean about the powers that it has clandestinely wielded as part of the constitution. And here the country's unwritten constitution needs to be viewed in a positive light. It presents us with a massive opportunity to create a new constitutional settlement fit for the twenty-first century: we can, in the words of Hennessy, 'make it up as [we] go along' in order to change our culture of politics for good.

Conclusion
Radical renewal or republican Britain?

Over the course of this book I've made the case for the renewal of the monarchy's role and purpose in modern Britain.

In so doing, I've suggested that we need to rethink other parts of our national culture connected to the royal family as well. This includes how we talk about and make sense of Britain's complex imperial history and the crown's symbolic role at the centre of empire. I've suggested that we need to reconsider the monarchy's ties to the established church at a time when the public are turning away from Anglicanism in growing numbers. I've raised concerns about the impact of royal philanthropy, including how it has worked to normalize a situation where the British state is no longer required to take primary responsibility for the welfare of the public. I've discussed the ways we actively remember those injured or killed fighting for their country, and how we might ensure that service people returning from warzones today get the support they need to reintegrate into society. I've criticized the UK's honours system, not least for the way it has been corrupted by political nepotism. And I've argued that we need to change how we engage with a news media which too often focuses on trivial royal celebrity stories to the detriment of a more serious debate about how the monarchy might modernize so that it can play a valuable role in the twenty-first century.

I have also demonstrated here how resolute modernization has, at certain points in time, been essential to the crown's survival – be it under Queen Victoria and Prince Albert, or during the transformative reign of George V. Indeed, it is by taking the long view of the monarchy's uneven evolution over the last 250 years that we're able to see that we have again entered a period characterized by malaise, where reinvention is urgently needed. The version of monarchy that King Charles inherited from his mother belongs, in essence, to the mid-twentieth century.

The fact that Queen Elizabeth avoided modernization – preferring instead to consolidate the style of constitutional monarchy popularized by her father and grandfather – means the crown is out of step with the fast-moving times and unable to help the UK overcome the serious challenges it currently faces. And, as it stands, the crown's future looks uncertain because of the profound loss of faith among younger sections of the public in the wider social, economic and political status quo. If the crown is to guarantee its survival, while also ensuring it plays a genuinely important part in national life, it will require root-and-branch reform comparable to what took place in the mid-nineteenth century and again after 1918. The Victorian royals embraced a new, more moral kind of monarchy that distanced them from their dissolute ancestors and which appealed to the pious (and powerful) British middle classes. Meanwhile, from the end of the First World War, the newly titled House of Windsor developed a new public relations strategy designed to woo the newly enfranchised working classes by emphasizing the monarchy's credentials as a national – and specifically British – institution.

It is worth restating that a monarchy which has, for too long, been too slow to embrace change will resist innovation unless it comes under significant public pressure to do so. The way the House of Windsor's greatest asset, Catherine, princess of Wales, is being repeatedly wheeled out as the beautiful (and relatively youthful) face of the new 'Carolean era' suggests that a certain degree of panic has set in among courtiers owing to the muted enthusiasm that has greeted King Charles since his accession. But, apart from this, there has been no indication that the royal household recognizes the scale of the challenge it faces or that it is ready to move out of its comfort zone in order to make the monarchy more meaningful to younger people. This has made it easy for republicans to criticize the king as out of touch. Meanwhile, the clumsy errors of officialdom at the 2023 coronation helped to crystallize the idea that the monarchy remains deeply hierarchical in character and its allies intolerant of opposition.

However, we must not allow the debate over the future of the crown to be two-sided: to stick with a stale status quo that is failing the country or to abandon kingship altogether in favour of a republic. There is a third way, rooted in progressive change, which is also pragmatic given the problems Britain faces. It would involve all sections of society as part of a national conversation that would ultimately lead to the creation of a new constitutional settlement. Such a settlement could not only secure the monarchy's future but also, more importantly, enable the strengthening of British democracy right at the moment when it is threatened by various existential forces from within and without.

Thus the straightforward answer to the question – 'Can the monarchy save itself?' – is yes, it can, provided it embraces a programme of radical transformation. But the more difficult question that we need to be asking ourselves in light of the fact that the Elizabethan impulse to avoid confronting hard realities still prevails in the palace is: 'How can the monarchy be saved from itself?'

Having dealt with this tricky question by expanding on how my programme for renewal might be implemented, I finally turn to the risk of failing to modernize: namely, the likelihood of republicanism gaining significant public support in the UK. If the monarchy fails to grasp the opportunity to modernize, we will see calls for a completely new political settlement – one without a hereditary crowned head of state – grow louder still. It is precisely because the arguments of republicans seem to offer hope via a total overhaul of a broken political system that they are gaining new followers among those who are (quite rightly) disenchanted with the current situation in Britain. However, I believe we have reason to be optimistic about a future where the monarchy remains in place, provided King Charles, his ministers and his people are ready to adopt the kind of constitutional settlement for democratic kingship that I set out here, whereby the crown would finally fully embrace its historic role as defender of our democratic values and institutions.

British politicians and the media have to lead the debate on what a twenty-first-century monarchy would look like. This is partly because the king himself is constitutionally prevented from simply announcing that he would welcome, for example, a reinterpretation of his role as protector of the UK's democratic freedoms. Convention dictates that the sovereign must only act on the advice of his or her ministers, although, as we saw in Part Four, Queen Elizabeth was more politically active behind the scenes than was widely assumed for most of her lifetime.

Indeed, it is because King Charles continues to wield the same kind of discretionary influence as his mother that he could quietly make it known through the channels that connect him to the government and civil service that he is amenable to innovation, provided there was broad public support for it. Such a move might give those with the power to effect significant constitutional change the confidence to speak out about the topic, safe in the knowledge that the monarchy would not seek to resist a programme of renewal. And, if it was secretly briefed to trusted figures in the press (as already happens so often with the House of Windsor today) that the king favoured change, it would signal to news editors that the monarchy would welcome a public discussion on the future of the crown.

Ultimately, if there is to be significant public support for changing the monarchy's role as part of a bigger programme of democratic renewal, then those institutions responsible for shaping opinion have to get to work explaining what is currently wrong with our political system and what a new vision of kingship might look like. While this book has gone some way to addressing both points, it is for our elected representatives and British journalists to make clear the pressing need for change as part of a national conversation about the monarchy.

There is an irony in having to rely on a broken political system to fix itself in this way. Likewise, if we are to have an honest conversation about the monarchy, then the media will also have to up its game by adopting a much more thoughtful (and less frivolous) approach to the royal family. As I suggested in Part Three, it is incumbent on the Windsors to disengage from the toxic media culture which they've helped to create if they want to avoid being the focus of scandalous headlines. If we begin a serious debate about what kind of monarchy we want, then newspapers will find they have to devote attention to such a discussion, and therefore reduce the column space they are able to dedicate to trivial celebrity stories about the royals.

More politicians will also need to stick their heads above the parapet if we are to see progress in this area. At the moment there are very few who are willing openly to criticize the royal status quo for fear of the damage it might do to their reputations and careers, despite the fact that in private many are scathing about how the monarchy operates. Some of those who have spoken out, such as the former Liberal Democrat MP Norman Baker and Labour's Clive Lewis, have developed followings among sections of the public which recognize that the time for change is now.

One of the UK's two main political parties will in the end need to take charge of the debate on the monarchy's future. This would involve explaining how the role of the sovereign and the royal family could be modernized, as per the kind of Monarchy Act that I outlined in Part Four. And it would also mean setting out the road map by which change would be constitutionally achieved: for example, through a general election or a referendum on the issue.

To reiterate, a Monarchy Act could, in short, help to create a better-informed public led by a more principled political class. It could do so by enshrining a new role for the crown whereby the sovereign and heir to the throne worked with a 'Crown Committee' tasked with a number of new political roles, including: upholding a higher code of ethics among elected politicians, especially for those wielding 'executive power', such as the prime minister and cabinet; promoting integrity, accountability and transparency in public life by, for example, tracking and challenging dis/misinformation, while also holding political officials responsible for what they say and do in public; championing a programme of democratic education designed to encourage active and thoughtful engagement with politics across the country; and building consensus through innovatory initiatives designed to develop long-term policymaking that addresses key areas of governance.

To get to a place where this kind of Monarchy Act might become a reality, we need to anticipate several years of public discussion and debate during which reform of the crown and Britain's constitution would become salient political issues. It takes time for a topic to gain traction, particularly when, at least on the surface, it can seem a bit abstract. But it is necessary that such a national conversation takes place because any vote on the issue of royal renewal must be based on a sound, fact-based understanding of the options facing the UK and its monarchy.

The most straightforward constitutional route by which a Monarchy Act could make it on to the statute book and into law would be via a UK-wide referendum where every member of the British public from across the four nations was invited to cast his or her vote either in favour of or against, royal reform. However, Britain's recent experience of referendums has not been good. The controversial 2016 plebiscite on the UK's membership of the European Union demonstrated spectacularly the problems that can emerge from such an experiment in what political scientists have termed 'direct democracy'. The public debate wasn't properly regulated, meaning it rapidly became contaminated with disinformation designed to mislead voters. Because no one political party backed Brexit, the victorious 'Vote Leave' campaign (a hotchpotch grouping of mainly right-wing politicians and public figures) had no formal constitutional platform through which to enact change, thus leading to years of destructive wrangling within Britain's governing Conservative Party over the kind of Brexit the country would pursue.

Equally, because no one party thought the public would actually back Brexit there was no clear plan formulated for the UK's departure from the EU. This subsequently made it impossible for voters to hold to account those responsible for the result and its consequences, such as the right-wing populist politician Nigel Farage. Finally, the 'winner takes all' nature of the 2016 referendum meant those government ministers navigating Britain's departure from Europe were left to interpret 'the will' of 52 per cent of the voting public, with no obligation to consider the opinions of the other 48 per cent, which has in turn fuelled division within the UK, as well as a loss of confidence in the country's political elite.

In order to ensure there was no repeat of the 2016 fiasco, a two-stage referendum process could be used to usher in the Monarchy Act. Presuming that public support for royal reform grew following several years of discussion and debate about the monarchy's future role, the governing political party could introduce legislation whereby the population would, first, as part of an 'advisory referendum', signal to parliament that they wanted change by voting in a majority for some form of Monarchy Act. After the public had signalled that they wanted change, it would then be the responsibility of each of the leading political parties to develop plans for what the Monarchy Act would look like, using the result of the first advisory referendum to determine how ambitious such legislation could be. There would need to be agreement among the parties that the outcome of any such advisory referendum was final: if the public determined that they wanted change, then politicians would have to respect the wishes of voters.

If the king tacitly signalled his agreement that such a referendum should take place, it might go some way to assuaging doubters who would rather a Monarchy Act wasn't up for public discussion at all, preferring instead to stick with the status quo. The most concerning thing would be if the doubters disputed the outcome of the advisory referendum and then sought to use the defence of the status quo (and the king's current position) to rally support to their cause. This could lead to serious problems: hence the need for some kind of discreet intervention from the royal household acknowledging that the democratic process must be allowed to unfold peacefully. It is worth remembering that the last time a King Charles defied the will of parliament it led to a military coup d'état, civil war and the eventual execution of the monarch.

Having time to plan out what the Monarchy Act would look like would enable the main political parties to engage in serious, detailed discussion before a second referendum took place, which would, this time, be legally binding. Each party could engage with other political parties and members of the public, especially in Scotland, Wales and Northern

Ireland, in order to draw up their own versions of the Monarchy Act, to be put to the British public in the legally binding referendum. Ensuring there was plenty of time for this consultation process to take place would mean that press and public could continue to feed into the debate as the different versions of the Monarchy Act were thrashed out. The public would therefore be in a strong position to make a well-informed decision when it came to the second referendum, and the civil service and royal household would have time to prepare for all eventualities.

Time for careful reflection prior to the legally binding referendum would be absolutely crucial, given that the transformation emanating from it would likely be profound and wide-ranging. Once the result had been determined, it would then be the legal responsibility of the governing political party (irrespective of whether or not the British public had voted for their particular version of the Monarchy Act) to work with civil servants in order to steer the Act through parliament, thus effecting the change desired by a majority of voters. Ensuring the wishes of the majority were respected would be a powerful symbolic act with which to begin a new phase of the UK's democratic development. There would be no turning back and no time for further quibbling.

If the kind of Monarchy Act that I've outlined in this book were to become a reality, then what would follow would be a significant 'airing' of the constitution as part of a shift to greater transparency in public life. Today's culture of royal secrecy would come to an end, and the historic political influence wielded by the sovereign and members of their family behind the scenes would be made visible by an opening up of the archives and a long overdue release of official documentation.

If the king is to truly embody – symbolically and in practice – our democratic values of integrity, accountability and transparency, then it is crucial that he set a positive example and that, as part of this process, we finally get to understand what powers his predecessors have, unbeknown to the public, exercised as part of our current opaque constitutional settlement. This period of amnesty would also ensure that such extra-constitutional behaviour becomes a thing of the past, while enabling King Charles to embrace fully his new role as defender of our democracy.

My Monarchy Act would also see the crown formally become a 'public' institution – as opposed to the 'public–private' entity that exists today. For too long our royal rulers have evaded proper scrutiny because they have been able to insist that they belong to a private family and are therefore not subject to the same kinds of checks and balances that apply to most other parts of the British state. As part of this transition to a public monarchy the number of royal family members in receipt of the Sovereign Grant would be dramatically cut as part of a broader civil service-led audit of the monarchy's personnel, finances and assets. The aim of such an audit would be to establish a clear division between what belongs to the crown (and thus the country) and what belongs to the Windsor dynasty in a private capacity.

Separating out public from private in this way would also ensure that there would be no future conflict of interests between a monarchy tasked with upholding moral standards in public life and a royal family intent on consolidating their social position and private wealth at the expense of other sections of society. Such an audit would also align with the changed role of the House of Windsor as it goes from being an institution that has sought, at significant cost (financial, social, political and cultural), to exercise influence in every area of national life to becoming an institution with a specific set of new roles within the constitution.

Significantly, the two-stage referendum process outlined here would, for the first time in the monarchy's history, confer a democratic legitimacy on the institution by way of the votes cast by a majority of the British public at the ballot box. There would be no need for the royal family to promote their old roles – ceremonial, dutiful, philanthropic, familial – in order to try to win the public's loyalty and affection, as has been the case for more than a century. Provided the sovereign and the heir to the throne took their new responsibilities seriously in working with the Crown Committee to uphold Britain's democracy, public support for the monarchy would be strengthened as it fulfilled its new roles as set out in the Monarchy Act.

Indeed, if the Windsors continued to devote attention to the old functions they once used to court the public, this would be a distraction from the monarchy's new constitutional roles and could lead to conflicts of interest. The crown could thus enable modernization by actively stepping back from its old roles, making clear to the public in the process how some of its past functions could be reimagined as part of its new constitutional remit. This could include older forms of religious ceremonial making way for the kind of secular 'King's Day' celebrations that I outlined in Part One. It could also see the royal family bring to an end the philanthropy discussed in Part

Two, which has seen them become so deeply entangled in the politics of health, environment and young people's welfare.

At the same time, though, the newly formed Crown Committee could work to identify solutions to these and other major issues as part of their long-term policy initiatives. And as already noted here, the Windsors would need to end their engagement with a toxic media culture that has thrived equally on the fantasy and failures of royal domesticity over the last hundred years. Instead, the king and his heir could lead a national education campaign designed to enhance both the British public's understanding of their political system and the critical thinking skills that will be essential to deliberative democratic decision-making.

One other obstacle to overcome would be the British crown's overseas commitments, not least the 14 Commonwealth realms where the king remains head of state. If he is to symbolize British democracy and spend his time overseeing its smooth functioning, King Charles can't be distracted by his political roles in other countries. Constitutionally speaking, the monarchy cannot unilaterally separate itself from the realms: the political impetus for change must come from the people and politicians of these countries. However, the sovereign could signal to these nations that his priority is the UK by discreetly acknowledging his reluctance to continue engaging in their political affairs, thus potentially hastening the process by which the publics in these countries vote to get rid of their crowned head of state.

It will be easier for King Charles to give up his role as head of the Commonwealth. This is not a constitutional position, nor is it a hereditary one. It is also a morally dubious position for a truly democratic monarch to occupy. In many of the 56 countries that comprise the modern Commonwealth there are severe constraints on democratic freedoms, as well as appalling human rights abuses. It would be much better for the king to distance himself from this morally wayward organization, so that he might act as an upright symbol of Britain's renewed democratic values on the international stage. Handing over the headship of the Commonwealth to an elected figure unconnected to the monarchy would also ensure there could be no further conflicts of interest between a House of Windsor which has, as we saw in Part Four, used the inter-governmental organization to pursue its own foreign policy goals, sometimes in direct opposition to the wishes of the democratically elected UK government.

If we assume that a Monarchy Act like the one I've set out here comes to pass, the patience of the public will be key during the transition period when the crown takes on its new roles as part of a new constitutional settlement. We might assume that, having received a vote of confidence from the public, the monarchy's position would be secure for another generation, or at least until there was a change of sovereign and heir to the throne. At the moment of succession it would make sense politically to hold a confirmatory referendum in which the British public could exercise their democratic right by voting to stick with the new constitutional settlement, thus conferring democratic legitimacy on the new king or queen, or by voting to 'twist' once more, should they decide that change is again required.

One final thing that King Charles should seriously consider is abdication. One of the reasons he has inherited such a difficult hand as monarch is that his mother's reign went on far too long, meaning that much-needed reinvention had to wait. Haunted by the very word 'abdication' because of what happened in 1936, Queen Elizabeth refused to countenance an idea that is popular among European monarchs, who tend to hand over their roles to the next (younger) generation so that they might inject new life and ideas into their dynasties, thus ensuring continuity through renewal.

We might envisage King Charles, having come to the throne at the age of 74, enjoying a reign of ten or so years in which he oversees, with the help of his son and heir, a dramatic overhaul of the monarchy's role and purpose in Britain, on the scale of what I've set out here. Then, in a sign of confidence about the future direction of his dynasty and the country, he could hand over the crown to Prince William, who, then aged about 50, would have plenty of time as king to continue the monarchy's evolution as it adjusts to the conditions of the mid-twenty-first century.

What if the monarchy refuses to modernize? Well, if republicanism might lead to the kind of democratic renewal which I've consistently argued for throughout this book, then so be it. There are good models of republican government that Britain could seek to emulate. These include Germany and Ireland, where the elected president is an almost entirely symbolic figure invested with special reserve powers which enable them to protect the democratic constitution in ways not dissimilar to what I've set out in my Monarchy Act. In both of these countries it is democratically elected politicians that wield almost all lawmaking power and who are held in check by the president as overseer.

There are also flawed republican systems from whose experience the UK could learn a lot, such as the USA and France, where arguably far too much decision-making power is invested in a single individual. The result in recent years has been similar levels of political polarization to that witnessed in Britain, with successive American and French presidents failing to unite deeply divided countries.

Britain's leading republicans have seized on the moment of King Charles's succession to publicize their arguments in books and interviews. As yet, we haven't seen any sea change in public opinion. But as a new generation of anti-monarchists take to the internet and our TV screens to argue their points of view, we will see republicanism gain traction, especially if life in Britain doesn't get any easier for younger people, who, as we know, are the ones most disillusioned with the state of the UK today.

The route to a republic is not dissimilar to the route to royal reform via a Monarchy Act as sketched out above. It would involve debate generated by the media; perhaps a new royal family scandal might accelerate a loss of public confidence in the monarchy, putting the wind in the sails of the republicans; there would need to be parliamentary, as well as public, support to get rid of the crowned head of state. But if popular opinion does suddenly shift, we can expect to see politicians follow; then one of the main political parties would need to table some kind of legislation for a new republican political settlement, setting out the constitutional mechanism – for example, a UK-wide referendum – that would enable such change.

The point is that all of this is ultimately unnecessary. A radically reformed monarchy at the centre of a renewed democratic settlement could do much to restore public confidence in Britain's political system. As I've said already, a new constitutional settlement could place greater emphasis on the democratic principles of integrity, accountability and transparency, while also working to create a better-informed and more engaged citizenry able to recognize the most serious political challenges facing the country in order to promote the changes and solutions needed for the UK to succeed in the coming years.

However, if Britain's fortunes are to improve, then the monarchy, politicians and public must first accept the need for real change. As far back as 1867, Walter Bagehot said of the UK that 'a Republic has insinuated itself beneath the folds of a Monarchy'. Shortly after this, the poet laureate, Alfred Tennyson, argued that the country had effectively become a 'crowned republic', combining the best aspects of both the monarchical and democratic republican systems. And yet, as we've seen throughout this study, these rose-tinted characterizations are far from the reality that confronts us today.

Under Queen Elizabeth the crown's subtle – sometimes insidious – influence became increasingly far-reaching in Britain. Meanwhile, the royal household complacently refused to contemplate concerted modernization. Now under new management, the House of Windsor finds itself leading a divided and dysfunctional nation. If the monarchy is to be rescued, then it is us – the *demos* – that must act to save it. Similarly, if the UK is to truly become a kind of 'crowned republic', then it is we who must push for such a political transformation.

My hope is that this book has helped to make clear the need for a deeper conversation about the monarchy's past, present and future. For without such a conversation it is not just the crown's future that will be in peril but the future of a democratic country that has progressed enormously in 250 years and which, crucially, has the potential to progress much further still.

Acknowledgements

I want to begin by thanking Bloomsbury's Robin Baird-Smith. This book would not exist without him. When he approached me with the idea of writing something about how younger Britons were growing increasingly disenchanted with the monarchy, the idea immediately struck a chord, resonating with what I'd seen and experienced first-hand since 2011. Robin is right. As opinion poll after opinion poll shows, the under-40s (me among them) are turning their backs on a socio-political status quo that simply doesn't reflect their ideals or aspirations. The House of Windsor is an integral part of this status quo. Thanks to Robin (and his indefatigable patience), I've had the time to think about the challenges Britain is facing today and the chance to set out a vision for change that might have some impact in shaping the politics of tomorrow.

I'm grateful to Robin's team at Bloomsbury and, in particular, to Sarah Jones and Sarah Head: their support and ideas in the final stages of writing were greatly appreciated. I owe special thanks to Matthew Taylor for his careful editing of the book. His discerning analysis of the first draft of the text has ensured greater accuracy and clarity of argument in the final version. And I must thank my agents at Northbank – Matilda Waring, Martin Redfern and Diane Banks – for their help in developing this project and other royal-related projects along the way.

Most of *After Elizabeth* was written in France. In 2019 I left a lecturing job in the UK in search of new opportunities. But I've continued to benefit from the generosity of the wider academic community back in Britain. Several conversations I've had with historians and other academics over the last couple of years have helped to shape the ideas contained in this book. I'd especially like to thank Philip Murphy, Penny Summerfield, Philip Williamson, Anna Whitelock, Richard Toye, Dominic Dean, Max Jones, Alistair Kefford, James Greenhalgh, Laura Clancy, Frank Mort and Heather Jones. Frank and Heather have recently written brilliant scholarly histories of the modern monarchy, and I've engaged with their work throughout this book.

It's also the case that without Frank Mort and Max Jones I would never have got the chance to begin researching the royal family back in 2011 as a doctoral student at the University of Manchester, and I wouldn't have subsequently ended up as a historian of the monarchy. The research for my PhD led to my first book, The Family Firm, in which, to my shame, I forgot to acknowledge the help of three people without whom I would never have made it to university in the first place. Beginning a new job in education in France, working with students aged 17 to 19, has brought into sharper focus the crucial contribution that Jeremy Crowhurst, Colin Gray and Eddie Falshaw made to my own schooling when I was that age. My sincere thanks to them all.

This book would not have been possible without the kindness of friends. I am grateful to all of our nouveaux amis in France who have welcomed us to their country and into their communities. My special thanks to Ivor Gemmell, who has been a great support ever since we arrived: our move was made much more difficult than it needed to be by the Covid-19 pandemic, but Ivor's friendship has helped to ease the transition to la vie en France. I am also grateful to old friends back in Britain who continued to ask challenging questions about this project as it developed, and who helped to guide my thinking on the changing relationship between the monarchy and public in a period marked by great change.

And, finally, a huge thank you to my family – the Owenses, Dillons, Prices and Evanses – who have all been caring, thoughtful and encouraging over the last couple of years. My mother and father, Debbie and Glyn, have been absolute champions since my wife and I moved to France, supporting our every decision and offering help wherever possible. Mum was exceptionally amazing at the time of the late Queen Elizabeth's death (a hectic time for royal historians like me), which coincided with the birth of our daughter, Emilie. The person responsible for bringing Emilie into the world was, of course, my incredible wife, Lisa. She has patiently and lovingly supported me through the evenings, weekends and holidays spent working on this book. She has happily engaged in lunchtime debates with our friends and family about the most recent royal drama. And, although we were sad to say a (temporary) farewell to the UK, Lisa more than anyone has made our move across the English Channel possible through her constant optimism and endeavour. This book is therefore dedicated to her: thank you.

Further Reading

INTRODUCTION

Bagehot, W. The English Constitution (London, 1867).
Billig, M. Talking of the Royal Family (London: Routledge, 1992).
Buettner, E. Europe after Empire: Decolonization, Society, and Culture (Amsterdam: CUP, 2016).
Harris, L.M. Long to Reign over Us? The Status of the Royal Family in the Sixties (London: William Kimber, 1966).
Jones, H. For King and Country: The British Monarchy and the First World War (Cambridge: CUP, 2021).
Mort, F. 'Safe for Democracy: Constitutional Politics, Popular Spectacle, and the British Monarchy, 1910–1914', Journal of British Studies 58:1 (2019), pp. 109–41.
Murphy, P. The Empire's New Clothes: The Myth of the Commonwealth (London: C Hurst & Co., 2018).
Olechnowicz, A. 'A Jealous Hatred: Royal Popularity and Social Inequality', in A. Olechnowicz (ed.), The Monarchy and the British Nation, 1780 to the Present (Cambridge: CUP, 2007), pp. 280–314.
Olechnowicz, A. 'Historians and the Modern British Monarchy', in A. Olechnowicz (ed.), The Monarchy and the British Nation, 1780 to the Present (Cambridge: CUP, 2007), pp. 6–44.
Pimlott, B. The Queen: Elizabeth II and the Monarchy (London: HarperCollins, 2002).
Ridley, J. George V: Never a Dull Moment (London: Chatto & Windus, 2021).
Smith, M. 'Where Does Public Opinion Stand on the Monarchy ahead of the Coronation?', YouGov (3 May 2023).
Steinfeld, J., et al. 'Crown Confidential: How Britain's Royals Censor Their Records', Index on Censorship 51:4 (2022).
Taylor, M. 'Introduction', in M. Taylor (ed.), Walter Bagehot: The English Constitution (Oxford: OUP, 2001), pp. vii–xxx.
Torrance, D. 'Research Briefing: The Coronation of King Charles III and Queen Camilla', House of Commons Library (London, 2023).

PART ONE: CEREMONY, SPECTACLE AND TRADITION

Atwal, P. Royals and Rebels: The Rise and Fall of the Sikh Empire (London: C Hurst & Co., 2020).
Bradley, I. God Save the Queen: The Spiritual Dimension of Monarchy (London: Darton, Longman & Todd Ltd, 2002).
Bradley, I. 'The Religious Dimensions of Monarchy', in R. Hazell and B. Morris (eds.), The Role of Monarchy in Modern Democracy: European Monarchies Compared (Oxford: Hart Publishing, 2022), pp. 102–6.
Cannadine, D. 'The Context, Performance and Meaning of Ritual: The British Monarchy and the "Invention of Tradition", c.1820–1977', in E. Hobsbawm and T. Ranger (eds.), The Invention of Tradition (Cambridge: CUP, 1983), pp. 101–64.
Cannadine, D. Class in Britain (New Haven, CT: Yale University Press, 1998).
Colley, L. Britons: Forging the Nation, 1707–1837 (London: Pimlico, 1994).
Cranmer, F. 'Monarchies and Religion in Europe', in R. Hazell and B. Morris (eds.), The Role of Monarchy in Modern Democracy: European Monarchies Compared (Oxford: Hart Publishing, 2022), pp. 94–101.

Dayan D., and Katz, E. Media Events: The Live Broadcasting of History (Cambridge, MA: Harvard University Press, 1992).

Dekavalla, M. 'Constructing the Public at the Royal Wedding', Media, Culture and Society 34:3 (2012), pp. 296–311.

Dimbleby, D. Keep Talking: A Broadcasting Life (London: Hodder & Stoughton, 2022).

Ellis, J. S. Investiture: Royal Ceremony and National Identity in Wales, 1911–1969 (Cardiff: University of Wales Press, 2008).

Hall, C. Civilizing Subjects: Metropole and Colony in the English Imagination, 1830–1867 (Cambridge: University of Chicago Press, 2002).

Hammerton, E., and Cannadine, D. 'Conflict and Consensus on a Ceremonial Occasion: The Diamond Jubilee in Cambridge in 1897', Historical Journal 24:1 (Cambridge: CUP, 1981), pp. 111–46.

Johnes, M. 'A Prince, a King, and a Referendum: Rugby, Politics, and Nationhood in Wales, 1969–1979', Journal of British Studies 47:1 (Cambridge: CUP, 2008), pp. 129–48.

Johnes, M. Wales since 1939 (Manchester: Manchester University Press, 2012).

Jordan, C. 'The British Monarchy and Royal Celebrations in the 21st Century', in C. Jordan and I. Polland (eds.), Realms of Royalty: New Directions in Researching Contemporary European Monarchies (New York: Transcript Verlag, 2020), pp. 233–50.

Kaul, C. Reporting the Raj: the British Press and India, c.1880–1922 (Manchester: Manchester University Press, 2003).

Kaul, C. 'Monarchical Display and the Politics of Empire: Princes of Wales and India, 1870–1920s', Twentieth Century British History 17:4 (Oxford: OUP, 2006), pp. 464–88.

Kuhn, W. Democratic Royalism: The Transformation of the British Monarchy, 1861–1914 (Basingstoke: Palgrave Macmillan, 1996).

Ledger–Lomas, M. Queen Victoria: This Thorny Crown (Oxford: OUP, 2021).

Loss, D. 'Missionaries, the Monarchy, and the Emergence of Anglican Pluralism in the 1960s and 1970s', Journal of British Studies 57:3 (2018), pp. 543–63.

McKernan, L. 'The Finest Cinema Performers We Possess: British Royalty and the Newsreels, 1910–37', Court Historian 8:1 (2003), pp. 59–71.

McKernan, L. '"The Modern Elixir of Life": Kinemacolor, Royalty and the Delhi Durbar', Film History 21:2 (2009), pp. 122–36.

Moran, J. Armchair Nation: An Intimate History of Britain in Front of the TV (London: Profile Books, 2013).

Morris, R. 'The Future of the Monarchy: The Reign of King Charles III', in R. Hazell (ed.), Constitutional Futures Revisited (London: Palgrave Macmillan, 2008), pp. 139–55.

Mortimore, R. 'Polls and Public Opinion', in R. Hazell and B. Morris (eds.), The Role of Monarchy in Modern Democracy: European Monarchies Compared (Oxford: Hart Publishing, 2022), pp. 220–235.

Murphy, P. Monarchy and the End of Empire: The House of Windsor, the British Government, and the Postwar Commonwealth (Oxford: OUP, 2013).

Murphy , P. 'Queen Elizabeth II and the Commonwealth: Time to Open the Archives', The Journal of Imperial and Commonwealth History 50:5 (2022), pp. 821–8.

Nairn, T. The Enchanted Glass: Britain and its Monarchy (London: Radius, 1988).

Owens, E. The Family Firm: Monarchy, Mass Media and the British Public, 1932–1953 (London: Institute of Historical Research, 2019).

Peplow, S. Race and Riots in Thatcher's Britain (Manchester: Manchester University Press, 2019).

Plunkett, J. Queen Victoria: First Media Monarch (Oxford: OUP, 2003).

Prochaska, F. 'George V and Republicanism, 1917–1919', Twentieth Century British History 10:1 (1999), pp. 27–51.

Reed, C. V. Royal Tourists, Colonial Subjects and the Making of a British World, 1860–1911 (Manchester: Manchester University Press, 2016).

Ridley, J. Bertie: A Life of Edward VII (London: Chatto & Windus, 2012).

Sapire, H. 'African Loyalism and Its Discontents: The Royal Tour of South Africa, 1947', The Historical Journal 54:1 (Cambridge: CUP, 2011), pp. 215–40.

Taylor, M. 'The Bicentenary of Queen Victoria', Journal of British Studies 59:1 (2020), pp. 121–35.

Tomlinson, J. 'De-Industrialization Not Decline: A New Meta-Narrative for Post-War British History', *Twentieth Century British History* 27:1 (2016), pp. 76–99.

Webster, W. *Englishness and Empire, 1939–1965* (Oxford: OUP, 2005).

Williamson, P. 'The Monarchy and Public Values, 1900–1953', in A. Olechnowicz (ed.), *The Monarchy and the British Nation, 1780 to the Present* (Cambridge: CUP, 2007), pp. 223–57.

Wilson, A. N. *Prince Albert: The Man Who Saved the Monarchy* (London: Atlantic Books, 2019).

Winter, J. *War and Remembrance in the Twentieth Century* (Cambridge: CUP, 1999).

Wolffe, J. *Great Deaths: Grieving, Religion, and Nationhood in Victorian and Edwardian Britain* (Oxford: OUP, 2000).

Wolffe, J. 'Protestantism, Monarchy and the Defence of Christian Britain, 1837–2005', in C. Brown and M. Snape (eds.), *Secularisation in the Christian World* (Farnham: Ashgate, 2010), pp. 57–74.

Ziegler, P. *Crown and People* (London: HarperCollins Distribution Services, 1978).

Ziegler, P. *King Edward VIII* (London: Fontana, 1990).

Zweiniger-Bargielowska, I. 'Royal Death and Living Memorials: The Funerals and Commemoration of George V and George VI, 1936–52', *Historical Research* 89:243 (2016) pp. 158–75.

PART TWO: DUTY, SERVICE AND PHILANTHROPY

Alcock, P. 'The History of Third Sector Service Delivery in the UK', in J. Rees and D. Mullins (eds.), *The Third Sector Delivering Public Services: Developments, Innovations and Challenges* (Bristol, 2016), pp. 21–40.

Bell, E., et al. 'Public Services in the UK: The Ongoing Challenges of Delivery and Public Accountability', *Revue Française de Civilisation Britannique* 26:2 (2021), pp. 1–12.

Bingham, A. *Family Newspapers? Sex, Private Life, and the British Popular Press, 1918–1978* (Oxford: OUP, 2009).

Calder, A. *The People's War: Britain 1939–45* (London: Pimlico, 1992).

Cannadine, D. *The Decline and Fall of the British Aristocracy* (New Haven, CT: Yale University Press, 1990).

Cannadine, D. *History in Our Time* (New Haven, CT: Yale University Press, 1998).

Clancy, L. *Running the Family Firm: How the Monarchy Manages Its Image and Our Money* (Manchester: Manchester University Press, 2021).

Dorey, P. 'The Legacy of Thatcherism: Public Sector Reform', *Observatoire de la Société Britannique* 17 (2015), pp. 33–60.

Edgerton, D. *The Rise and Fall of the British Nation: A Twentieth Century History* (London: Penguin, 2019).

Harper, T. *From Servants of the Empire to Everyday Heroes: The British Honours System in the Twentieth Century* (Oxford: OUP, 2020).

Harrison, B. *The Transformation of British Politics, 1860–1995* (Oxford: OUP, 1996).

Hay, C. *The Failure of Anglo-Liberal Capitalism* (Basingstoke: Palgrave Pivot UK, 2013).

Hay, C., and Wincott, D. *The Political Economy of European Welfare Capitalism* (Basingstoke: Red Globe Press, 2012).

HRH Prince Charles, *A Vision of Britain: A Personal View of Architecture* (London: Doubleday, 1989).

HRH Prince Philip, *Men, Machines and Sacred Cows* (London: H. Hamilton, 1984).

Irvine, S., et al. 'Research Briefing: Food Banks in the UK', *House of Commons Library* (London, 2022).

Kefford, A. *The Life and Death of the Shopping City: Public Planning and Private Redevelopment in Britain since 1945* (Cambridge: CUP, 2022).

Krunke, H. 'Day-to-Day Political Functions of the Monarch in Denmark', in R. Hazell and B. Morris (eds.), *The Role of Monarchy in Modern Democracy: European Monarchies Compared* (Oxford: Hart Publishing, 2022), pp. 74–9.

Langhamer, C. *The English in Love: The Intimate Story of an Emotional Revolution* (Oxford: OUP, 2013).

Lowe, R. 'The Second World War, Consensus, and the Foundation of the Welfare State', *Twentieth Century British History* 1:2 (1990), pp. 152–82.

Lownie, A. *Traitor King: The Scandalous Exile of the Duke and Duchess of Windsor* (London: Blink Publishing, 2021).

McClure, D. The Queen's True Worth: Unravelling the Public & Private Finances of Elizabeth II (London: Lume Books, 2020)

Morrah, D. The Work of the Queen (London: William Kimber, 1958).

Prochaska, F. Royal Bounty: The Making of a Welfare Monarchy (New Haven, CT: Yale University Press, 1995).

Prochaska, F. 'Monarchy and Charities', in J. Grogan (ed.), UK in a Changing Europe: The British Monarchy (London, 2023).

Rose, S. O. Which People's War? National Identity and Citizenship in Wartime Britain, 1939–1945 (Oxford: OUP, 2003).

Rose, S. O. 'From the "New Jerusalem" to the "Decline" of the "New Elizabethan Age": National Identity and Citizenship in Britain, 1945–56', in F. Biess and R. G. Moeller (eds.), Histories of the Aftermath: The Legacies of the Second World War in Europe (Oxford, 2010), pp. 231–51.

Seward, I. Prince Philip Revealed: A Man of His Century (London: Simon & Schuster, 2020).

Warwick, C. Princess Margaret: A Life of Contrasts (London: Andre Deutsch Ltd, 2002).

Wenander, H. 'The King and Public Power in the Minimalist Monarchy of Sweden', in R. Hazell and B. Morris (eds.), The Role of Monarchy in Modern Democracy: European Monarchies Compared (Oxford: Hart Publishing, 2022), pp. 32–6.

Williams, B. 'The "New Right" and its Legacy for British Conservatism', Journal of Political Ideologies (2021), pp. 1–24.

Ziegler, P. George VI: The Dutiful King (London: Allen Lane, 2014).

Zweiniger-Bargielowska, I. 'Royal Rations', History Today 43:12 (1993), pp. 13–15.

Zweiniger-Bargielowska, I. 'Keep Fit and Play the Game: George VI, Outdoor Recreation and Social Cohesion in Interwar Britain', Cultural and Social History 11:1 (2014), pp. 111–29.

PART THREE: FAMILY, CELEBRITY AND SCANDAL

Adekoya, R. Biracial Britain: A Different Way of Looking at Race (London: Constable, 2021).

Bingham, A., and Conboy, M. Tabloid Century: The Popular Press in Britain, 1896 to the Present (Oxford: Peter Lang Ltd, 2015).

Brown, S. 'Cecil Beaton and the Iconography of the House of Windsor', Photography & Culture 4:3 (2011), pp. 293–307.

Clancy, L. '"If You Move in the Same Circles as the Royals, Then You'll Get Stories about Them": Royal Correspondents, Cultural Intermediaries and Class', Cultural Sociology (2022), pp. 1–20.

Collins, M. The Beatles and Sixties Britain (Cambridge: CUP, 2020).

Crawford, M. The Little Princesses (London: Cassell & Co. Ltd., 1950).

Dimbleby, J. The Prince of Wales: A Biography (London: William Morrow & Co., 1994).

Dunlop, T. Elizabeth & Philip: A Story of Young Love, Marriage, and Monarchy (London: Headline, 2022).

Finch, J., and Summerfield, P. 'Social Reconstruction and the Emergence of Companionate Marriage, 1945–1959', in D. Clark (ed.), Marriage, Domestic Life and Social Change: Writings for Jacqueline Burgoyne (London: Routledge, 1991), pp. 7–32.

Fleming, T. Voices Out of the Air: The Royal Christmas Day Broadcasts, 1932–1981 (London: Williams Heinemann Ltd., 1981).

Hiley, N. 'The Candid Camera of the Edwardian Tabloids', History Today 43:8 (1993), pp. 16–22.

HRH the Duke of Windsor, A King's Story (London: Cassell & Co., 1951).

King, L. Family Men: Fatherhood and Masculinity in Britain, 1914–1960 (Oxford: OUP, 2015).

Langhamer, C. 'The Meanings of Home in Postwar Britain', Journal of Contemporary History 40:2 (2005), pp. 341–62.

Mantel, H. 'Royal Bodies', London Review of Books 35:4 (2013).

Mass Observation, May the Twelfth: Mass-Observation Day Surveys 1937: By Over Two Hundred Observers (London: Faber & Faber, 1987).

Mayhall, L. N. 'The Prince of Wales versus Clark Gable: Anglophone Celebrity and Citizenship between the Wars', Cultural and Social History 4:4 (2007), pp. 529–43.

Mort, F. 'Love in a Cold Climate: Letters, Public Opinion and Monarchy in the 1936 Abdication Crisis', *Twentieth Century British History* 25:1 (2014), pp. 30–62.

Morton, A. *Diana: Her True Story* (London: Simon & Schuster, 1992).

Paulmann, J. 'Searching for a "Royal International": The Mechanics of Monarchical Relations in Nineteenth-Century Europe', in M. Geyer and J. Paulmann (eds.), *The Mechanics of Internationalism: Culture, Society and Politics from the 1840s to the First World War* (Oxford: OUP, 2001), pp. 145–76.

Phillips, A. *The First Royal Media War: Edward VIII, the Abdication and the Press* (Barnsley: Pen & Sword History, 2023)

Prince Harry, *Spare* (London: Bantam, 2023).

Samuel, R. 'Mrs Thatcher's Return to Victorian Values', *Victorian Values* (1992), pp. 9–29.

Schwarzenbach, A. 'Royal Photographs: Emotions for the People', *Contemporary European History* 13:3 (2004), pp. 255–80.

Schwarzenbach, A. 'Love, Marriage and Divorce: American and European Reaction to the Abdication of Edward', in L. Passerini et al. (eds.), *New Dangerous Liaisons: Discourses on Europe and Love in the Twentieth Century* (New York: Berghahn Books, 2010), pp. 137–57.

Seaton, J. 'The Monarchy, "Popularity", Legitimacy and the Media', in R. Hazell and B. Morris (eds.), *The Role of Monarchy in Modern Democracy: European Monarchies Compared* (Oxford: Hart Publishing, 2022), pp. 255–64.

Smart, C. 'Divorce in England, 1950–2000: A Moral Tale?' in Sanford N. Katz et al. (eds.), *Cross Currents: Family Law and Policy in the US and England* (Oxford, 2000), pp. 363–85.

PART FOUR: NATION, DEMOCRACY AND THE CONSTITUTION

Aldrich, R. J., and Cormac, R. *The Secret Royals: Spying and the Crown, from Victoria to Diana* (London: Atlantic Books, 2021).

Baker, N. ... *And What Do You Do? What the Royal Family Don't Want You to Know* (London: Biteback Publishing, 2020).

Ball, S. 'The Reform Act of 1918 – The Advent of Democracy', *Parliamentary History* 37:1 (2018), pp. 1–22.

Bentley, M. 'Power and Authority in the Late Victorian and Edwardian Court', in A. Olechnowicz (ed.), *The Monarchy and the British Nation, 1780 to the Present* (Cambridge: CUP, 2007), pp. 163–87.

Blick, A., and Hennessy, P. 'Good Chaps No More? Safeguarding the Constitution in Stressful Times', Constitution Society Report (London, 2019), pp. 1–35.

Bogdanor, V. *The Monarchy and the Constitution* (Oxford: OUP, 1995).

Bradford, S. *King George VI* (London: Penguin, 2011).

Brazier, R. 'The Monarchy', in V. Bogdanor (ed.), *The British Constitution in the Twentieth Century* (Oxford, 2003), pp. 69–98.

Burch, M., and Holliday, I. 'The Blair Government and the Core Executive', *Government and Opposition* 39:1 (2004), pp. 1–21.

Cannadine, D. 'The Last Hanoverian Sovereign?: the Victorian Monarchy in Historical Perspective, 1688–1988', in A. Beier, D. Cannadine and J. M. Rosenheim (eds.), *The First Modern Society* (Cambridge, 1989), pp. 127–65.

Craig, D. M. 'Bagehot's Republicanism', in A. Olechnowicz (ed.), *The Monarchy and the British Nation, 1780 to the Present* (Cambridge: CUP, 2007), pp. 139–62.

Economist Intelligence Unit, 'Democracy Index 2021: The China Challenge' (London, 2022).

Hames, T., and Leonard, M. 'Modernising the Monarchy', Demos Report (London, 1998).

Harris, J. 'War and Social History: Britain and the Home Front during the Second World War', *Contemporary European History* 1:1 (Cambridge: CUP, 1992), pp. 17–35.

Hennessy, P. *The Hidden Wiring: Unearthing the British Constitution* (London: W&N, 1995).

Kumarasingham, H. 'The Role and Powers of the Queen in the 2019 Brexit Political Crises – Reflections from British and Commonwealth History', *The Journal of Imperial and Commonwealth History* 48:1 (2020), pp. 1–14.

Loughlin, J. 'Crown, Spectacle and Identity: The British Monarchy and Ireland under the
Union 1800–1922', in A. Olechnowicz (ed.), *The Monarchy and the British Nation, 1780 to the
Present* (Cambridge: CUP, 2007), pp. 108–38.

Mokrosinska, D. (ed.) *Transparency and Secrecy in European Democracies: Contested Trade-Offs* (London:
Routledge, 2020).

Morgan, K.O. *Britain since 1945: The People's Peace* (Oxford: OUP, USA, 2001).

Morgan, K.O. 'The Labour Party and British Republicanism', *Revue Électronique d'Études sur le Monde
Anglophone* 1:2 (2003).

Parry, J. 'Whig Monarchy, Whig Nation: Crown Politics and Representativeness, 1800–2000',
in A. Olechnowicz (ed.), *The Monarchy and the British Nation, 1780 to the Present* (Cambridge:
CUP, 2007), pp. 47–75.

Payne, S. *The Fall of Boris Johnson: The Full Story* (London: Pan, 2023).

Rappaport, H. *Queen Victoria: A Biographical Companion* (London: ABC-CLIO Ltd., 2003).

Richards, D., and Smith, M. J. 'In Defence of British Politics against the British Political
Tradition', *The Political Quarterly* 86:1 (2015), pp. 41–51.

Russell, M., et al. 'Rebuilding and Renewing the Constitution: Options for Reform', *Institute for
Government and The Constitution Unit* (London, 2023).

Thane, P. 'The Impact of Mass Democracy on British Political Culture, 1918–1939', in
J. Gottlieb and R. Toye (eds.), *The Aftermath of Suffrage: Women, Gender, and Politics in Britain,
1918–1945* (Basingstoke: Palgrave Macmillan, 2013), pp. 70–86.

Twomey, A. 'The Exercise of Soft Power by Female Monarchs in the United Kingdom', *Royal
Studies Journal* 7:2 (2020), pp. 31–48.

UK Government Cabinet Office, 'The Cabinet Manual' (London, 2011).

Williamson, P. '1931 Revisited: The Political Realities', *Twentieth Century British History* 2:3
(1991), pp. 328–43.

CONCLUSION

Craig, D. M. 'The Crowned Republic? Monarchy and Anti-Monarchy in Britain, 1760–1901',
Historical Journal 46:1 (Cambridge: CUP, 2003), pp. 167–85.

Hazell, R. 'The Royal Family's Lack of Human Rights', in R. Hazell and B. Morris (eds.), *The
Role of Monarchy in Modern Democracy: European Monarchies Compared* (Oxford: Hart Publishing,
2022), pp. 194–201.

Jungclaussen, J. F., et al. (eds.) *Republic vs. Monarchy: How Sound Is Your Constitution?* (London:
KE7.net Publishing, 2012).

Loft, P. 'Research Briefing: The Commonwealth and Human Rights', *The House of Commons Library*
(London, 2023), pp. 1–30.

Index